Learning Abroad

Learning Abroad:
A History of the Commonwealth Scholarship and Fellowship Plan

By

Hilary Perraton

CAMBRIDGE SCHOLARS

PUBLISHING

Learning Abroad: A History of the Commonwealth Scholarship and Fellowship Plan, by Hilary Perraton

This book first published 2009

Cambridge Scholars Publishing

12 Back Chapman Street, Newcastle upon Tyne, NE6 2XX, UK

British Library Cataloguing in Publication Data
A catalogue record for this book is available from the British Library

Copyright © 2009 by Hilary Perraton

All rights for this book reserved. No part of this book may be reproduced, stored in a retrieval system, or transmitted, in any form or by any means, electronic, mechanical, photocopying, recording or otherwise, without the prior permission of the copyright owner.

ISBN (10): 1-4438-0600-5, ISBN (13): 978-1-4438-0600-8

Table of Contents

List of Tables vii

Acknowledgments ix

Abbreviations xi

Introduction 1

Chapter One 5
Launch: Planning and Implementing

Chapter Two 19
Purposes: The Plan in its Context

Chapter Three 35
Britain: Establishing the Plan

Chapter Four 59
Britain: Adapting and Surviving

Chapter Five 81
Commonwealth: The Plan in the North

Chapter Six 101
Universities: Expansion in the South

Chapter Seven 123
Experience: The Scholars' and Fellows' Story

Chapter Eight 155
Impact: What they did next

Chapter Nine 179
Conclusion

Appendix: Statistical tables 187
Notes.. 197
Sources 213
References 217
Index.. 225

LIST OF TABLES

1.1	New awards of scholarships, by awarding country	13
1.2	Fellowship programmes	16
2.1	Commonwealth universities in the south 1960	20
2.2	Higher education enrolments: some Commonwealth countries	25
2.3	Foreign students in selected countries	29
3.1	New awards made by Britain 1961-2008	47
3.2	Commonwealth Scholarship Commission budget 1961-2008	56
4.1	Fees and costs per award	63
4.2	British awards 2002–8	77
6.1	Plan alumni at Barbados campus	111
7.1	Numbers of scholars and fellows	124
7.2	Ages of scholars	126
7.3	Percentage of female scholars by nominating region	126
7.4	Subject areas of scholars coming to Britain	138
7.5	British scholarship monthly stipends	144
7.6	Scholars' doctoral success rates in Britain	152
8.1	Estimates of proportion of scholars returning home after award	156
A 1	Scholarships taken up by nominating country	187
A 2	Scholarships taken up by hosting country	190
A 3	Fellowships taken up by nominating country	192
A 4	Fellowships taken up by hosting country	194
A 5	Total number of awards held by awarding country—selected years	195

ACKNOWLEDGMENTS

I am indebted to the Commonwealth Secretariat, the Nuffield Foundation, the British Academy with the Association of Commonwealth Universities, and the Department of Foreign Affairs and International Trade of the government of Canada, who together funded the research reported here. I am also grateful for the support of the von Hügel Institute of St Edmund's College, Cambridge where it was based.

Without the encouragement of my wife, Jean, the book would have been much more difficult to write, without her company my life immeasurably less rich. Many others have provided help, support, critique, and advice. First among these are the research colleagues who worked with me: Suzanne Lawrence, appointed by the government of Canada as the George Curtis Memorial Commonwealth Fellow to work on the project, who did all the hard work in Cambridge; Helen Connell, Candice Harrison-Train, Surinder Jodhka, Charles Levi, Reehana Raza and Pat Stafford, who wrote country studies, and Monica Darnbrough who looked at the British programme of medical awards. I have a particular debt to those who welcomed and supported the idea of the project from its early stages; they include David Bridges, Trudy Harpham, John Kirkland, Don McKinnon and Rémi Tremblay. Colleagues at the Commonwealth Scholarship Commission and the Association of Commonwealth Universities helped with information and with their interest; an incomplete list includes Rachel Day, Sabina Ebbols, Jonathan Jenkins, Jocelyn Law, Natasha Lockhun, Anna O'Flynn, Tim Shaw, Julie Stackhouse and Tim Unwin. Nick Mulhern, the ACU librarian, consistently went the extra league in a way that marks his profession and I have also benefited from the help of librarians and archivists at the National Archives, Senate House Library of the University of London, the Institute of Education, and the Cambridge University Library. The book would not exist without the comments of all those whom we interviewed and with whom we corresponded. I am also grateful for help, at home and abroad, and in various ways, from others who include in particular Charlotte Creed, Kate Crofts, Pat Gouldstone, Peter Hetherington, Jennifer Humphries, Gail Larose, Brian Long, Woodville Marshall, Kees Maxey, Jasbir Singh, Malcolm Skilbeck, Edgar Temple, and Peter Williams. All those mentioned are, of course, absolved from responsibility for errors which are all my own.

ABBREVIATIONS

ACU	Association of Commonwealth Universities
agm	agendum
AUBC	Association of Universities of the British Commonwealth
AUCC	Association of Universities and Colleges of Canada
CASF	Commonwealth Academic Staff Fellowship
CASS	Commonwealth Academic Staff Scholarship
CBIE	Canadian Bureau for International Education
CEM	Report of Commonwealth Education Meeting/Conference of Education Ministers
CIDA	Canadian International Development Agency
CRO	Commonwealth Relations Office
CSC	Commonwealth Scholarship Commission in the UK
CSCAR	Annual report of Commonwealth Scholarship Commission
CSCM	Minutes of Commonwealth Scholarship Commission
CSFP	Commonwealth Scholarship and Fellowship Plan
CSFPAR	Annual report of CSFP
DfID	Department for International Development
FCO	Foreign and Commonwealth Office
FRS	Fellow of the Royal Society
LAC	Library and Archives Canada
LP	Logan papers
NA	National Archives
ODA	Overseas Development Administration
ODM	Ministry of Overseas Development
ODNB	*Oxford dictionary of national biography*
OECD	Organisation for Economic Cooperation and Development
PDC	Parliamentary debates—House of Commons
PDL	Parliamentary debates—House of Lords
PhD	Doctor of philosophy
Rev	Ten-year review
SCSM	Report of Commonwealth Standing Committee on Student Mobility
UDI	Unilateral Declaration of Independence
UTA	University of Toronto Archives
WW	*Who's Who; Who was Who*

Introduction

In 1960, 297 young men and 38 young women left home to study abroad under the newly launched Commonwealth Scholarship and Fellowship Plan. Most of them went to Britain, Canada or Australia, smaller numbers to Hong Kong, Malaya, New Zealand, South Africa and the Central African Federation; they included a future Sri Lankan astronomer, a South African judge, a West Indian pro-vice-chancellor, and future professors by the dozen. Some 25,000 have since followed their examples. Many went on to academic careers; a smaller number have become ministers and prime ministers; others have attained fame or notoriety in journalism and the arts; some became political prisoners, some poets; a few have combined several of these achievements. This book tells their story.

The scholarship plan (CSFP) was set up in the afterglow of empire and at the dawn of the new Commonwealth. A meeting of Commonwealth trade ministers, held in Montreal in 1958, and a Commonwealth education conference in Oxford a year later, agreed that a reciprocal programme of scholarships would bind Commonwealth countries so that "their people should be able to share as widely as possible in the advantages of education". This was described as "the first occasion on which a concerted effort at mutual help has been made by all the Commonwealth countries in collaboration". The aim was to make awards to "men and women of high intellectual promise who may be expected to make a significant contribution to life in their own countries on their return from study overseas".[1]

The idea was a simple one. Under a vaguely defined, but much vaunted, Commonwealth umbrella, individual Commonwealth countries would offer scholarships to young people, or fellowships to people in mid-career, from other Commonwealth countries. Most of the scholars were to be postgraduates with undergraduate awards generally reserved for countries with no home university. The country offering awards would pay all the costs for the scholars it was hosting, including transport, subsistence and university fees. The country nominating scholars was to identify short lists of applicants and send these to the awarding countries which would make the final selection—a responsibility they closely guarded. There was no central mechanism so that, while the plan was multilateral in its scope, and its intentions, it was bilateral in its operation. Each awarding country decided how many scholars or fellows it wanted to invite from each other

Commonwealth country. A Commonwealth Education Liaison Committee in London kept the statistics, until it handed the job over to the newly established Commonwealth Secretariat in 1967. It had nothing to do with policy which remained with individual governments.

Each country set up its own arrangements to administer the plan. This was done at arm's length from government in the four rich Commonwealth countries. Britain set up a Commonwealth Scholarship Commission while Australia, Canada and New Zealand appointed committees, mainly of university representatives, to choose scholars and fellows and to guide or determine policy. In most other countries the ministry of education took on the job of selecting nominees and, for countries offering them, of placing scholars for their own awards.

The plan began with a flourish. By 1965 some eighteen Commonwealth countries had given awards and just over 1,000 scholars and fellows were holding them. Since then Britain, Canada and India have offered the largest number of awards, followed by Australia and New Zealand. Most scholars have travelled from the south to the north, but about a quarter of the total have travelled between the four industrialised countries.[2] Smaller numbers have travelled, within the south, between Commonwealth developing countries, or from the north to the south. The plan grew in scale till the mid-1990s, even as the Commonwealth changed and as the costs of international study increased in response to widespread inflation in the 1970s and policy changes on university funding in the 1980s. The number of award holders reached a peak in the 1990s after which totals declined and the number of countries offering awards fell to six. In the present century numbers have risen again, encouraging Commonwealth education ministers to agree new targets for the plan's expansion, despite a withdrawal by Australia and proposals to cut funding in turn by Canada and Britain.

The plan has always had its critics and sceptics who have brought three main charges against it. The first is that it has been dominated by the north and contributed to the brain drain, enabling the best scholars to study and then to stay in the north. A series of studies attempting to discover how far scholars returned home demonstrates the seriousness with which the charge has been taken. Second, it has been accused of elitism and irrelevance, of meeting the needs of an elite, or easing access to one, rather than addressing greater national needs. In the early years of the plan, for example, rich countries insisted on giving postgraduate awards when many in the south wanted lower-level scholarships. Third, bias has been suspected or identified. Accusations of bias have been made against nominating countries and their agencies, and of favouring those drawn from existing elites, with selection influenced by cronyism, class, region or ethnicity. More generally, the plan has never achieved gender balance, and has been steadily criticised for this, as the proportion of women given awards has slowly risen from less than 12 to more than 40 per cent.

Against these criticisms, and against major changes in the Commonwealth and its university systems, the plan's survival as an oddly uncoordinated set of bilateral programmes, with a shared name and even purpose, provoke three questions about its history: what is it for, how has it changed, and what has it achieved? Their answers, the theme of this book, illuminate the politics of the Commonwealth, as well as the sociology and educational history of individual member countries.

The next chapter examines how the plan was set up and describes the various programmes of scholarships and fellowships that have been offered, by Commonwealth member countries, as it has evolved. Chapter 2 then looks at the development of the plan, and the resolution of tensions within it, in the context of Commonwealth universities and of international student mobility. The next three chapters set out the history of the plan within its political environment, examining the plan's purposes as well as its achievements . As Britain has been the largest player, chapters 3 and 4 do this by examining the British record, and the nature and work of the Commonwealth Scholarship Commission, in the light of British policy towards the Commonwealth, towards aid, and towards its own universities. Chapter 5 looks in the same way at the Commonwealth itself and at the changing policies of the other rich Commonwealth countries, Australia, Canada and New Zealand, exploring the interplay between national and Commonwealth priorities. Chapter 6 moves south to examine policies in the developing Commonwealth and at the role and achievements of the plan in university development. Case studies of two regions, India and the eastern Caribbean, and of one unusual mode of scholarships, using distance learning, illuminate the record. Study abroad is likely to be a formative experience, important for its process as well as its structure and paper trail of qualifications: these are the themes of chapter 7 which asks who the scholars and fellows were, and examines what they studied, and what it was like to do so, as they went on their travels. Chapter 8 then follows them home, or explores why they did not go home, in asking about the effects of international study on their careers, a necessary part of any assessment. That general assessment is then made in the concluding chapter 9.

CHAPTER ONE

LAUNCH: PLANNING AND IMPLEMENTING

The story begins in Canada. To general surprise John Diefenbaker, a lawyer from the prairies of Saskatchewan, won the 1957 election, becoming the first conservative Canadian prime minister in twenty-two years. He was lucky in his timing; Canada's economy was to flourish in the last years of the 1950s, encouraging the false hope that it had emerged from a lacklustre cycle. To sustain the prosperity Diefenbaker needed to find a role for a country of only 20 million in a world dominated by markets of 100 million or more.[1]

With America an unsettling giant to the south, Britain still the custodian of sterling and of much of the empire across the Atlantic, and the Common Market an unknown quantity six months away, the Commonwealth had economic as well as political appeal. Joe Garner, then British high commissioner in Ottawa and later to chair the Commonwealth Scholarship Commission, saw this time as,

> the apogee of the Commonwealth idea. The [Commonwealth Prime Ministers'] meeting in the summer of 1957 was held in circumstances of easy familiarity and some enthusiasm, engendered by the apocalyptic appearance of Diefenbaker, breathless from his surprise electoral triumph in Canada. Eager to exploit the full potentiality of Commonwealth collaboration, Diefenbaker invited a special Conference to meet in Montreal in 1958 which registered a high point in post-war cooperation. Not only Ghana (now a full member) but also many Colonial Territories attended and the Conference looked forward hopefully to a steady expansion of Commonwealth membership.[2]

The Commonwealth trade and economic conference had grand ambitions. Diefenbaker hoped that some variant of imperial preference could preserve a Commonwealth trading block and protect Canadian sales of wheat. He took to the conference a series of economic proposals, all of which the British treasury disliked. Three of them, more Canadian technical assistance, aid to the West Indies, and expansion of the Colombo plan, were dismissed as "chicken feed". The fourth, about setting up a Commonwealth development bank was worse, involving the investment of more British than Canadian funds so that "we pay the price for the success of their conference".[3] The lack of agreement meant that the conference's long-term achievements were different and more modest. One was to agree on an international coaxial-cable network, which had been considered by a Commonwealth telecommunications conference, and crept on to the agenda even though the British thought it not worth discussing.[4] Another was to conceive of a Commonwealth Scholarship and Fellowship Plan. The British went along with this idea; education was safer and cheaper than Diefenbaker's grander plans. The scholarship plan was to be approved by trade ministers in Montreal and established the following year, this time by a Commonwealth educational conference.

In Britain, Harold Macmillan's government was enjoying a similar interlude of prosperity which was to lead him to an election victory in October 1959 on the prospectus that "you've never had it so good". The Commonwealth was demanding his attention too, as twenty-four colonies and protectorates were to leave British rule between Ghana in 1957 and Aden ten years later. Cabinet meetings, with a secretary of state for Commonwealth affairs alongside the foreign secretary and colonial secretary, regularly considered Commonwealth matters. Macmillan had a patrician air, with his cleverness concealed behind drooping eyelids, and his complexity revealed by his balanced references to his crofter grandfather and his links to the Duke of Devonshire. As prime minister he was willing to preside over the dismantling of the British empire, which Churchill had foresworn, and was persuaded by his colonial secretary, Iain Macleod, to do so at breathtaking speed and with unexpected skill. Macleod had sharpened his skills of calculation as a professional bridge player and gambler in the 1930s and of negotiation at the ministry of labour in the 1950s. He later claimed that, "the change of policy that I introduced in October 1959 was, on the surface, merely a change of timing. In reality, of course, it was a true change of policy, but I telescoped events rather than created new ones".[5]

Like Diefenbaker, Macmillan started out with an attachment to the Commonwealth though he stopped enjoying its meetings when they shifted from being a "small and pleasant country-house party" to a "sort of miniature United Nations".[6] Relations with America needed to recover from the Suez crisis. Europe did not seem that important. The Commonwealth still did. In the cold war of the late 1950s, it was seen, despite India's neutrality, as ideologically part of the west. "Indeed this was the major function of the Commonwealth fifteen years after the war: keeping out of the 'Communist clutches' a large part of 'the world's more backward populations'".[7] The cold war seeped into educational politics: George Curtis, a Canadian academic who was floating the idea of a scholarship plan in 1958, argued for expanding postgraduate education as a response to Russia's launch of the first-ever satellite, sputnik.[8]

Britain's position in the world, or at least her self-importance, flowed from her imperial past and it was confidently and naively expected that these would be sustained by the creation of an independent Commonwealth. It was not to be. Hoping to retain the cosiness of Commonwealth meetings, attended by a handful of countries, the British tried to find a formula for a two-tier Commonwealth. The formula could not be made to fit Cyprus which, with a population of less than 600,000, joined the Commonwealth on its independence in 1960. Macmillan grumbled that this precedent would change its nature: "was it to be the R.A.C. or Boodles?" If Cyprus was admitted "all the other tiddlers would demand this treatment".[9] Worse was to come as:

> It was splendid when India, Pakistan, Ceylon, Ghana, Malaya and Nigeria joined the Commonwealth, hitherto a white man's club. But far from the Commonwealth proving to be a buttress in its post-colonial era, as was confidently expected, it turned out to be instead a new, unplanned, and quite major area in which Britain found itself pilloried.[10]

But this is to anticipate. In 1959, as the brides of the Commonwealth were shopping for their gowns, their beauty was admired from the right, because of their imperial past, and from the left, because of their radiant and independent future. It was a good time for a party and a wedding present.

Setting up the plan

The Earl of Halifax, as chancellor of the university, hosted the party held in Oxford in July 1959. Labelled the first Commonwealth education conference in Commonwealth mythology, which conveniently forgets imperial educational conferences in the 1920s, it brought together delegates from the eleven Commonwealth member countries and representatives—a subtle difference—from the colonial empire, from Aden through Northern Borneo and Sarawak, to Zanzibar. They were mainly educators, and nearly all men. The conference received from the Montreal trade ministers the proposal for a scholarship plan to which Britain and Canada were already committed. It had taken time and diplomacy to widen support for it. Early discussions suggested there was only lukewarm interest in a plan concentrating on university exchanges. Australia and New Zealand had different priorities that included training for the civil service. India did not want it limited to university staff; it too wanted awards for civil servants and more and better teachers. Malaya's priorities were for temporary staff for new universities, teacher trainers, and scientists. The Canadians at this point wanted to use some of their funds to send Canadians abroad: nobody else seemed to like this idea.[11] Despite the various reservations, by the summer of 1959 Britain had pledged 500 awards, Canada 250, Australia 100 and India 50.[12]

The origins of the proposal are contested with at least four Canadian academics having or laying a claim to its paternity. Sidney Smith, the foreign minister and former president of Toronto University, launched the idea in Montreal. He talked about university exchange in an address to a Commonwealth universities' congress on 1 September 1958 but in such general terms that his audience did not realise there was a specific proposal for activity.[13] Within two weeks he made the same proposal to the trade conference in much more specific terms. In an interview in 2005 George Curtis, who had been dean of law at the University of British Columbia, talked about his discussions with other academics and with civil servants and claimed, of the plan, "it was thought up by me in 1958". His claim may be weakened by his mistaken recollection that it had got into the Montreal report because of a casual remark by one of the Canadian civil servants to Sir Henry Lintott of the British delegation; Lintott had in fact been at the centre of extensive earlier discussions (see chapter 3). Curtis went on to chair the 1959 conference committee that shaped the plan.[14] His own vice-chancellor, Norman Mackenzie, had staked his claim in 1959, explaining that "it was he who produced the Canadian plan and sold it to 'his ex-fellow Vice-Chancellor' Sidney Smith". As he went on to complain about the presence of 500 undergraduates from Trinidad in his own university, his commitment to student mobility looks thinner than Curtis's.[15] Tom Symons, who was to become the founding vice-chancellor of Trent University, has a stronger claim. He was a friend and adviser to Sidney Smith and at his request drafted a brief for him in May 1958. It contained many of the features that were to find their way into the plan: bilateral exchanges, support from both governments and universities, open competition for "excellence in any field", its value as a means of strengthening universities and its potential for fostering "knowledge and understanding of the Commonwealth itself".[16] After fifty years paternity may not matter. The various claims demonstrate both early enthusiasm for the plan and the fact that the promotion of international university exchange was then a shared part of academic discourse.

Smith, Symons and Curtis had similar views of the plan's purpose. Both Curtis and Symons had benefited from scholarships as postgraduate students, which had taken them to Europe and sent them back with a common commitment to internationalism. In his speech to Commonwealth universities Smith spoke of the role of Commonwealth universities in the "acquisition of common attitudes by students and potential leaders from dissimilar and diverse origins" and went on to argue:

> that the free flow and exchange of ideas has been and will continue to be one of the strongest bonds among the Commonwealth's members. To encourage and facilitate this flow even further, I believe that a programme of exchange of Commonwealth university and staff, particularly at the graduate level, should be promoted. Such a programme should reflect the pattern already established; rather than the one-way traffic of an earlier time, our exchanges must be multilateral in character.[17]

Symons and Smith had earlier agreed how important it was to "enlarge the concept of the numbers and range of student exchange and that every country and every society had a big stake in this". Symons recalled Smith arguing that "what we need ... is something that will involve many countries, many continents and many cultures, and the best vehicle to have is the Commonwealth".[18]

These were the ideas that were carried from Montreal to Oxford. Alongside a British pledge to support teacher training in the developing Commonwealth, the conference endorsed the Montreal recommendations, arguing that:

> The Commonwealth is a new experiment in human relationship. It is founded on a belief in the worth and dignity of the human individual and a recognition of the value of freedom and cooperative action. The end of all our Commonwealth endeavour is the good life—material and spiritual—and the happiness of the 600 million individuals who are its citizens.
>
> The good life and happiness can be attained only through education in the deeper and wider sense. Freedom from want demands the application of technical skills of ever-increasing complexity. The stability of our democratic way of life requires maturity of judgment in the citizen that can come only from a good general education. The increasing pace of development and the growing interdependence of modern society call for the highest intellectual and moral qualities. Above all it is through a sound and balanced education that the individual must seek the fulfilment of his personality and the enrichment of his life.[19]

The aim was to establish 1,000 scholarships with the British providing half and the Canadians a quarter of the total and the rest made up by Australia, India, Pakistan, New Zealand, Malaya, Ghana, the Central African Federation, Ceylon and East Africa. It had to be multilateral:

It is of special importance that the CSFP should pay great attention to the needs of the economically less developed countries, where educational facilities and opportunities are at present less amply provided. But educational interchange between all the countries of the Commonwealth is essential if we are to get the best out of the Plan and to share to the full the benefits of the special experience and facilities which our countries possess. Each has something to learn from the others; each has something to give. If the Plan is to achieve its purpose, we must bring the widest possible variety of cultural exchange between all parts of the Commonwealth and so facilitate the development of a multilateral trade in ideas.[20]

With this in mind, the Oxford conference identified five principles for the plan, which have remained as a formal commitment ever since:

the Plan should be additional to, and distinct from, any other plan in operation;

the Plan should be based on mutual cooperation and the sharing of educational experience among all the nations of the Commonwealth;

the Plan should be sufficiently flexible, to take account of the diverse and changing needs of Commonwealth countries;

while the Plan will be Commonwealth-wide, it should be operated on the basis of a series of bilateral agreements to allow for the necessary flexibility;

awards should be designed to recognise and promote the highest standards of intellectual achievement.[21]

Scholarship programmes may have one or more distinct raisons d'être. Some have aimed for educational redistribution, seeking the most disadvantaged students. (This was never a purpose of CSFP and there is no evidence that any of the agencies involved with it wanted the job of means testing applicants for awards.) Some have been overtly political, hoping to influence scholars and their attitudes throughout their working life. Some have been concerned with the interests of the institution or country from which scholars are drawn, others with those of the institution to which they are going. Some have been limited, concentrating on particular disciplines or institutions, others open to all comers. The Oxford principles did not explore any of these and left further policy decisions to individual Commonwealth countries.

The statements of high purpose also left undecided who should run the plan. As the Commonwealth Secretariat was still seven years in the future there were no Commonwealth mechanisms to implement conference recommendations. Smith had worried about the danger of setting up a large bureaucracy for the plan and instead welcomed a suggestion of Symons' "using the phrase of the president of Harvard ... 'Each tub on its own bottom'; good philosophy I think".[22] Following that precept, practical arrangements were to rest with individual member states. Each member country would fund the awards it was offering, would determine how many there should be, and how it should identify and nominate scholars for awards offered by other countries. "Special agencies should be set up in the various Commonwealth countries to select scholars for their own awards and to nominate scholars for awards to other countries".[23] Most countries arranged for the ministry of education to be the nominating agency which selected the first, long-list, of applicants to be forwarded to the awarding country in the two-stage selection process. Canada gave the job to the Association of Universities and Colleges of Canada and created a committee of academics to guide policy. Australia and New Zealand set up advisory committees of university teachers. Britain set up a freestanding scholarship commission. This followed the precedent of the Marshall commission, set up in 1953 to manage scholarships commemorating the Marshall Plan, and was perhaps the only possibility: government did not want the plan to belong to the universities, which ruled out a university agency, while the ministry of education at that time had minimal responsibilities in higher education. By 1960 the first scholars were on their way, by plane or ship. The largest cohort came to Britain where the scholarship commission sent welcoming parties to Heathrow and Tilbury.

The Oxford conference agreed there might be two kinds of award. Most would be scholarships, generally for those working towards a degree. But the conference also agreed that "a limited number of awards should be made to senior scholars of established reputation and achievement. These we call Commonwealth Visiting Fellowships". Scholarships and fellowships have had differing histories.

Scholarships

The programme of scholarships developed on the lines agreed at Oxford though on a slightly reduced scale. In its first decade Britain usually awarded between 200 and 250 scholarships a year, Canada about a hundred, Australia thirty to forty, India about twenty and New Zealand about twelve. At any one time there were between 500 and 1,000 scholars and fellows holding awards. From the outset Britain has been the largest player with its contribution to the plan managed by the Commonwealth Scholarship Commission. While numbers have changed, scholarships to individual students have continued to this day as the mainstay of the plan.

Alongside the general scholarships, a number of more specialist programmes have been established within the framework of the plan. In 1965 Britain hosted a Commonwealth medical conference in Edinburgh and, flushed with the apparent success of the scholarship plan, announced a set of medical awards to strengthen medical education, particularly, but not solely, in the developing Commonwealth. Alongside a new programme of medical fellowships, medical scholars were for doctors seeking a postgraduate qualification.[24] The programme ran till a government review of the commission's work in 1993 could find no strong case for medicine to be separated out from other disciplines. Britain was still in an expansionist mood in 1968 when, at a Commonwealth education conference in Lagos, it announced a set of awards targeted at universities. Again these were at two levels, Commonwealth Academic Staff Scholarships (CASS) and Commonwealth Academic Staff Fellowships (CASF). The scholarships were targeted at young university staff in developing-country universities who needed a PhD. Candidates were nominated directly by universities, rather than through the nominating agencies which, by this time, were mainly ministries of education. As set out in table 1.1, Britain usually funded up to thirty medical scholars and thirty to sixty CASS scholars each year.

No new scholarship programmes were to be introduced for another thirty years until in 1998 Canada launched a small programme of distance-learning scholarships. The programme ran for four years and allowed seventy-seven students in the Caribbean to follow Canadian undergraduate degrees in computer science, teacher education and tourism management. For the most part they studied at a distance but all came to Canada for one semester of full-time study. Britain followed this Canadian lead and launched a distance-learning programme in 2002, like Canada seeking to base this on partnerships between home and overseas universities. Although launched with a "new initiative" label and dubbed experimental, the distance-learning programme seemed by 2008 to have become a regular part of the commission's work. In contrast there has been no successor to the Canadian programme.[25]

Throughout the history of the plan Britain, Canada, Australia and India have been the largest awarding countries. New Zealand and Trinidad have consistently offered awards, as did Hong Kong till it left the Commonwealth in 1997. Others have come and gone. South Africa, Pakistan and Nigeria all offered awards until they left the Commonwealth—Pakistan has

Table 1.1 New awards of scholarships, by awarding country

	Average number of new awards made per annum				
	1960s	1970s	1980s	1990s	2000s[a]
Britain – general scholars	199	179	216	206	196
academic scholars	n/a	36	63	57	29
medical scholars	30	29	19	12	
distance learning scholars					161
split-site scholars					24
Canada	92	81	116	88	57
Australia	35	32	38	13	2
India	19	25	20	22	28
New Zealand	9	10	14	14	14
Nigeria	4	5	3	2	
Hong Kong	2	3	4	2	
Malaysia	3	2	1		9
Sri Lanka	2	3	2	<1	
Ghana	<1	3		0	<1
Trinidad		<1	1	1	2
Pakistan	3				
Jamaica	<1	<1	<1	<1	<1
Brunei				3	4
Malta	<1	<1	<1		<1
South Africa	<1				<1
Mauritius					<1
Botswana					<1
Sierra Leone	<1		<1		
East Africa	1		<1		
Zimbabwe	2				
Total	404	409	500	420	523

Source: CSFPAR, CEM, various dates, ACU database
Note. Years not reported are not included in averages
a. Generally for awards to 2005 but taking account only of years specialised programmes were running.

done it more than once—but only South Africa began offering awards again after its return. The small states of the Commonwealth have offered a small number of awards on a sporadic basis. Despite Trinidad's example, Jamaica has followed suit sometimes, Barbados never. Before a handful of new awards from Botswana, Ghana, Mauritius and South Africa, Africa had almost fallen away as an awarding continent whereas, in the first decades, Ghana, Nigeria, Sierra Leone and Uganda were all making awards.

The total number of scholars rose from the early 1960s and remained at about same level through much of the 1970s and 1980s, despite changes in member states, in the Commonwealth, and in the pattern of funding for higher education. Industrialised Commonwealth countries began to charge full-cost fees for overseas students in the 1980s but budgets generally were adjusted to match (see chapter 4). At the 1984 conference of Commonwealth education ministers Canada offered to increase her awards from 300 to 500 and thirteen countries pledged to offer awards for the first time or increase the number on offer. While these did not all materialise—education ministers propose but finance ministers dispose—the total effect was an increase in the size of the plan which reached a new high of 1,594 people holding awards in 1986 and was to reach a peak of 1,809 in 1993.

Despite this, there were warning signs by 1990 when ministers noted that there had been a decline in the uptake of awards in the last three years.[26] Numbers fell in the 1990s. Britain cut its funding to the commission; Australian national policy increasingly put its links with Asia ahead of those with the Commonwealth; Canada reduced the number of awards; Nigeria was suspended from the Commonwealth and Hong Kong left. In the mid-1990s both the Australian and the New Zealand governments decided to stop awarding Commonwealth scholarships, although they continued in New Zealand under university auspices. Canada and Britain were next to falter in their support for the scheme. In August 2006 the Canadian government halted recruitment of scholars for the next year but reversed the policy in time for Christmas. Two years later, the British foreign secretary announced that his department was cutting off funding for scholarships to the industrialised Commonwealth, though awards to developing countries were to continue. Again there was a partial reversal with the government department responsible for universities agreeing to fund a reduced number of awards at doctoral level (see chapter 4). Against this pattern of reverses, ministers of education agreed new targets for the plan at their meeting in Cape Town in 2006, while the number of countries offering awards rose to fourteen from its low point of six.

Fellowships

Alongside their scholarships, five countries set up fellowship programmes of various kinds, set out in table 1.2.

Australia ran a programme of visiting professorships from 1962 until 1986 and visiting fellowships from 1962 to 1995. The visiting professors came for a year with the programme meeting their travel costs and others being absorbed by the universities; visiting fellows generally came for three months. They seem to have attracted people of the distinction argued for in 1959: the composer Peter Maxwell Davies went to Australia in 1965 and the doyen of British educators Alec Clegg, chief education officer for the West Riding county council, in 1970.[27] Budget cuts ended the professorial programme in 1986 with a claim that it was no longer working effectively. Canada introduced fellowships in 1964, initially with three research fellowships and five visiting fellowships, for "persons prominent in various fields of education including universities, colleges, primary and secondary schools and technical institutions".[28] Awards were held at a variety of institutions, including local departments of education as well as universities, and were usually for two to four months. A year after these awards Canada introduced a programme of research fellowships which ran from 1965 to 1997. Fellows were to carry out their own research, though some found themselves teaching, for a period of up to one academic year, with the aim that the award would benefit both Canada and the nominating country. Up to the early 1990s, about three-quarters of the awards went to the old Commonwealth.

New Zealand offered two programmes from 1960 to 1988: prestige fellowships brought academics to tour the New Zealand universities and carry out research; the original awards were for up to a year but the period was reduced to a maximum of two months in 1972/3. Over the same period, it offered a small number of administrative awards annually for educational administrators who came for up to a year. In principle up to three awards were available each year but in practice there appear to have been only eleven administrators in twenty-five years.

Education was also the theme of awards in India and in Central Africa. India introduced awards for visiting fellows in 1962 to encourage the sharing of ideas on educational development and methodology. Awards were originally for three to six months, later cut to a standard three. They ran till 1978, and were resumed in 1984, but only for a couple of years. Between 1960 and 1964 the ill-fated Central African Federation offered one fellowship to a senior inspector of schools in England, to look at the secondary school system and another to Howard Sheath, the head of the external

Table 1.2 Fellowship programmes

Country and type of fellowship	Dates	Purpose	Numbers
Australia			
Visiting fellowships	1960-96	For persons prominent in education	Usually 4 p.a.
Visiting professorships	1964-86	Research and teaching	Usually 2-3 p.a.
Britain			
Fellowships	1960-80	To support research	2-7 awards p.a.
Medical and senior medical fellowships	1965-95	Capacity building in overseas medical schools	Usually 40-60 p.a.
Academic Fellowships	1968-	To strengthen developing-country universities	50 p.a.
Professional fellowships	2003-	Short-term awards for mid-career professionals	60-70 p.a.
Canada			
Visiting fellowships	1960-97	Various fields in education	About 4 p.a.
Research fellowships	1965-97	Bring scholars of established reputation for research with mutual benefits	Usually 3 – 7 p.a.
India			
Visiting fellowships later short-term visits by senior educationalists	1962-78, 1988-89	Encourage exchange of experience among senior educators	31 awards in total
New Zealand			
Prestige fellowships	1960-88	Bring scholars of eminence to research and lecture	About 3 awards p.a. in total in both categories
Administrative awards	1960-88	For administrators in education expected to occupy key role	
Zimbabwe/Central African Federation	1960-64	To support education in the Federation	2 in total

studies programme from the University of New England in Australia. Sheath served as a member of the Lockwood Commission which planned the post-federation University of Zambia whose department of correspondence studies was modelled on University of New England practice.[29]

Britain has offered four kinds of fellowship programme, two of which have survived. The first category of fellows were for the "scholars of high distinction" referred to in the 1959 Oxford conference. Fellows came for a year, tended to bring their families with them, and usually cost more than scholars. They balanced, in different ways, their own interests and those of their host universities. One Canadian professor of English who spent a year in Oxford gave four lectures, completed a novel, and described it as an *annus mirabilis* that included twenty plays, three concerts, six ballets and nine operas. An Australian professor at the University of Sussex reported that, with his host, they had transformed the faculty; the latter confirmed that he had "engaged himself in the affairs of the ... Faculty with quite extraordinary enthusiasm".[30] With reductions in the budget, and rising costs, the commission suspended them in 1980; the suspension became permanent. The last of the fellows, who travelled from Perth to Hull, reported gratefully and wistfully on their value in enabling "links to be forged between members of departments separated by many thousands of miles". He regretted their ending but with almost British restraint thought it would be discourteous to comment on this publicly.[31]

Medical fellowships were instituted alongside the medical scholarships launched in 1965 and were initially at three levels: visiting professors were expected to be playing a leading role in education within their own countries; senior medical fellows would hold chairs or be heads of department; medical fellowships were for clinicians with a postgraduate degree who needed a course to help their development as teachers and researchers.[32] They were available to both the industrialised and the developing Commonwealth. The programme was later simplified so that there was a single category of medical fellows. Usually between forty and sixty medical awards were offered each year between 1968 and 1995, with the largest numbers coming from India. Like the medical scholarships, these were swept away in the mid-1990s. In contrast the academic staff fellowships, introduced for mid-career university staff in 1968, have remained part of the commission's programmes although restrictions have been placed from time to time on the universities eligible to nominate candidates. In 2000 the commission introduced a new brand of professional awards for people in occupations other than higher education. Awards were in six areas: education, engineering, environment, governance, public health and technology. Professional fellows were nominated by, and attached to, an agency within Britain with the idea of benefiting both host and fellow.[33] In 2003, for example, Wilson Tamakloe, of the Ghanaian Protection Agency spent three months attached to the Environment Agency in Britain to look at their information systems. He was able to apply what he had seen to coastal zone and oil spill management at home, and more broadly when he was promoted two years later. For its part the Environment Agency was sufficiently convinced of the interest and value of the scheme to continue bidding for fellowships in succeeding years. Similarly, Paul Chunga went from his job as an environmental health office Malawi to the Scottish Environmental Protection Agency and other Scottish bodies working in public health. Despite the differences between Scotland and Malawi he concluded that "The knowledge and skills gained in all fields are very relevant to the Malawian situation and they will be used to develop the environmental health profession in Malawi in order to raise the environmental health status of all Malawians".[34]

Fellowship schemes proved less robust than scholarships: university teachers have probably needed them less in the academic small world created by the rapid fall in the real costs of communication and travel.[35] Whereas scholarships were designed primarily to benefit the nominating country, the reverse seems to have been true of many fellowships. Conceived as a device for sharing experience throughout the Commonwealth they seem in practice, and with the important exception of the British academic and medical awards, to have been used to bring distinction into the institutions of the awarding country, with a high percentage of awards going to fellows from the north rather than the south.

The next chapter sets these stories in the context of Commonwealth universities and of international student mobility.

CHAPTER TWO

PURPOSES: THE PLAN IN ITS CONTEXT

The Oxford conference recommended that awards should be mainly in the academic field and that "an important role in the selection and placing [of scholars and fellows] should be played by institutions of higher learning and by members of the academic community who work in them".[1] These communities were small and the education ministers' vision of academic self-help throughout the Commonwealth was a bold one at a time when its universities were, by twenty-first century standards, modest in size and even aspiration. Britain had twenty-nine universities, enrolling 4 per cent of the age group. Canada had 114,000 university-level students, or 11 per cent, but had only eight universities with over 5,000 students, and limited opportunities for postgraduate study. In the south, India had less than forty universities and just over a million students; Pakistan about 125,000. In the rest of the developing Commonwealth, outside South Africa, a dozen universities had less than 10,000 students between them (table 2.1). But despite these modest numbers, pledges were made from east and west Africa and southeast Asia alongside India.[2] Commonwealth universities and the patterns of international student mobility were about to change, and in their turn those changes were to shape the scholarship plan.

Universities in the Commonwealth

While the Commonwealth has developed and adapted as a political institution, its systems of higher education have changed just as dramatically. As well as being modest in scale, higher education had what now look like modest expectations. It had been neglected in the colonial period so that, in 1950, for example, "with one exception in Tanganyika, there [were] no African officers holding higher administrative, professional or technical posts in any of the African territories outside West Africa". Malaysia and Singapore had moved further, with 15 and 23 per cent of senior posts localised, while the figures in the West Indies were between 50 and 60 per cent.[3] One explanation of the neglect lays responsibility on colonial officials:

Table 2.1 Commonwealth universities in the south 1960

University or college	Students			Staff	
	men	women	total	total	of whom local
Africa					
University College, Ghana	638	47	685	175	34
Royal Technical College, Nairobi, Kenya	285	48	333	60	4
University College, Ibadan, Nigeria	1,173	79	1,252	205	57
University of Nigeria, Nsukka [a]	222	33	255	n/a	n/a
University College of Rhodesia and Nyasaland	136	73	209	70	5
Fourah Bay College, Sierra Leone	269	33	302	65	16
South Africa - 6 universities [a,b]	14,043	4,808	18,851	n/a	n/a
Makerere University College, Uganda	844	68	912	136	14
Africa total	17,610	5,189	22,799	n/a	n/a
Asia					
University of Ceylon [a]	2,548	1,136	3,684	n/a	n/a
University of Hong Kong	1,035	370	1,405	218	53
India 37 universities [a]	n/a	n/a	1,042,269	54,615	n/a
University of Malaya (Kuala Lumpur)	505	149	654	75	29
University of Malaya (Singapore)	1,259	443	1,702	164	74
East Pakistan - 2 universities [a,c]	53,929	3,738	57,667	n/a	n/a
West Pakistan - 4 universities [a,d]	n/a	n/a	67,473	n/a	n/a
Asia total	n/a	n/a	1,174,854	n/a	n/a
Caribbean					
University College of the West Indies, Jamaica	577	315	892	167	61
University College of the West Indies, Trinidad	67		67	n/a	n/a
Caribbean total	644	315	959	n/a	n/a
Europe					
Royal University of Malta	224	19	243	66	62
Total			1,198,855		

Source: Carr-Saunders, *New universities*, table 1 and appendix 9 except where shown

Notes: a. Source is *Commonwealth universities yearbook*; b. omitting University of South Africa as figures are generally for full-time students; c. including constituent and affiliated colleges; d. including Islamia College, recognised, affiliated, and constituent colleges

They had usually graduated at one of the older universities from which they carried away agreeable memories rather than professional accomplishments or enduring intellectual interests. They had little understanding of the part played in the modern world by universities and of the importance of the professions for which universities are a preparation, and to them the idea of transplanting to the regions where they worked the only type of university known to them doubtless seemed fantastic. Between British officials with this background and the young and ambitious local intellectual elite there was little or nothing in common; certain virtues, probity, justice and devotion to duty, were widely exhibited by the former, but understanding of, and sympathy with, the student class were not among them.[4]

Changes in policy came slowly. There had been a shift in British policy with the Asquith commission on higher education in the colonies, set up in 1943. It argued not only for the expansion of higher education but also for a broad, rather than narrowly instrumental, educational process. "Pride of place is given by Asquith to the quality of education to be provided and the standard of the degree" with the aim of producing "men and women with the standards of public service and capacity for leadership which self-rule requires".[5] The commission wanted universities that would produce "not only doctors, but educated doctors; not only agriculturalists, but educated agriculturalists; and to this end Universities minister far more effectively than specialised institutions".[6] Sir Christopher Cox, education adviser at the colonial office, wanted them modelled on Oxbridge;[7] in its early years undergraduates at the University of Ghana sweated appropriately in their gowns. More instrumental voices were sometimes heard. When the House of Lords discussed the work of the scholarship commission in 1963, Lord Peddie, chairman of the cooperative party, argued that "it is not the lawyer or the politician or the budding Prime Minister that they want: I imagine they have as many of these as they need at the moment. They need technicians, agriculturalists, people versed in the simple rudiments of business and administration. And they must have these coming to this country, not in their hundreds but in their thousands". (His preference for technicians may have been a narrow view but it was prescient: by the 1990s some 12,500 students were coming to Britain under just such a technical cooperation and training programme.)[8]

The creation of universities to develop a local elite did not imply such numbers and the British government did not see this as an appropriate function for the scholarship plan. In 1961 Carr-Saunders, who had served on the Asquith commission, saw a quite limited need for university expansion:

the obvious policy is rapidly to expand numbers in the existing colleges and universities. If this were done in Hong Kong, Malaya (with the possibility of two universities), and in the West Indies (with two branches for its college) there seems to be no immediate need for new foundations. In Ghana there is the problem of the Kumasi College of Technology, which is recognized by London University as preparing for degrees in engineering; the College might be brought within a federal university along with the University College. If the University of East Africa were to come into being with three constituent colleges, there would be no need for more university provision for some time to come. The future of Central Africa is clouded by uncertainty about its political organization, but owing to the paucity of secondary schools for Africans, there will be for some years ahead an insufficient supply of African candidates, with qualifications for admission to a university, to justify a new foundation. Only in Nigeria is it urgent that new universities should be founded at once.[9]

Bolder views were soon heard. Sir Arthur Lewis, later to win the Nobel prize for economics, was vice-chancellor of the University of the West Indies from 1960 to 63. "He was not an easy man, nor did he pretend to be. ... He used a speed-boat whose ripples sometimes rocked the canoes in which we followed, but how good it was to move with him as captain from the sheltered anchorage of colonial dependence to an implacable Atlantic".[10] He steered the university from being a single, residential, campus, associated with the University of London, to a freestanding institution, serving all the territories across its region and saw its expansion as a necessity for the economic development of the region. He criticised the view that

> Here in the West Indies our ideas of university numbers still belong to eighteenth century thinking. Great Britain has the smallest proportion of university students of any advanced country in the world, and yet, if we had in the University College the same proportion of university students as Great Britain our number would be 20,000 students, instead of our present number of less than 1,000. Even when we achieve the current target of 2,000 students, we shall be taking in only one-half of one per cent of each generation. We do not, of course, need to have the British target, which is 6 per cent in universities, but experience shows that countries at our level of development need to have an absolute minimum of 1 per cent university trained, accompanied by 10 per cent in secondary schools—the richer countries ranging from 20 to 40 per cent in secondary schools ... It is pretty clear that even, if looking ten years ahead, we set ourselves a target of 5,000 students by 1970, that figure would prove much too small.[11]

In response to views of this kind, higher education was to grow rapidly across the Commonwealth. In India it "enjoyed its golden period during the 1960s (with the real expenditure increasing at an annual rate of 11 per cent)".[12] By 1975 Commonwealth Africa had twenty-five universities with some 56,000 students. (South Africa had 70,000.) But the oil price rise of the mid-1970s and the depression of the 1980s checked this advance. Even in India, where enrolments have tended to rise inexorably, undergraduate numbers fell from 2.8 million in 1970 to 2.4 million in 1980.[13] Quality suffered too. By the early 1990s most of Africa's universities were "a mere shadow of their former glory: drained of teaching staff, lacking in equipment and teaching materials, housed in degenerate infrastructure, surrounded by an air of demoralization and incipient decay".[14] The World Bank was arguing for a reduction in university enrolments.[15] By 2005 the Commission for Africa looked more positively at universities "which ought to be the breeding grounds for the skilled individuals whom the continent needs", though it gave them only about three pages of attention in 400. But it again reported that "many of Africa's higher education institutions are in a state of crisis. They lack physical infrastructure, such as internet access, libraries, textbooks, equipment, laboratories and classroom space. ... They lack human resources, such as teachers, lecturers, and administrative and managerial systems".[16] Much of the Indian picture is brighter: "the country is self-sufficient in higher learning. Indians do not have to go abroad to study in order to qualify for high positions in government. .... What is more, professionals trained at Indian universities can easily secure employment in any of the developing and developed countries of the world".[17] At the same time numbers have grown faster than budgets, faster than the national economy, and concerns about quality have remained consistently high.

Universities face a paradox. They need to expand in order to respond to the growing demands of society for teaching, research and service; but with limited resources expansion jeopardises their quality. More does not inexorably mean worse; more with the same resources is likely to.

The process of university expansion has been driven partly by demand, partly by changing expectations of what universities can do for society. The rate of expansion can be inferred from tables 2.1 and 2.2: over less than half a century India's students grew from one million to over 10 million, Uganda's 912 to 88,000 despite a civil war, and Trinidad's from 67 to more than 16,000. Enrolments of women, starting from a lower base, have risen faster than those of men. The demand for expansion has come from several directions. As secondary education expands, growing numbers of school leavers want to go on to university. They, and their parents—

voters—see this as the royal road to prosperity. Public and private employers alike want an educated workforce. Politicians need and want to respond to these pressures; over the last half century the former colonies wanted to localise jobs held by expatriates. (India had largely finished this job by 1947 but old colonialists take time to fade away: in the mid-1970s there were still old India hands in the expatriate civil service in Botswana.) Demand could run ahead of planning:

> The hallmark of Indian higher education since independence has been growth. Student numbers have grown from 174,000 in twenty-eight universities and 695 colleges in 1950 to 3,948,000 in 144 universities and 6,912 colleges in 1989 - a growth rate of almost 10 per cent a year for a forty year period. ... Expansion has continued despite a variety of policy statements and reports that have indicated that continued growth is not necessary and results in a misallocation of resources. Virtually every official commission has recommended against further expansion.[18]

A new orthodoxy was to reinforce the demands for expansion. By the 1990s it was widely assumed that a network of national universities was needed in the interests of locally based research, to meet the demand for higher education, and as a driver of economic development. Knowledge was increasingly seen as a driver of growth and a factor of production alongside the more traditional land, labour and capital. The dialogue shifted over ten years. In a report concentrating mainly on the problems of higher education, the World Bank made a strong but essentially narrow case in 1994:

> Higher education contributes to human resource development in many ways. Investment in higher education can be a key contributor to a country's economic growth. Higher education institutions have the main responsibility for training a country's professional personnel, including the managers, scientists, engineers, and technicians who participate in the development, adaptation, and diffusion of innovations in the economy. Such institutions should create new knowledge through research and advanced training and serve as a conduit for its transfer, adaptation and dissemination.[19]

This view of the purposes of higher education reflects what was happening at the time at least in middle-income countries. Both Malaysia and Singapore, for example, have vigorously expanded higher education as one route towards creating advanced industrialised economies, with a heavy emphasis on science and technology. By 2002, the World Bank was taking a broader view and not only reaffirmed "the emerging role of know-

Table 2.2 Higher education enrolments: some Commonwealth countries

all in thousands

	1960		1970		1980		1990		2000	
	total	f%	total	f%	total	f%	Total	f%	total	f%
Ghana	2.7	18	5.4	14	16.4[a]	21	9.6[b]	22	54.1	34
Kenya	0.3	n/a	7.8	n/a	13.0	n/a	31.3[b]	n/a	98.6	44
Nigeria	2.7	7	15.6	15	150.1	n/a	335.8[c]	24	699.1	43
South Africa	51.9	32	82.7	n/a	n/a	n/a	439.0	44	644.8	55
Zambia	0	0	1.4	15	8.1[c]	22	15.3	n/a	24.6	32
Hong Kong	8.5	40	25.5	30	38.2	26	85.2[d]	40	n/a	n/a
India	1097.2	17	2903.6	n/a	3545.3	26	4951.0	33	9404.5	39
Malaysia	2.6	26	17.4	27	57.7	39	121.4	45	549.2	51
Pakistan[e]	149.1	12	221.7	21	156.6	27	336.7	33	385.5	43
Australia	80.7	27	179.7	33	323.7	45	485.1[a]	53	845.1	54
Britain	178.8	c35	601.3	33	827.1	37	1258.2	48	2024.1	55
Canada	142.1	n/a	642.0	40	888.4	50	1196.8	54	1212.2	56
New Zealand	19.9	34	n/a	n/a	76.6	41	111.5	52	172.0	59

Source: UNESCO *Statistical yearbook*, various years, UIS online database
Notes: f% is percentage of women; Some figures are for nearest available year. a. 1981; b. universities only; c. 1989/90; d. 1991; e. 1979, 1989/90, 2002/3

ledge as a major driver of economic development" but also argued for "a balanced and comprehensive view of education ... that includes not only the human capital contribution of tertiary education but also its critical humanistic and social capital building dimensions and its role as an important global public good".[20] University expansion in the interest of the knowledge economy has become the new mantra.

In fifty years higher education in the developing as in the industrialised world has moved from being an elite activity to something seen as a necessity for economically competitive societies and good governance. The proportions of the age group now going on to university in some countries of the south are similar to those entering secondary education half a century back. Universities themselves have changed. We go on, in later chapters, to examine how far the work of Commonwealth scholars has reflected, or contributed to, those changes.

Student mobility

Most universities are set up to meet national needs. But, from their medieval beginnings, they have attracted students from across national borders, who have travelled abroad to study either as a matter of personal choice or as a response to institutional or national policy. Individuals have been attracted by better courses than those available at home, or ones that were simply different. Specialist courses, available only in metropolitan or large countries, have attracted students for their intrinsic interest and for their value as a career path. At the same time, one of the enduring features of universities across the centuries has been to provide an enjoyable lifestyle for a minority of privileged young people;[21] student mobility offers an extra international frisson. For my own generation a postgraduate year in America was a rite of passage. (Not universal: I went to look after refuse containers at London County Council instead.)

Universities have their own institutional reasons for attracting international students: to recruit the brightest, to seek international cross-fertilisation, to keep up the numbers in their own particular specialisms. Some courses are viable only if they recruit internationally. Universities have, historically, sought universality. The structure of university funding may help encourage international recruitment. In Britain and Australia, for example, universities have since the 1980s enjoyed a freedom to determine their own fees for international postgraduate students even though governments have retained control over the level of fees for home students studying for a first degree.

Governments in their turn may share their universities' wish to attract able students. Just as its predecessor backed the creation of Commonwealth scholarships in 1959 so in 2004 the British government set up a new programme of Dorothy Hodgkin awards in the sciences in the interest of its own universities. Sometimes, despite their rhetoric, countries had national interests for wanting foreign students to stay. Canada saw itself as benefiting from the Commonwealth plan because it attracted able British graduate students into its universities who then never went home.[22] Countries sending scholars overseas, too, have done so for reasons of national educational interest, to acquire skills not available in their own institutions.

Governments have used scholarships within a political agenda that goes beyond the educational one. In the early discussions about CSFP, Commonwealth cohesion was seen as one of its driving forces. Both Britain and Canada have demonstrated their continuing commitment to Commonwealth ties by recruiting students from the industrialised as well as the developing Commonwealth, treating the plan for much of its history as being in some ways different from an aid programme (see chapter 5). History, along with politics, has helped determine the patterns of student mobility. India has attracted cohorts of foreign students from its own diaspora in Fiji, Malaysia and Mauritius. Broader political objectives have led governments to fund scholarships: governments want friends. This was always implicit in British support for the plan, eventually made explicit by the foreign and Commonwealth Office when it told the scholarship commission in 1995, in relation to the old Commonwealth, "specifically to identify ... future leaders, decision makers and opinion formers from around the world. Thereby to further the UK's long-term political, diplomatic, commercial and other interests through the cultivation of influential friends overseas".[23]

Until 1990 the politics of student mobility have to be seen against the backdrop of the cold war. Cultural policies aimed to keep newly independent countries aligned with the west, not the east. A review of British policy commented, for example, that alongside the need "to attract the best students and to secure influence abroad, there are also common responsibilities towards Third World nations and a shared interest in winning 'the battle for the minds of men' against totalitarian regimes and military dictatorships".[24] For Australia, support for the Colombo plan of educational aid, originally set up in 1950, was seen as a way of checking the influence of China in Asia with the added benefit of colourwashing the white Australia policy, in place till 1967.[25] In the United States it was argued in Congress in 1985 that there was a need for a scholarship programme "that could tell the world that the U.S. was interested in educating Third World children of the poor, and that this activity was not a monopoly of the Soviet bloc countries".[26] The Soviet Union made much of its scholarship programme and boasted that its African and Asian students returned home in contrast with common American practice. Despite western concerns, UNESCO figures show that the Soviet programme was in fact modest in size; in 1980, for example, the USSR had 63,000 foreign students against USA's 312,000.[27]

Scholarship programmes, like CSFP, provide one mechanism for encouraging student mobility. Many students now manage without them: figures from both Australia and Britain suggest that self-funding students, with their costs met mainly by their families, may outnumber those funded through scholarship schemes.[28] With public or private funding, just as universities have expanded, so their overseas student numbers have grown over the last fifty years. Numbers in Britain doubled in three decades out of four; in the 1990s they increased almost threefold. Australian numbers have increased even more rapidly in the last fifteen years as the country has marketed its international education with aggressive success. (See table 2.3.) At the same time there have been geographical changes in student movement which mean that, while Commonwealth flows of students are a consistent part of the story, mobility within regions has become steadily more important.

Tensions and intentions

The scholarship plan has formed a part, though never the major part, of student mobility within the Commonwealth. Its functions, which have changed and developed over its history, can be examined from the standpoint of the Commonwealth itself, of the universities and other institutions that have administered and benefited from it, of individual scholars and fellows, and of national governments. The plan has been shaped by the interplay between these various actors. We look at each of them in turn.

The plan has consistently attracted Commonwealth interest. It started with grand hopes and high aspirations. The language of the 1960s has a lost visionary tinge that reflected a particular sense of the Commonwealth: "We should think of these scholarships not simply as part of a method of technical assistance, but as a means of increasing our knowledge of one another and strengthening our mutual appreciation".[29] As proposals for the plan were being negotiated, the British made much of Commonwealth cohesion and the Canadians much of the principle of reciprocity.

The 1959 conference has been followed by a sequence of Commonwealth education conferences, from New Delhi in 1962 to Cape Town in 2006, at which education ministers have looked regularly and benignly on the plan. They commissioned three reviews of its progress, at ten-yearly intervals. But its achievements are more modest than the early hopes. Inevitably it has not held together a quite different Commonwealth from the one imagined by Diefenbaker and Macmillan in the 1950s. Nor has it expanded in pace with the growth of higher education in the north or the south; rather, it has become steadily more exclusive. At the time of writing it sits alongside vastly bigger, regional, programmes: 71,000 students come to Britain from Europe each year, only 69,000 from the Commonwealth. The European Union's ERASMUS programme reaches 144,000

Table 2.3: Foreign students in selected countries

	Britain	Canada	Australia	New Zealand	India	United States	France	USSR	Russian Federation
1960	12,410	7,251	4,991	514	3,606	53,107	27,123	n/a	
1970	24,606	22,263	7,525	2,495	7,804	144,708	34,500	27,918	
Decadal increase (%)	98	207	51	385	116	172	27	n/a	
1980	56,003	28,443	8,737	2,404	14,710	311,882	110,763	62,942	
Decadal increase (%)	128	28	16	-4	88	116	221	125	
1990	80,183	35,187	28,993	3,229	12,802	407,528	136,015	n/a	
Decadal increase (%)	43	24	232	34	-13	31	23		
2000	222,936	40,404	105,764	8,210	6,988	475,169	137,085		41,210
Decadal increase (%)	178	15	265	154	-45	17	1		

Source: UNESCO, *Statistical yearbook*, various years, UIS online database

students a year across Europe, in contrast with the 1,500 Commonwealth scholars across the whole of the Commonwealth. Australia, Canada and New Zealand now recruit most of their international students from outside the Commonwealth.

Two kinds of institution have shaped the history of the plan—universities and the commissions, committees and ministries that have administered it. With its quest for "academic excellence" the plan has had a resonance for universities in both the south and the north. University expansion within the newly independent Commonwealth created an immediate demand for its alumni. The British academic scholarships and fellowships represented one additional response to that demand. The institutions administering the plan have borne even more directly upon it than the universities. Ministries of education, in their capacity as nominating agencies, have determined whose names should be put forward as potential scholars. As the industrialised countries have provided the great majority of awards so the committees' and commission's policies have been all-important in the south as well as in the north.

Commonwealth scholarships and fellowships have usually been made to individuals, and not to targeted groups of them, so that much of the story is of individual aspiration and achievement. This scattergun approach means that, from an individual perspective, the function of the plan can be defined simply as "to study abroad" and often "to get a degree". Unlike more targeted scholarship programmes it has not aimed to lift able students out of poverty or to train a cadre of staff for a particular institution. To see how it worked we therefore need to examine what common factors there were in the selection of scholars and fellows, what they wanted to study, and where they wanted to do so, and to look at these in the light of their experience while they were studying abroad. The record of individual careers makes it possible to look at the achievements of the plan and to gauge the strengths of the various charges made against it.

Government decisions, and shifting policies, have been all-important in determining the nature and scale of the plan. From the outset, governments differed in their expectations with tensions between the north and the south about the plan's key purposes. Within the south governments have interpreted it in a variety of different ways, some seeing it as a means for training the civil service, some as a mechanism for university development, and some as a scheme essentially for individuals, of little national importance. They were initially enthusiastic to offer awards—an enthusiasm that has fallen away, partly for reasons of cost, partly for lack of demand. In the north, Canada assumed that scholars in the humanities would dominate the early exchanges as the natural missionaries for internationalism. For its part Britain started by emphasising academic excellence as the criterion for selecting scholars and treating study within Britain as such a valuable experience that scholars were expected to stay there throughout their award, even in the extreme case of anthropologists wanting to do field work as part of a doctorate. Priorities have shifted to the extent that Britain now favours split-site degrees, demands evidence of development potential, and funds some scholars who do not get to visit the country.

For many years the British tried to finesse issues about the purpose of the plan, and possible conflicts between excellence and relevance, by arguing that they were seeking academic excellence and leaving it to member countries to determine any balance between the types of applicants they put forward. For Eric Ashby, who was heavily involved in setting up the commission in Britain, "The prime purpose of the scholarships is to consolidate the Commonwealth and in particular to establish a greater cohesion among educated people in the Commonwealth".[30] It quickly became clear that there were tensions between this idea and the immediate demands for higher education in the interest of economic development.

Skirmishes were fought over undergraduate awards and over the practical relevance of scholarships. The British brief for the Commonwealth education ministers' conference in 1962 recognised that the smaller colonies were getting little out of the plan and needed undergraduate awards, which Britain did not want to fund through the plan.[31] At the conference itself Ghana argued on similar lines for awards to be available at undergraduate level and in technical colleges, with support not just from small territories but from India, Kenya and Pakistan among others. But the minority group of Australia, Britain and Canada refused to change, kept hold of the purse strings, and justified their position on grounds of flexibility and of university autonomy.[32] Tensions continued between the idea of academic excellence and the claims of developmental priority. In 1974 the Canadians still saw the plan "as it was originally conceived ... namely as an exchange of young people of high intellectual promise among members of the Commonwealth, serving to promote human development at a cultural and scientific level". It saw "a danger in the intrusion of questions of 'relevance' into scholarly areas" and argued that "the aims of technical training and middle-management, however relevant to developmental assistance, should not be met at the expense of the intellectual and human side of the present Commonwealth and Scholarship Plan".[33] Twenty years later the British reaffirmed their long-standing position: "The Commission tries in its selections and placements, to effect a proper balance between excellence and pertinence. Of its own initiative it places no limits upon the subjects in which overseas countries make their nominations, believing that they are the best arbiter of their own need".[34] Britain formally adopted developmental relevance as a criterion for selection only after 2000.

Debates about purpose spilt over into issues of control. Repeatedly countries nominating candidates wanted awarding countries to accept their order of preference among them. Within a programme of medical awards, Britain and India consistently disagreed about the mechanisms for identifying and selecting candidates. The main awarding countries have rarely been prepared to cede the principle that the awarding country had the final say on the selection of candidates from among the applicants put forward.

Alongside the tensions about purpose and control there has been an ambivalence about its main target audiences. University staff were always part of the audience. By 1982 one of the plan's functions was formally defined as to "assist universities and other leading tertiary institutions in developing countries of the Commonwealth to build their own capacity for post-graduate study and research".[35] But this was not the sole purpose and, at the outset, in the Commonwealth relations office in London, "The general feeling was that the scholarships should be used to attract potential leaders—whether in the educational field or more generally in public life—in the same way as the Rhodes, Harkness, Fulbright, etc schemes".[36] Industry and commerce were little mentioned in the early documents but later accounts begin to talk of people like Chittaranjan Debnath who had been improving jute technology in India since his scholarship in 1978 or Joram Mewsigye, a Ugandan banker, who had worked for his bank on rural credit since gaining his master's in 1993. In Barbados solar roof panels were successfully developed by one Commonwealth alumnus, the university's professor of chemistry, and marketed by another who had moved from a doctorate in statistics to running a business consultancy.[37]

Analysis of the plan in terms of purpose, audience, control and outcomes needs to take account of three consistent lines of criticism of northern domination, of elitism, and of bias, particularly against women.

From the outset the plan's administrators tried to encourage award holders to go home once they graduated. Commonwealth ministers of education in 1964 identified, "the recurrent difficulty of inducing some scholars to return home on completion of their tenure" and commented that the industrialised countries had "complained most strongly about this problem". One critic from the University of New South Wales claimed that, "for Australia the net result has been loss rather than gain: good men had not returned to Australia and Britain had done a very good thing in buying these brains".[38] The brief for the British delegation at the same meeting noticed that "Some disquiet has been expressed by representatives of overseas universities at a tendency of their best graduates to pursue their postgraduate work in Britain, with or without the aid of the Plan, with the result that the building up of strong schools of research in their own universities is being hampered".[39] The evidence from a number of surveys is assessed in chapter 8.

It is difficult to weigh charges of elitism and the extent to which membership of an elite has been a condition or a consequence of gaining a scholarship. Most Commonwealth scholars travel from the south to the north and the proportions doing so have increased over the years. The reputations of Oxbridge, Toronto and Sydney have acted as a powerful magnet. A significant minority have travelled between the rich countries of the Commonwealth. Some have travelled within the south, between developing countries, but numbers declined from the plan's first decade to its fifth. Far fewer scholars have travelled from the north to the south, often numbered in their ones and twos rather than the tens and twenties moving in the other direction. Ministers of education, even in the enthusiastic early days of the plan, noticed that "full advantage had not so far been taken of the awards offered by some of the developing countries".[40] Limited academic opportunity is one explanation. When Alastair Niven, as a young Cambridge graduate went to Ghana in 1967, he was the only student in the English faculty doing a master's course in African literature. Scepticism and active discouragement may be another: one Barbadian historian of Africa felt that he had been discouraged from applying for a scholarship to Nigeria.[41] There have been practical and financial difficulties too. Host countries pay a living allowance to overseas students which the latter may find inadequate: the commission in Britain, for example, for many years subsidised the stipend paid to British scholars in India and Sri Lanka who claimed they could not make ends meet. (Niven was luckier and found himself well off on his grant paid in Ghanaian cedis.) We come back in chapters 7 and 8 to questions of elitism, and of scholars' experience as they travelled north or south.

Women, or their neglect, have been a problem from the beginning. When the house of commons was debating the Commonwealth scholarship bill, Joan Vickers, the conservative MP for Devonport, made the point that

> Women from Colonial Territories were not present at the Oxford conference. I believe that there were four women from this country, one from Pakistan and one from Canada. I understand that those present commented that it was a great pity that women from the Colonies were not represented.[42]

The conference had started with even fewer. A circular letter to British high commissioners reporting on the conference explained:

> At the beginning of the Conference the U.K. delegation was the only one in which any women were included. (There was a rather acid comment on this in "The Times".) Two delegations were somewhat shamed by this—Canada and Pakistan—and telegraphed for women to be sent. It became a race as to which would arrive first, but the Canadian woman's plane was held up and the Pakistani woman beat her to the post. They were both very good.[43]

To give the founding fathers—with hardly any mothers—their due, Britain and Canada made awards to men and women from the beginning, and paid marriage allowances, at a time when Rhodes scholarships were restricted to single men. In the first ten years, of nearly 4,000 awards, only 11 per cent went to women.[44] Numbers rose slowly, particularly for fellowships where the low proportion of applicants reflected the gender balance within developing-country universities. Even by 2006 "the proportion of awards held by women remained stubbornly low ... accounting for an average of 44 per cent of the scholarships awarded".[45] In later chapters we look at the plan's stated policies and actual achievements on gender, setting this against the general evidence on women's participation in higher education, and in travel to study abroad.

The plan's change, scale and survival tell us something about the roles it has played within the Commonwealth's changing universities and the ways in which it has resolved its inherent tensions about purpose, control, and audience. They help us towards answers, from various standpoints, to questions about the plan's changing functions and achievements. Those answers need to come from across the Commonwealth. But Britain has been the largest actor; it originally agreed to offer half the total number of awards and has in practice exceeded that proportion. Chapters 3 and 4 pick up the British story.

CHAPTER THREE

BRITAIN: ESTABLISHING THE PLAN

As he sailed back from the Commonwealth universities' congress in Montreal, Sir Douglas Logan, principal of the University of London, got talking with the South African high commissioner to London who was on the same ship, but had been at the trade conference in the same city. Logan learned from him about the proposal for Commonwealth scholarships that had been launched at the trade conference. The British ministerial delegation was apparently unaware that Commonwealth universities had been meeting in the same town only a week before, just as the universities had not picked up the seriousness of Smith's ideas. Logan, an idiosyncratic principal at the heart of the British university system, busied himself, found his colleagues knew little about the proposal, and wrote to the Commonwealth relations office asking how they proposed to move ahead and urging contact with the Association of Universities of the British Commonwealth (AUBC) and the Committee of Vice Chancellors and Principals, the two bodies representing university interests.[1]

Whitehall was already familiar with the proposal. In wanting something positive out of the trade conference, civil servants and ministers were aware of

> the Prime Minister's insistence on some new "institution" emerging from Montreal. He presumably wants this as a demonstration to the U.K. public of the closeness of our economic relations with Commonwealth Governments and particularly as evidence that a Free Trade Area in Europe does not mean that we would be drawing away from the Commonwealth economically. The trouble is that the Commonwealth very largely operates on the "old boy net" and there is pretty strong aversion in most Commonwealth countries to institutionalising our flexible arrangements, unless there is real practical advantage in doing so.[2]

In seeking something to have on show in Montreal, Whitehall wanted credit for what Britain was already doing for Commonwealth education, considered expanding teacher education in the Commonwealth, and with some reluctance decided to go along with the Canadian proposal for scholarships. This might be cheaper than simply asking universities and colleges to expand the number of places available to overseas students, which could lead to a demand for increased government funding. At the same time there were reservations about a Commonwealth-wide scheme. Officials thought that it was "of doubtful value to provide places in the United Kingdom for Commonwealth students who are likely to fail to achieve the qualifications they seek—as many do already".[3] India, too, was already recruiting African students with the "risk of Africans so educated becoming, on their return, focuses of discontent". Eventually, and more positively, it was argued that "for presentational reasons, the United Kingdom's aim should be to assume at least half the burden of any reasonable scholarship scheme which might be agreed upon at Montreal".[4] The Commonwealth relations office, which was making the running, had not, at this stage, considered in detail how the scholarships would be run, or consulted either universities or, it appears, the respected and influential education adviser to the colonial office.[5]

Setting up the plan

The British delegation came back from the Montreal trade conference with two jobs: to set up a Commonwealth conference on education in 1959 and to develop plans for educational cooperation within the Commonwealth including the scholarship plan. It was not seen as the most important proposal: early in 1959 it was estimated that Britain might spend £500,000 on its Commonwealth scholarships but £1.1 million on training Commonwealth teachers and subsidising British teachers who went to work abroad.[6] The Commonwealth relations office had to carry all these ideas forward. In doing so it needed to clarify the purpose of the proposed scholarships, to agree the mechanics for operating them in Britain and throughout the Commonwealth, and to identify the people who would do the work. The British academic community, mobilised by Logan, had ideas on most of these. From the beginning the plan had its political ends. Before the Montreal conference the government saw the possibility of "presenting the overall project as an important educational initiative in the West in the educational field, comparing favourably with the facilities offered by the Communist bloc in this sphere".[7] Civil servants and academics alike saw the plan as bringing benefits to the Commonwealth as an institution. Officials preparing for the Oxford conference considered "that there would be great advantage if a form of words could be agreed between all Commonwealth countries which would link the scholarships with our aim of strengthening Commonwealth relationships generally".[8] In the 1950s Commonwealth cohesion was seen as a political good and a phrase that tripped off ministerial and civil service tongues. Eden was worried about it in 1952.[9] Government reviews of policy in 1959 examined threats to Commonwealth cohesion at some length leading Norman Brook, then cabinet secretary, to define the need "to preserve and strengthen the cohesion of the Commonwealth" as one of the three aims of foreign policy, alongside countering the influence of the Soviet bloc and the maintenance of sterling and British trade.[10] Academics took it for granted that the plan would recruit the ablest students but beyond that stressed its value for the Commonwealth. Robert Aitken, vice-chancellor of the University of Birmingham, for example, reminded the Commonwealth relations office "that the main purpose of the scholarships was to strengthen Commonwealth cohesion".[11]

The mechanics of the plan turned out to be more contentious than its purpose. The first idea was that a committee of civil servants and university representatives should run the scheme but civil servants and ministers then changed track and decided a commission would be more appropriate.[12] Once it was agreed that a commission should be set up by statute, and work at arm's length from the government, it was necessary to decide who should provide its administration. One of the key players at this stage was Eric Ashby, master of Clare College, Cambridge, and vice-chairman of the AUBC who was to chair the planning committee that preceded the commission. He saw three possibilities: the British Council, the postgraduate awards committee of the Department of Scientific and Industrial Research or the AUBC. He rejected the first on the grounds that it was seen as an organisation for interpreting the British way of life and "as such regarded with some suspicion in the so-called under-developed Commonwealth countries". The second was concerned mainly with research. This left the AUBC which had the advantage of dealing with the whole Commonwealth on "terms of complete equality".[13] (That equality was to be emphasised when it changed its name to the Association of Commonwealth Universities (ACU) in 1963.) But it was not that easy and civil servants were divided on the choice between the British Council and the AUBC. They raised doubts about the AUBC's capacity, about its relations with colleges of advanced technology that were outside its membership, and about the appropriateness of the AUBC administering British money as it had a non-British chairman. The AUBC dismissed these arguments, pointing out that the foreign office was quite happy with its administration of Marshall scholarships.[14] A meeting in the Commonwealth Relations Office (CRO) resolved the problem, though at the cost of the vice-chancellors' present conceding that the British Council would have some functions and look after the money. Ten years after the event Logan remembered it like this:

> I am afraid that there is inevitably a certain amount of suspicion between the staff of the Association of Commonwealth Universities and the British Council which stems back to a major controversy in 1959 before the first Commonwealth Education Conference when the civil servants involved, principally Harry Lintott [Deputy Under Secretary, Commonwealth Relations Office], were undecided whether to trust the administration of the Commonwealth Scholarship Scheme to the Association or to the Council. We had a ding-dong battle one evening in the old CRO building from 9 pm until midnight when the combined forces of Eric Ashby [Cambridge], Rob Aitken [VC, Birmingham], Philip Morris [VC, Bristol] and myself carried the day against Paul Sinker [Director General, British Council] and Nancy Parkinson [Controller, Home Division, British Council]. I harbour no suspicion that the higher officers of the British Council have any improper designs about displacing the Association but there is undoubted friction in the lower ranks.[15]

Either his memory or the contemporary record was at fault as it does not show Nancy Parkinson as being present. She was there to fight the council's corner at other encounters and may have overplayed her hand at the time as she irritated civil servants by telling them how they should run their conference.[16]

Decisions about mechanics could be taken by civil servants while those about people went to ministers. In the autumn of 1959 they began to identify a chairman for the commission, with suggestions coming from Commonwealth relations, the colonial office, the board of trade and the ministry of education. The Commonwealth relations view was that:

> We want a distinguished figure (preferably not an academic) who will give prestige and authority to the scheme; but we do not want a pure figurehead, since the Commission will certainly have difficult questions of policy to determine and we want them to take full responsibility for the running of this large and complicated plan. ... Whoever we have must, of course, be acceptable to university opinion.

Iain Macleod, at the colonial office agreed about the qualities and floated the "rather unexpected name" of Herbert Morrison, the former labour home secretary, which "might go down well and would certainly attract some attention to the scheme, which is part of what we want". Eventually Lord Home, the Commonwealth relations secretary, put four names to the prime minister who duly selected Lord Scarbrough, the only fellow old Etonian on the list.[17]

The eleventh earl of Scarbrough brought the necessary prestige and authority buttressed by four knighthoods as well as a hereditary peerage. His day job was lord chamberlain, a post which combined looking after the Queen's household with censoring plays. Like seven of his thirteen colleagues on the commission he had served in the first world war. He then went on to an unremarkable career as a conservative member of parliament, while continuing to serve as an officer in the Yorkshire dragoons, building up a reputation as an efficient and decisive administrator. He left parliament in 1937 and went to India as governor of Bombay, returning to Britain and the army in 1943. But Scarbrough was more than a colonel, or in his case major-general, Blimp. While in India he was forced to respond to the Congress party's "Quit India" campaign by arresting its leaders but went on repeatedly and rightly to warn that it would be catastrophic for Gandhi to die in gaol. Neither the viceroy nor the prime minister were to be moved; Gandhi survived but the governor's career was blocked when Churchill promptly crossed him off his list of potential viceroys. As lord chamberlain Scarbrough went on to display more independence than his predecessors, easing restrictions on acceptable language in the theatre and lifting the ban on references to homosexuality. He even had more than a toehold in the academic world, serving as chairman of a postwar commission on African, Asian and Slavonic studies and of the governors of the School of Oriental and African Studies.[18]

Ministers went on to identify his colleagues and the constituencies that they should represent, ranging from universities to industry and trade unions and a single representative woman.[19] With a requirement that four should hold high academic office, and a limit of fifteen members, some had to represent more than one constituency. A suggestion in parliament that the commission should include some young men made things more difficult and had Lord Home minuting that in the interest of prestige the commission must,

> in my view, be composed of people who will carry weight in their own particular circles and command respect generally. The academic representatives must be experienced people with executive responsibilities, who can ensure that the scholars are accepted and properly treated by the universities, and this really limits us to Vice-Chancellors, Heads of Houses and the like.

He thought a young man in the arts might be acceptable and suggested Peter Hall, director of the Memorial Theatre at Stratford. Iain Macleod, at the colonial office dismissed that idea: "He is no doubt an excellent fellow, but I cannot see that he would bring anything of value to the Commission, and I feel that the appointment would arouse surprise without any compensating advantage".[20]

By February the list was agreed. Of the fourteen members, nine had studied at Oxford or Cambridge, two at Imperial and one at the Royal Technical College, Glasgow (now Strathclyde University). Their average age was 61. The representatives of industry and of the trade unions were non-graduates; as Sir Julian Pode had to leap from one ship to another while serving in the first world war, his education at HMS Conway may have been more relevant. As well as doubling for Wales and industry he could have done agriculture as well, if it had been on the list, as the owner of a pedigree herd of Guernsey cows as well as racehorses. Sir Cyril Hinshelwood brought academic distinction, as a Nobel Laureate and FRS. The vice-chancellors of Birmingham and Glasgow universities, the heads of two Oxbridge colleges, the principals of London University and the Battersea College of Technology together with the former director of the Glasgow Royal Technical College, provided the academic weight that Lord Home had sought. In terms of international experience two had served in India (and were soon to be joined by a third), two had experience of Australia and New Zealand, while Ashby was concurrently chairing a commission on higher education in Africa. One place was left vacant. Together there were four to represent universities, two from technical colleges, two from industry, one trade unionist, one scientist, one from the local education authorities, one from the British Council, and the lone woman.[21]

With the AUBC approved as the administering agency, its secretary-general headhunted an administrator from Manchester University, Edgar Temple, who was to stay with the plan for the next quarter century. He was able to put in place the framework of the plan in the light of the discussions at the Montreal and Oxford conferences and at an interim planning committee which met from September to November 1959. He later claimed:

> In effect they just handed me the Oxford Conference Report and said "please go and do it!" That's really what it was. And I had already on going back from Eric Ashby to Manchester via Chesterfield—I remember the leaning spire which I had never seen before that day—I had already used the old envelope in my pocket to work out how to run the scheme if I was involved and I used that envelope ever since.[22]

Following Oxford, and the envelope, it was agreed that Britain would offer awards throughout the Commonwealth, mainly but not exclusively at postgraduate level, in all disciplines, and to men and women, with marriage allowances for male scholars. The interim committee recommended that a panel of academic advisers should be set up to read and assess scholarship applications.[23] The Commonwealth Relations Office decided that, of 500 British awards, 150 would go to the old Commonwealth, 150 to the new, 150 to colonial territories with fifty in reserve, soon reduced to forty to allow an extra ten to Pakistan. High commissioners were given a provisional allocation on this basis. The £500,000 budget was confirmed.[24] There was no fixed quota by country. A rough allocation, based on population and region, was worked out for individual countries which were invited to nominate twice that number of candidates, but without any commitment by the British to a particular number of awards. The preparatory work was followed by the publication of a white paper in November, debates in parliament in November and December, and the passage of the Commonwealth Scholarships Act on 17 December 1959, only six months after the Oxford conference. The act quoted the conference report setting that as the context for the commission's work.

The legislation reflects the speed at which this had all happened. Through an oversight it left out any reference to the Channel Islands and the Isle of Man and, more seriously, capped British awards at 500 in number. An amending act was to follow in 1963 when the limit became a constraint; awards were made annually, for differing lengths of time, so that it was awkward to administer a cap on the total permitted number of award holders. The chairman and fourteen other commission members were to be appointed by the secretary of state and would have four jobs: to select scholars or fellows coming to Britain, to place them in universities and colleges, to select outward award holders, and to discharge other functions assigned to it. They would report to parliament annually. The commission had to comply with directions given by the secretary of state "provided that no direction shall be given for the selection or rejection of any particular person". (Curiously the act did not spell out which secretary of state was meant to direct the commission—Commonwealth relations or colonies.)

A set of directions was drafted by the Commonwealth relations and colonial offices, discussed with the chairman of the commission, and issued in March 1960. They referred to the conference's priority of finding "men and women who are capable of reaching the highest standard of intellectual achievement and who may be expected to make a significant contribution to life in their own countries". They emphasised postgraduate rather than undergraduate study, referred to adult education colleges, whose cause had been argued in parliament, and required "a reasonable balance between the arts and the sciences generally". Detailed allocation of awards round the Commonwealth was left to the commission subject to a "reasonable apportionment" among member countries and dependent territories. The directions specified that the AUBC would provide the secretariat and that the British Council would look after money and welfare.[25]

The Oxford conference had agreed that each independent Commonwealth country, and the remaining colonies and protectorates, would set up agencies to manage the plan. In order to get scholars in place by the new academic year in the autumn of 1960 it was necessary to make contact with all these agencies, to set up arrangements for selecting scholars, and to make contact with British universities. All this fell to the AUBC, and particularly to Temple. He moved into an office in Marlborough House, a grand if inconvenient palace in central London, despite hesitation by Ashby who was concerned that the absence of a lift would make things difficult for some commission members.[26] A booklet of *Information for 1960 scholars* was produced setting out, among other detail, the allowances to which they were entitled: £51 10s 0d (£51.50) (2008£878) per month for maintenance with an additional £16 13s 4d (£16.67) (2008£284) as a marriage allowance although that was balanced by a ruling that a scholar must pay for his wife's passage. Scholars could bring 100 kg or 16 cubic feet of baggage by sea or the free baggage allowance by air.[27]

The first five years

The commission settled into a regular pattern of activity. Applications for scholarships were received in the early year and sent to academic advisers for their comments. The commission established a selection committee from its own membership; generally the university-based commissioners sat on the committee but Scarbrough made a point of doing so himself. Boxes of applications were then delivered to committee members who met to make the final decisions, weighing advice from nominating agencies about their own priorities and recommendations from academic advisers, but making their own decisions on academic merit. Scarbrough had his boxes by hand as Temple would carry them across the road from Marlborough House to St James's Palace.[28] The administrative staff then placed scholars at universities throughout the country, told them of their good fortune, and left the British Council to get them to Britain. Once a year scholars, and their supervisors, reported on progress and the commission considered a digest of what they had said. An annual welcome programme was arranged for new scholars, later replaced for some years by regional conferences, but then reinstated. And, at least once a year, a group of commissioners met to interview applicants for outward scholarships.

In its early meetings the commission felt the need to make few decisions of policy. At the opening meeting members considered the draft directions from the secretary of state, which the chairman, Ashby and Logan had already seen, but after a brief discussion decided they had no comments to make.[29] There appears to have been a simple consensus that the quest for academic excellence and Commonwealth cohesion was an adequate guide for policy. Much of the business of meetings was taken up with detailed issues raised by individual scholars that in later years were to be dealt with by the secretariat. Minor issues ranged from the late arrival of forms delayed at London airport to Australian requests for a clothing allowance, eventually approved for scholars from Queensland and Northern Territories only.[30] Early in 1961 the commission appointed a medical adviser to be paid an annual honorarium of 25 guineas (£26.25) and a fee of 3 guineas (£3.15) per medical examination.[31] His job and his successors' were to grow. Despite these cautious beginnings, the civil service were worried that an autonomous body was using its autonomy. Only six months after the commission began its work a note from the cabinet office complained that

> there seems to be some evidence that the CSC are tending to regard themselves as trustees of the whole scholarship scheme as far as the United Kingdom is concerned, instead of being merely the selection and placing authority as specified in the Act. ... I imagine that it is the intention to keep the policy control in the hand of the Government, and in wording my minute of last week's meeting on the subject I have angled it this way.[32]

The commission's independence gave it freedom of action but this was subject to the same tensions about its purpose that were to be played out in CSFP as a whole: between serving as a practical demonstration of Commonwealth cohesion, or a means of rewarding intellectual promise, or a route towards development in the south (see chapter 2). Although debates about purpose were to be a recurrent theme in the development of the plan there were few overt discussions about them in the early years. They crept on to the agenda from an unexpected direction when scholars began to ask for authority to spend part of their time outside Britain. The Commonwealth relations office advised that there was nothing in the act to bar this but that if it increased costs then the commission should consult with them or with the colonial office, suggesting that "there would not be very many of these cases and that reference to the Department concerned would not be too burdensome for you".[33] A series of requests from scholars followed, particularly about field work, and it became clear that they raised issues that went beyond finance. Anthropologists and geographers argued that they were a necessary part of their academic disciplines. In contrast, at least one commissioner, who had spent most of his working life in India, thought this at variance with the plan's intentions, arguing that "much of the value of the scholarships lies in the fact that they bring scholars into close contact with the British way of life and thought. The period of such contact is all too short and I do not think we should very readily allow it to be shortened". With some difficulty, and against his advice, the commission managed to adopt a restricted policy by 1964: permission to do field work abroad would be given in quite exceptional circumstances, for a substantial period of more than six months and in neither the first nor the last term.[34]

Three other policy issues demanded the commission's attention and continued to do so for some years: the match between supply and demand of scholarships, allowances, and the duration of awards.

In looking at the match between supply and demand the commission was concerned with both the inward and the outward competitions—about scholars and fellows who came to Britain and about those whom it nominated to go abroad. Advice from Britons abroad could be discouraging. The British Council regional controller in Bombay thought that

> the main problem will be to pull these scholars up out of the ruck of foreign student life in England and the processes of student welfare: to give them standing and let them fend for themselves on the strength of it: to exact Rhodes-Scholar standards of conduct from them while allowing that many of them will not be Rhodes material and will in fact need the welfare which would be an impertinence to a Rhodes man.[35]

The commission found no reason to express doubts about the quality of its scholars in its early meetings and the selection committee commented specifically on the high standard of applicants from Australia and New Zealand. As supervisors' reports came in they were generally positive although with occasional reservations. Comments in 1962 on two scholars, for example, said in one case that his performance was "disappointing especially in relation to the strong reputation with which he came" to the university and another that he had "not shown the initiative expected of a PhD student".[36] But negative comments were in a minority and did not lead the commission to change its policies or its geographical allocation of scholarships. Logan was disappointed, however, with the first list of fellows to be invited to Britain who should have been "distinguished scholars of established reputation and achievement", nominated by British universities. He wanted publicity to make clearer the calibre of person to be nominated.[37] More often there was a mismatch in number for either the inward or the outward competition. In 1960 there were only three applicants for outward awards to east Africa and none for Malaysia; two years later there were none for awards to Ceylon. Even after five years, there were only thirty good candidates for thirty-six scholarships offered by Canada.[38]

Marriage and children's allowances were to trouble the commission for fifteen years. They were not paid within most government-funded scholarships in 1959, but were written into the Commonwealth plan from the outset. Despite treasury objections, civil servants agreed that:

> From the wider aspect of Commonwealth relations the majority of the Official Committee consider that there would be great advantage in providing a marriage allowance to Commonwealth scholars. Many of these will be coming to a completely new way of life and would be greatly helped to settle down and so get the most out of their stay here if they were able to bring their wives. It is important too not only from the personal aspect but also for the social structure of the country concerned that the wives of students from the newly independent and dependent territories should be enabled to develop socially and intellectually alongside their husbands.[39]

Allowances for the industrialised Commonwealth were necessary to compete with America. They were paid to men, provided that their wives were neither working nor themselves holding a scholarship. There seems to have been no discussion of allowances for husbands. Initially children's allowances were not paid as it was not considered "desirable to attract the married overseas student with family commitments to apply for an award, since he might be unable to benefit to the fullest extent from his stay in Britain".[40] The children might not benefit either. Parliament was warned that there was no point in spending money on "a whole lot of little children who will catch cold, and throw their brussels sprouts on the floor and will not remember a single thing about their journey to this country a few years after".[41] A dozen years later a Commonwealth academic fellow had the answer to that when she explained to the commission:

> As a woman Fellow I was not given the children's allowance. In spite of this I brought my children here and they have been in schools and college here and have enjoyed themselves in general. This has been such an enormous benefit to them that I think it was worth the expense. It has given them a knowledge of the world which is not limited to one small country. Although it has been a bit difficult for me ... it has also given me an opportunity to meet people and see part of the British way of life which I would never have seen otherwise.[42]

The commission was told that the treasury would not approve of allowances for dependants of women award holders. The regime was eased slightly after three years when evidence of hardship was used to increase the marriage allowance from a third to a half of the scholar's stipend and to introduce children's allowances. Gradually, too, the commission relaxed its rules on the date of marriage where, initially, men who married after applying for the scholarship would have to wait a year for the allowance.[43]

The commission was rapidly forced to address issues about the length of awards. It had originally expected that most PhD students would gain advanced standing, so that they could graduate in two years; in practice, by 1962 half the first cohort had applied to extend their award.[44] Undergraduate awards necessarily took three years and the commission was reluctant to provide awards for people to read medicine with a five-year commitment. Scholars, and university teachers, began to argue that three years was in practice too little for a doctorate: the case continued to be made and debated for the next half century, with no clear resolution.

Meanwhile, the commission made steady progress. Numbers on award rose from 178 in 1960 to 523 in 1964/65. (The increasing numbers of new awards are shown in table 3.1.) The commission got its amending act so that it might have more than 500 people on award at any one time, and applicants from the Channel Islands and the Isle of Man could apply. (The only one located to date was a Manxman, working for the Bechuanaland Protectorate civil service, who went to do a master's in economics in Canada; see chapter 8.) Despite initial concerns about the pressure on universities, it was proving possible to place students. Government confidence in the scheme, and a desire to have something to display at meetings of Commonwealth ministers, led to the new academic and medical programmes. The commission seemed confident about its priorities. In response to suggestions that there might be more, but shorter, awards the chairman wrote in 1962:

> The task entrusted to the Commission is to provide the best which this country has to offer in the way of higher education for those from Commonwealth countries selected for awards. It is for this high purpose that the Commission has received full co-operation from the Universities in this country, particularly in the giving of places to Commonwealth Scholars and in the interest in these scholars taken by university teachers.
>
> If we give in to the demands of Commonwealth governments for a quicker turn round of scholars—a demand which in certain cases we can well understand—we shall impair the prestige which Commonwealth Scholarships have already acquired and run the risk of a fall in the general quality of candidates for them.[45]

Table 3.1 New awards made by Britain 1961-2008

Year ending	New scholars	New fellows	Year ending	New scholars	New Fellows
1961	178	0	1985	319	94
1962	232	3	1986	381	118
1963	187	2	1987	318	132
1964	219	5	1988	263	97
1965	241	3	1989	369	113
1966	191	4	1990	286	102
1967	257	50	1991	309	106
1968	217	47	1992	314	82
1969	238	74	1993	297	99
1970	237	54	1994	261	79
1971	242	91	1995	297	106
1972	229	100	1996	264	75
1973	230	101	1997	223	64
1974	238	118	1998	242	81
1975	292	112	1999	249	88
1976	218	107	2000	255	87
1977	190	79	2001	165	75
1978	258	84	2002	231	69
1979	264	83	2003	374	100
1980	218	81	2004	451	125
1981	182	68	2005	445	132
1982	281	92	2006	384	118
1983	271	81	2007	405	132
1984	362	115	2008	524	118

Source: Appendix, ACU database
Note. From 2002 new categories of award, shown in table 4.2. are included in the totals but shared scholarships are excluded

People, politics and policies

With the number of awards and the budget relatively stable, Scarbrough was able to tell the secretary of state when he retired that "My successor will, I think, find that the Plan has got into its stride and that with the help of the other members of the Commission it will not present him with a very exacting task".[46] While his successor had, formally, to be appointed by the secretary of state, decisions this time were in practice left to civil servants. Various names were canvassed within the Commonwealth relations office but the choice was effectively made over dinner at the Athenaeum. In November 1962 the CRO consulted Logan "who really is the key man in all this". Sir Cecil Syers, secretary of the University Grants Committee, then rang to report on discussions at dinner with his chairman and the vice-chancellors of Bristol and Manchester. "All were agreed that Lord Kilmuir would be outstandingly good as the first choice".[47] He was duly appointed and took office in February 1963.

As Sir David Maxwell Fyfe he had been a successful lawyer, building up a reputation for immense hard work, and enhancing it with his performance as deputy chief prosecutor at the Nuremberg trials. He was home secretary from 1951 to 1954 when he became lord chancellor. In that job he was one of the few lawyers who argued that the Suez war was legal. Macmillan was then to dump him unceremoniously from his post, along with six other cabinet ministers, on his night of the long knives in July 1962. At this point, therefore, Kilmuir was 62, with excellent political connections, and time on his hands. His international experience, other than that in Germany, seems to have been limited to chairing the Malta round table conference in 1955 unless one includes the time when he was known as Dai Bananas as a Scottish secretary of state for Welsh affairs.

The commission membership was beginning to change. Civil servants noticed that it would be helpful if the commission "had at least one member with experience in an overseas university".[48] Logan, now deputy chairman, was playing a more active role in identifying members which he would go on doing for the next twenty years. In 1964, for example, he sounded out the Royal Society for a biologist to succeed Ashby, explaining that he had "a suspicion that the Commonwealth Relations Office ... usually consults the Royal Society when a place formerly held by a scientist on the Commission falls vacant". He wanted its help in identifying and encouraging a first-class scientist who was "not already burdened with commitments".[49] He made his views on commission membership clear in talking to the CRO:

> Some of the members, he said, were distinguished public figures. Some, though distinguished, were hard working academics. It was, in his view, important that there should be a sufficient number of the second class on the Commission to take on the paper work of selection of candidates, finding of places, oversight of progress etc. The merely distinguished could not be looked to for this important chore.

He wanted at least eight of the fourteen to be working academics "to take part in some of the grassroots work of the Commission and not simply involve attendance at its bi-monthly formal meetings".[50] His influence steadily took effect and the proportion of university teachers on the commission increased. One commissioner recalled his style of recruitment:

> Well I know how I was nominated and then appointed. I don't know about anybody else but I think I know exactly how I came into the frame. The person responsible was Jock Logan. He was in search of, not primarily a commissioner though this person would have to be a commissioner. He was in search of somebody to be on the selection committee, to do the work, and he wanted somebody in the humanities. And I think he decided that it would be useful to have a woman because at that particular stage, I think, the selection committee that did most of the work—incoming and outgoing—was otherwise going to be all male. And he was visiting All Souls, here in Oxford and talking with people he knew there and he said, "Who is there around the place who is in the humanities, and is a woman, and is sensible, and would be willing to put some real work into this?" and that's when my name came up and so they rang me up and said, "Can I come and talk to you?".[51]

Changes of government can bring changes of policy, people or style. A labour government was elected in 1964, bringing to power Harold Wilson, who had a reputation as a strong supporter of the Commonwealth which he dated back to a childhood holiday visiting relatives in Australia.[52] He immediately created a new ministry of overseas development with a powerful minister, Barbara Castle, in charge. It took over responsibility for the commission from the Commonwealth relations office. She was unimpressed with Kilmuir only to find that no term had been set to his appointment. The civil servants had little more to say in his favour than that he was "a most agreeable Chairman and made an excellent speech of welcome to the last intake of scholars" and that the case for keeping him was that he got on well with Logan who was "the de facto Chairman already".[53] Kilmuir died early in 1967, Logan ruled himself out of the succession, and the civil servants duly produced a long list of names only to be trumped by the junior minister who produced the name of Douglas Houghton, a former labour minister. The civil service were edgy about the appointment, particularly as Houghton was likely to become chairman of the parliamentary labour party, but the prime minister gave his approval and Houghton took up the post in May 1967.[54]

Houghton was very different from his predecessors. Like them he had served in the first world war but as a private soldier, enlisting and fighting in the trenches alongside Henry Moore, who became a lifelong friend.

After the war he had moved from a civil service post through trade union activity into politics. He acquired a national reputation during and after the second world war as a regular speaker on social security questions in a radio series entitled *"Can I help you?"*. Temple thought he was the best of the five chairmen he had served.[55] Houghton became chairman just as the government moved unhappily towards budget cuts in July, a run on sterling, and devaluation in November. He soon found himself out of sympathy with the commission's concentration on academic excellence alone as a criterion for awards. By this time he had become chairman of the parliamentary party, which gave him a reason to go because of his work load, while the occasion of his doing so was a disagreement about marriage allowances. In a bad-tempered and handwritten letter to Reg Prentice, who was now minister of overseas development, he explained:

> If I stayed as Chairman I would want to spend much more time than I can now spare on what we are supposed to be doing, & why.
>
> I am not an academic & I am impatient with too much learning for its own sake. Some of the things students are coming here to study are not justified as a form of economic aid. Some are even ridiculous. It is a world of "flannel" and I said so in an outburst of annoyance at the last meeting when it was decided on a vote (& against my view) to extend marriage allowances to students who hurried to marry after they are notified of the award but before leaving to take up the award. (The Indian mothers apparently want their sons to be properly wed before coming to England to study.)
>
> Are we in desperate straits or aren't we?
>
> Anyway, I'd rather not continue but do not wish to make it too difficult for others. I have the reason to give up as soon as you are ready with someone else.[56]

Prentice tried to mollify him, without success and his office expressed slightly defensive surprise:

> What is more to the point is Mr H's apparent view that it is invidious for us, in the present financial climate, to go on contributing to a scheme which goes much wider than the field of immediate economic development. This is a criticism which we, and the other overseas departments, in consultation with whom we take our policy decisions in respect of the scheme, must obviously take very seriously. There are strong arguments for the scheme as it stands. The long-term good-will it earns us, the "civilising" effect on overseas countries of having their young people mix with ours at post-graduate level, and the fact that our contribution helps to bring forth contributions from Canada and Australia, can all be cited. So can the very great technical skill with which Sir Douglas Logan and his academics op-

erate the scheme. When all is said and done, however this still remains on the face of it a somewhat "plushy" scheme, with more immediate appeal to those concerned with political aspects of policy than to managers of aid.

Given the commission's autonomy it was difficult to make changes, such us excluding certain subjects, or changing the character of the commission, or bearing down on its budget.[57] Houghton's brief challenge to the plan's main purpose brought no changes. Rather than attempting any, ministers reached for a safer candidate than an active politician and appointed Sir Saville Garner who was on the point of retiring as permanent under-secretary in the Commonwealth office and a former high commissioner to Canada. The only hesitation, on the part of civil servants rather than ministers, was that "he was not as eminent a public figure as Mr Houghton or … Lord Kilmuir, and that a good deal of importance was attached to a publicly known name"; his reputation in the Commonwealth outweighed that disadvantage.[58]

Garner had worked briefly as a schoolteacher after graduating from Cambridge but joined the dominions office in 1930 at the age of 22. He worked for J. H. Thomas, dominions secretary in the mid-1930s, who refused to call him Saville ("What sort of a fancy name is that?") and called him Joe instead, the name he used for the rest of his life. He had gone to Canada as British high commissioner

> at a nadir in Anglo-Canadian relations, caused by the Suez crisis and its aftermath. Suez horrified Garner and prompted him to offer his resignation, but he was persuaded to stay. His integrity, informality, and friendliness endeared him to Canadians, and enabled him to do much to repair the damage.[59]

He became chairman of the commission in May 1968 and was to stay there for nearly ten years.

By the mid-1960s the political context was changing and a different Commonwealth emerging. South Africa had left in 1961; setting a useful precedent the commission agreed that South African scholars could retain their awards till they graduated. (Two of them went on to distinguished careers in the law that illustrate the dilemmas faced by the South African diaspora. One returned and in due course became a high court judge, upholding the legal system in the dark years. He recalled that at Oxford "I realised what I, and we as a society, had lost through dividing people as part of the apartheid system". Another found his experience "made me unwilling to participate in the apartheid system" and led him to a career as an academic lawyer outside South Africa.[60])

The labour government continued the process of decolonisation; by the 1970s this was effectively over with the important exception of Southern Rhodesia and anomalous spots of pink on the map like the Falklands. At home, new institutions, including twenty-two universities and even a national plan, were created despite a balance of payments crisis in 1964, devaluation in 1967, and a pervading concern about the level of government expenditure. The commission's budget steadily increased during ten or more years of social hope punctuated by economic gloom.

The Commonwealth came back into the headlines in 1965 when Southern Rhodesia's unilateral declaration of independence left it within the Commonwealth but under an illegal regime. As with their South African predecessors, the existing eleven scholars were allowed to stay provided that they "did not participate in any political activity in support of the illegal regime".[61] Ad-hoc arrangements, which were to continue for the next fifteen years, had to be made for the selection of Zimbabwean scholars with nominations being made through the ministry of overseas development rather than direct from an agency within the country. Zimbabwe may have received more awards than might have been expected: Temple wrote to ODM in March 1969 expressing surprise at there being twenty-eight nominations with a few more on the way, above the notional quota.[62] The commission also had to relax its policy of encouraging scholars to return home while the illegal regime remained in power.

Alongside these crimes and tragedies, British relations with Tanzania had an element of farce. Tanzania had broken off diplomatic relations with Britain in 1966, in protest against Britain's policy on Southern Rhodesia, though these were restored in 1968 and it was intended that British aid to Tanzania would resume. But a dispute now arose about pensions. After independence Tanzania stopped paying the pensions of the former colonial civil servants who had worked there and Britain responded by again suspending aid. (Judith Hart, then minister of overseas development, got this tit-for-tat policy reversed in 1970 but immediately lost office in the general election.) The commission was first encouraged to withdraw awards which it had already offered, but successfully resisted doing so in a rare discussion recorded as being acrimonious; it was then formally directed to stop new awards to Tanzania.[63] Again this set precedents for later directions against awards to Uganda, during the Amin regime, Pakistan on its leaving the Commonwealth in 1972 (although not in 2007 when it was suspended from the councils of the Commonwealth, without technically leaving it), and Nigeria in 1995.

The ministry of overseas development's doubts about CSFP were revived in 1969 when it reviewed its training activities generally and concluded that, while at least some of its staff did not much like the plan, little could be done about it:

> (a) viewed in the light of the new thinking, this scheme was awkward. It cost the ODM a great deal of money but the O.D.M. had no positive say in who was trained, why, and for what.
> (b) on the other hand, its origins were political and not developmental (even though recently its application had become more developmental than before); and to try to change it now would cause a monumental row.[64]

Questions about priorities were also being asked within the commission, in particular by Jack Butterworth vice-chancellor of Warwick, who joined it in 1968. He also chaired the Inter-University Council for Higher Education Overseas which had been set up in 1946 to promote links between British and overseas universities. It had a difficult relationship with the commission where it unsuccessfully claimed a say in the use of CASS and CASF funds targeted to overseas university teachers.[65] He asked about the balance between developing-country needs and scholars' individual preferences, which set off alarms in the ministry of overseas development. Sir Christopher Cox, now chief education adviser to ODM, vigorously defended the status quo. He did so in much warmer tones than those of the departmental discussion a year before, possibly reflecting, for neither the first nor the last time, a difference between the views of administrators and educators within the ministry. Quoting his involvement in the early stages of the plan he reminded Butterworth that the "whole emphasis was on making the Commonwealth a significant reality". He insisted "that the developmental criterion, to the best of my recollection was never emphasized in the inception of the scheme and that this historical factor is embedded in the scheme as it is today and cannot be forgotten or lightly overridden".[66] The commission went on to review the issues in a paper on the "Relevance of studies to the needs of developing countries". Any change of policy raised a series of difficulties. Britain might be accused of neo-colonialism if it were to judge other countries' priorities; the commission would not want to prefer indifferent candidates on the ground of the relevance of their area of study; and any short-term preference of practical and applied subjects might not meet long-term needs. Logan argued, as in previous discussions on the same point, that

> If Scholars' studies were not thought relevant to their countries' requirements, the solution lay entirely with their home authorities who had the responsibility for nominating them for consideration for awards; it was difficult for the authorities responsible for the final selection in an awarding country to assess the needs of the candidates' own country.[67]

The commission was gradually evolving its policy on time outside Britain. By 1971, commissioners were slightly more relaxed about field work and appear to have been concerned as much about the risk of increasing expenditure as about reductions in the time available to "study in Britain and to have close contact with British life and thought". They decided against making any formal change in policy but agreed to regularise it by setting up a standing committee to consider applications. They showed little more enthusiasm when considering the ten-year review of the plan carried out for the Commonwealth secretariat in 1972. In contrast with later practice, when the secretariat usually assembled a Commonwealth-wide group to draft its reports, this was the work of a single author, Arthur Loveridge, a lecturer in education in tropical countries at the University of London Institute of Education. The report is more individual, but more tentative in its conclusions, than two later reviews. It favoured greater flexibility, looked forward to what would be called split-site degrees, and was sympathetic to the idea of scholars' doing field work in their own country (see chapter 5). Commissioners noted the proposals in the review but thought that there had been little demand for scholars to spend time in Britain working for an overseas degree while there was concern that periods of field work might breach the three-year maximum for doctorates.[68] Scholars were not happy with the position and comments made by them at a regional conference brought it back to the commission's attention three years later. Commissioners heard that there were only about twenty applications a year, and that "by one device or another most succeed in finding the finance for the visit". They saw no reason to consider a change in their practice but did discuss a request from Bangladesh to consider funding a "split location award" based on cooperation between a British and an overseas university. There were a few ad-hoc precedents and the commission did not rule out developments on these lines.[69]

Policy on marriage allowances began to shift in the 1970s. The schemes for academic scholars and fellows (CASS and CASF) stuck to the old rules; the 1969 prospectus, for example, referred to marriage allowances for men but excluded air fares for their wives. By 1971, three years after *les évènements* and the heyday of student protest, scholars were questioning the logic of paying allowances but not fares and arguing for marriage allowances for women. Logan was cautious or unsympathetic and reminded the commission that marriage allowances just for men had been a concession by the treasury, but it was agreed to consult the department for education and science. It proved unsympathetic and did not provide marriage allowances for women on state studentships as its "philosophy hinges on the fact that by common law the man is normally expected to provide a home for his wife and would be her main source of financial support".[70]

Policy changes were to come not from the commission but from legislation. The sex discrimination act of 1975 forced the commission into line. Extending allowances from men to women does not seem to have been discussed in a commission meeting but the annual *Information for scholars leaflet* tells the changing story. In 1973 and 1974 scholars got £81 per month as a maintenance allowance with an extra £32 for male scholars accompanied by their wives and a further £7, £5 and £4 for each child up to a maximum of three. By 1975, when the maintenance allowance had gone up to £84, a widow or divorced female scholar, legally responsible for her children, would get a children's allowance. The basic allowance went up to £110 the next year while in 1976 the rubric changed: the personal allowance was increased to £132 and there was a marriage allowance of £66 for all married scholars, male or female, provided they were living together.[71]

Finance

Whitehall originally expected that an annual budget of £500,000 would meet the costs of a steady state of 500 award holders. An additional £50,000 was also available for supplementing awards for scholars travelling to other Commonwealth countries. (Expenditure never rose to this level.)[72] The budget rose with the number of awards and negotiations appear to have been about numbers on award rather than about the actual size of the budget. The £500,000 figure was to be reached by 1964, the year of the third Commonwealth education conference (see table 3.2). At this point government was reluctant to let the scheme expand in terms of numbers or of expenditure, although it was prepared to accept a ten per cent increase if other member countries announced at the conference that they were increasing their awards. Two reasons for the reluctance were cited. First, Britain was "under strong pressure to increase her contribution to Commonwealth educational co-operation in other ways" particularly by supplying and training teachers. Second, Sir Edward Boyle, the education minister who would lead the conference delegation, thought that before considering any expansion, the plan should redress the balance between popular awards in the industrialised Commonwealth and under-subscribed offers in the developing Commonwealth.[73] The policy remained one of modest expansion but with no dramatic change in the number of scholars

Table 3.2 Commonwealth Scholarship Commission budget 1960-2008

all in ££ '000

Year ending	Current ££	Constant 2008 ££	Year ending	Current ££	Constant 2008 ££
1961	121.8	2,027.4	1985	7,787.4	17,682.3
1962	290.3	4,619.1	1986	8,877.0	19,496.8
1963	429.5	6,733.5	1987	9,597.5	20,230.9
1964	507.7	7,734.8	1988	9,411.5	18,911.0
1965	555.5	8,061.5	1989	10,406.6	19,404.0
1966	547.3	7,633.9	1990	10,935.9	18,628.3
1967	555.5	7,551.3	1991	12,485.0	20,088.2
1968	675.8	8,797.2	1992	13,077.0	20,281.2
1969	810.0	9,998.8	1993	14,169.0	21,631.1
1970	902.6	10,479.0	1994	14,209.0	21,180.4
1971	1,025.2	10,847.9	1995	13,809.3	19,894.3
1972	1,191.7	11,796.6	1996	13,918.5	19,578.9
1973	1,191.7	10,801.1	1997	12,275.3	16,741.2
1974	1,280.6	10,002.5	1998	12,271.2	16,180.8
1975	1,610.9	10,117.5	1999	11,934.9	15,499.5
1976	1,959.1	10,573.0	2000	12,255.7	15,458.2
1977	1,960.7	9,135.6	2001	12,021.9	14,900.8
1978	2,402.6	10,321.5	2002	11,857.5	14,455.1
1979	2,757.4	10,446.0	2003	13,112.8	15,535.7
1980	3,405.0	10,949.1	2004	13,655.6	15,710.9
1981	3,685.0	10,582.1	2005	14,188.1	15,873.0
1982	4,773.9	12,628.6	2006[a]	16,249.4	17,619.2
1983	5,278.6	13,355.1	2007[a]	16,300.5	16,947.5
1984	6,844.3	16,500.0	2008[a]	16,921.4	16,921.4

Source: CSCAR
Note: a. Includes shared scholarships at c£2m

and fellows to be funded. The plan remained a fairly small part of aid expenditure on education. Estimates for the Canberra ministers' conference in 1971 showed CSFP expenditure at £910,000 out of a total of £7,950,000 on overseas training and higher education.[74]

University fees were a modest proportion of the total expenditure. In its review of British higher education, the Robbins committee had noted in 1963 that as student fees were set at below full cost, overseas students received a subsidy, which came from educational, rather than aid, funds.[75] Four years later, in a round of expenditure cuts, the secretary of state for education, Tony Crosland, introduced a differential between home and overseas student fees. While there was some logic on his side, the conservative opposition attacked him vigorously and effectively and seem to have had the best of the day.[76] Universities were united in opposing the policy but without success. Fees remained relatively low, at £250 for overseas students as compared with £85 for home fees, and the differential does not seem to have held back increasing numbers.

Inflation and a shift in government policy were to have more immediate effects on the commission. The early 1970s were years of rapid inflation so that, while the commission's budget rose in cash terms by 78 per cent from 1970 to 1975, this represented a fall of 4 per cent in real terms. Although numbers of scholars had been rising in the mid-1970s, increasing costs made continuing expansion unsustainable; the number of new scholarships fell from 264 in 1978/9 to 218 a year later. In 1976 government introduced cash limits. Until this time expenditure seems to have been determined and constrained by the number of award holders rather than by a fixed budget. At this point the ministry of overseas development wrote to Lord Garner to advise that cash limits would now be applied to expenditure outside the aid programme. The commission was given its budget for 1976/77 in two elements—£1,475,000 from the aid programme and £400,000 from FCO sources outside aid. The commission did not like this split and:

> It was noted that in past years the Commission had never been formally notified that its funds came from other than a single source and Sir Douglas Logan expressed the hope that the revised arrangements could be reviewed at a later date when the financial position of the country improved since any division of the budget such as was now required would, in his view, complicate the administration of the whole Commonwealth Scholarship and Fellowship Plan to an unfortunate extent.[77]

It came back to the charge in the next meeting, arguing that "Differential between 'old' and 'new' Commonwealth countries was objectionable in principle" and may have been contrary to the spirit of undertakings given at the Oxford conference. The foreign office was unmoved. If the identification of two funding streams meant reduced rich-country awards then "other Commonwealth contributors to the plan should be invited to consider whether they might accept some increase in their own provision to compensate for any reduction in UK awards for old Commonwealth countries". Funding streams were to remain separate from this time on.[78]

The first twenty years

The context of the commission's work was about to change with the election of Margaret Thatcher's conservative government in 1979. By this time the commission had twenty years' experience. Despite the academic turmoil of the universities in the 1960s, and the world's economic turmoil of the 1970s, it had continued quietly on its chosen path. While it had survived budget cuts and cash limits, it had not changed its own policy direction, or expanded in pace with the expansion of higher education, in the north or the south, or of international aid. The unresolved problems of South Africa and Zimbabwe kept the Commonwealth in the news but it did not demand the attention that it had two decades before. The commission had not changed its own policies in any serious way and discussed them only rarely. It rejected proposals for changes in its priorities whether these came from the ministry of overseas development, or from the Commonwealth, or from its own members. Time in Britain was still valued so highly that field work was discouraged or restricted. Marriage allowances had been extended to husbands as well as wives following a change in the law. A change in the balance between dignified and efficient members of the commission did not bring policy changes, though it may have resulted in a fairer work load for the efficient. The commission remained committed to its twin ideas of Commonwealth cohesion, though fewer people now talked about that, and academic excellence. It had a new chairman in 1977 in Sir Michael Walker, a retired diplomat who had previously been British high commissioner in Delhi and looked unlikely to seek dramatic change. But the next thirty years were to be quite different from the previous twenty.

CHAPTER FOUR

BRITAIN: ADAPTING AND SURVIVING

During the first twenty years of the commission's existence, overseas students attracted little political attention. In the 1960s higher education was expanding, faster than any major national enterprises apart from electronics and natural gas.[1] Overseas student numbers, usually around 10 per cent of the total, kept pace with the growth. But

> overseas students were not a distinct policy issue in Britain. They paid fees at the same rate as those nominally paid by British students, their education was subsidised out of public funds and enrolment was entirely unregulated. ... National policy remained essentially one of *laissez-faire*.[2]

Ministers edged towards a policy in the late 1970s. Overseas student numbers in higher education grew to over 90,000 leading the ministers concerned, Shirley Williams and Fred Mulley, to seek a way of restricting their recruitment, initially by the use of quotas. The growing number of overseas students, and the quest for a policy response to it, was

> part of a world-wide phenomenon. By 1979 a number of countries, including Britain, had become concerned about this rapid growth, either on grounds of the cost of public subsidies for overseas students or because of fears that their growing numbers would displace home students or cause imbalances to develop, particularly in the most popular courses and institutions.[3]

But there was no general policy; a parliamentary committee in 1980 agreed that, "successive governments have been at fault in failing to respond adequately to initiatives from Robbins and the Expenditure Committee and to formulate any clear principles on which to base a policy for overseas students".[4]

All change in the 1980s

The 1979 election changed the government and the atmosphere. The ministry of overseas development lost its independence and was absorbed into the FCO.[5] In its first year in power the new Thatcher administration acted decisively, announcing that it would impose cost limits on most public expenditure and charge full-cost fees for overseas students, who promptly became the stuff of political debate. As in 1967 there was some logic to the argument that educational funds should not be used to subsidise overseas students. But the abruptness of the change, the severity of a shift from fees of £320 to £2,000 in the arts or £3,000 in the sciences, and the lack of consultation, all drew protest. Universities were told only after the event. The evidence suggested "that neither the ODA nor the FCO were properly consulted" and that the "decision was taken by the Department of Education and Science in the context of an emergency cost-cutting exercise and presented as a *fait-accompli* to the FCO".[6] Commonwealth member countries protested with a double sense of grievance: the decision disregarded the history of university cooperation while allowing European students to pay home fees in accordance with the treaty of Rome. It was assumed that increased fees would reduce international student mobility.

The Commonwealth lumbered into action. In 1981, Commonwealth ministers of education and heads of government argued that "student mobility and educational interchange within the Commonwealth were important to the national development efforts of Commonwealth countries and to maintaining Commonwealth links". Sonny Ramphal, the secretary general, ratcheted up the argument in talking about "the implication of significantly reduced educational interchange ... for the future character, if not indeed the future, of the Commonwealth itself".[7] He set up a Commonwealth Standing Committee on Student Mobility which tried, over seven meetings, to find a way of mitigating the drive towards increased or full-cost fees. The title of the seventh report, *The final frustration*, will do as a précis (see also chapter 5). With Commonwealth students making up 40,000 out of the total of 86,000 from overseas in 1980, the government was not likely to make a general concession and proved unwilling to bend for particular categories such as Commonwealth scholars.

Protests from home and abroad brought some concessions. Malaysia, Hong Kong and Nigeria were in the lead with Malaysia introducing a "buy British last" policy in retaliation.[8] Government introduced a new Overseas Students Awards Scheme (ORSAS) in 1980; the foreign secretary, Francis Pym announced a "Pym package" in 1983 to soften the impact of full-cost fees. The package, which was funded by the foreign office, included a new tranche of scholarships, later renamed the Chevening awards after the foreign secretary's official country house. These were to be run by the FCO itself with ambassadors selecting scholars, rather than leaving that to a commission working with overseas nominating agencies and at arm's length from government. Some of the additional funding also went to the scholarship commission.

The terms of the debate in the early 1980s had moved away from the internationalist enthusiasm of the early 1960s. Much of the British opposition to the full-cost fee policy stressed the national benefit from the presence of overseas students. Awkward calculations were made to gauge the effect of studying in Britain on future export orders; there was a warning example from Sierra Leone where doctors trained in Germany went home to order medical equipment from there rather than from Britain. Arguments about development were rarer, and those about the Commonwealth tended to come only from its own institutions. By 1987 it was possible to discern a national policy:

> (i) Britain welcomes overseas students for a variety of reasons—educational, political, commercial and developmental;
> (ii) in general, their education should not be subsidised by the British taxpayer;
> (iii) however, in accordance with perceived national priorities, carefully targeted awards should be made available to selected individuals and categories of students.
>
> In practical and financial terms, therefore, national overseas student policy in Britain is now based upon full-cost fees and targeted scholarship support.[9]

During the great overseas student fee war the commission wisely kept its head down. At its first meeting after the announcement of full-cost fees, in March 1980, it agreed to write to the foreign secretary. The commission argued that it was being doubly penalised by tighter cash limits and by the increase in fees. It went on to bring together national interest, the Commonwealth, and the needs of development in explaining that,

> It will fall to the lot of the British Delegation at the Eighth Commonwealth Education Conference which is to be held in Sri Lanka in August of this year to explain why the resources at the disposal of the Commission have been singled out for what amounts to a double cut—despite these commitments to our Commonwealth partners.
>
> It is the deep conviction of the Commission that the educational links between the countries of the Commonwealth are still firm and that the importance of these links, particularly with the developing countries, in-

creases as the political ties become less strong. Indeed in many areas of the third world it is now the case that educational links provide the remaining source for developing the pattern of subsequent political and economic association with Britain. The significance of these links is shown by the interest of foreign countries in trying to attract students from the developing countries; the decrease in the awards at the disposal of the Commission will inevitably increase the number of students going to foreign countries—to the manifest disadvantage of the Commonwealth connection.[10]

The restrained approach seems to have done the trick. The minister's reply explained that the commission could not be entirely shielded, but funding would be increased for the next year.[11] (At this time the chief education adviser to the overseas development administration, Bill Dodd, was a member of the commission; it is possible that he wrote at least one side of the correspondence; he would have enjoyed writing both.) The reassurances may have helped the British at the ministers' conference where, as Dodd later reported, there had not been too sharp a clash or division of opinion over the issue of overseas student fees.[12] The Pym package meant that the commission received a promise of up to £800,000 extra in 1983/4 and an additional £6 million over three years. Without any formal direction, ODA explained that "we leave to the Commission the allocation of this funding to the several categories of awards, but we should wish them to be in 'developmental' disciplines".[13]

The short-term effect of the introduction of full-cost fees was to increase the cost per student and inevitably to decrease the number of new awards, which fell from 347 in 1979 to 250 two years later (see table 3.1). The cost per award now began to rise, in cash as well as real terms, and was to continue to do so, as set out in table 4.1. In the medium term, however, the years of the student-fee debate were surprisingly good for the commission: between 1981 and 1986 its annual expenditure rose by 91 per cent in real terms and award numbers rose again, reaching 477 new awards in 1983/84. In part this may have been a response to the strength of the Commonwealth reaction. In part, in the view of Dodd's successor as chief education adviser, Roger Iredale, it was that government "didn't want to take on the commission. There were heavyweights there. I think that there would have been so much trouble from people like Sloman [vice-chancellor of the University of Essex] and his fellow academics if they'd tried to cut the scheme". Partly it was skill on the part of Dodd and Iredale, both of whom supported the plan: Dodd seems to have successfully guided funds from the Pym package to the commission while Iredale tried to keep the scheme uncontroversial in the annual spending round so that it would not attract the beady eyes of functional departments whose budgets were

Table 4.1 Fees and costs per award

Annual average Current ££	Year ending				
	1966	1971	1981	1991	2001
Fee	85	250			
Fee—arts			2,000	4,560	6,895
Fee—science			3,000	6,050	8,700
Cost per award	1,035	1,544	6,375	12,871	19,937
Constant 2008££					
Fee	1,186	2,645			
Fee—arts			5,743	7,337	8,546
Fee—science			8,615	9,734	10,783
Cost per award	14,431	16,337	18,308	20,710	24,711

Source: CSCAR
Note: These are necessarily crude calculations, with expenditure divided by the total number of award holders, without any allowance for the different costs associated with different types of award.

also under pressure.[14]

During the 1980s the commission's work was scrutinised externally, by the Commonwealth and by the FCO, which led it to carrying out an internal review of its own. At their conference in 1980, ministers of education asked the Commonwealth Secretariat to set up a second ten-year review. Unlike the first it was carried out, not by a single British scholar, but by a team led by the director-general of education of New Zealand which included Temple from the commission secretariat and Dodd, who was then still both chief education adviser at ODA and a commission member. The report, published in 1982, is less quirky but more definite than its predecessor and ended with a set of recommendations. Most of these were uncontentious: to increase the number of awards, including undergraduate awards and academic fellowships, to nominate more women, and to strengthen procedures on information. It encouraged nominating countries to specify their priorities and awarding countries to respect them. The report argued for more third-country awards in which industrialised Commonwealth countries would fund south–south scholarships. (The word "more" is theirs but, if there had already been any, they have left little trace in the records.) A proposal to amend the plan's fifth principle of rewarding "the highest standards of intellectual achievement" was more contentious. The review team wanted to broaden the principle by adding the words "as well as of technical and professional performance and have regard to any expressed manpower or development needs of nominating countries".[15] The commission noted the report but did not feel the need to take any particular notice of the recommendations or change their practices.

Five years later the British government published a *Financial management review* of the commission. The new administration had committed itself to cutting back quangos and pursuing value for money in government expenditure. Reports on the efficiency of all government-funded bodies were decreed, with a deadline of April 1987, met with a month to spare for the commission. The report described the commission's activities, found it worked efficiently, noticed the free contribution made by advisers and commissioners, and recommended no major changes. It thought that the commission was already taking adequate note of ODA and development priorities and saw no need for closer contact with the ODA. The commission had deployed evidence of its influence so that the report ends with a list of distinguished alumni from the ministers of education in Nigeria and foreign affairs in Sierra Leone to the directors of the Palm Oil Research Institute of Malaysia and of finance and planning in the government of Barbados. Some twenty-seven vice-chancellors were claimed without being listed: for this audience ministers and directors were more important.[16]

There was both encouragement, from ODA, and a warning, from the diplomatic wing of the FCO, in the review's financial comments. The encouragement came in ODA's explanation that it had rejected the idea of financing "the Plan under country technical cooperation programmes rather than as a functional scheme" on the grounds that this would reduce flexibility and add complications.[17] At the same time the diplomatic wing of the foreign and Commonwealth office was concerned about the scale of the British contribution to the plan. Britain had continued to provide half the total number of awards, as these had grown from the original 1,000 to 1,700. It concluded that "It is perhaps time for the FCO to consider whether the British contribution to the Plan is now large enough and whether future British contributions could be pegged at this year's number of awards".[18]

The commission noted these encouragements and threats but spent little time discussing them. It had in the meantime carried out its own internal assessment of its work. In looking at "pointers to quality" it quoted success rates and supervisors' reports and argued for the strength of what it was doing by citing the success of plan alumni. Echoing the contemporary debates about student mobility, it quoted and applauded a government statement about the "long-term mutual benefits [brought by overseas students] through better understanding, goodwill, increased commercial exchange and improved diplomatic relations".[19] The assessment referred to the commission's funding difficulties: it could not switch between its ODA and diplomatic wing votes, lived on one-year funding against commitments of up to three years, and found its calculations complicated by uncertainties about the proportion of scholars offered awards who would in practice take them up. It was still concerned about the shortage of women applicants for awards. But for the rest the report is mainly about procedures and not about aims and policies, either for the commission or for the plan as a whole.[20]

These three reviews, by the Commonwealth, the FCO's financial managers and the commission itself, were of greater long-term significance than of immediate impact. In the late 1980s the commission had to deal with more urgent financial problems. It had originally been funded in terms of numbers of scholars and fellows rather than of finance, with a budget calculated by reference to the average cost per scholar/month. The introduction of cash limits meant that a new budgetary system had to be developed, which soon went badly wrong. In July 1987 the commission was under pressure to reduce the number of awards, in order to avoid overexpenditure; six months later it proved to be in danger of underexpenditure of over £500,000 on the ODA vote and £200,000 on the diplomatic wing.[21] Worse was to follow eighteen months later when forecasts again proved unreliable; ODA now expressed alarm that the total number of award holders would not reflect the increased funding it had provided. In October 1989 a forecast overspend of £1.3 million led the secretariat to consider postponing awards, even to scholars and fellows who were on the verge of travelling to Britain. The chairman required "strong and immediate measures to bring expenditure into line with financial resources" and that it should not happen again. The British Council argued that its "own financial system was not at fault" and that "it was not so much the Council's procedures alone that needed review, as the joint and several responsibilities of the Secretariat and the Council". By December damage had been limited with the aid of an additional £57,000 from the British Council's own resources and £700,000 from ODA.[22]

The commission was to enter the 1990s with uncertainties about its funding and its efficiency.

By the 1980s its character had begun to change. Sir Michael Walker served as chairman for ten years from 1977 to 1987. His colleagues seem to have found him a remote character who played a low-key role during his ten years in the post. His chief administrator recalled him as

> austere but friendly. I remember going up on a Sunday night in a train to Newcastle with him and the train was over heated and I was over dressed and sweating like a damp wall. Michael sat there with a metabolic system that had been trained not to perspire; he sat there immaculately groomed over four and a half hours of a hot journey. He exercised no control over internal process. He wanted things to happen immediately and every so often he would come and you would have to come and give an account of your stewardship; I used to take him into the card room in the Athenaeum and he would go through it, "Well, you seem to have got hold of this rather quickly, don't you?" I liked him.[23]

In 1986, Logan retired as the longest-serving commissioner—a record that stands and, given later rules on official appointments, one that is likely to stay—and was replaced by Sir Albert Sloman, the founding vice-chancellor of Essex University, who was to look after the selection process for the next nine years. His approach was to be different:

> Also the contrast between Jock and Albert Sloman was very striking just in the kind of style too, so in long days of doing the selection, in the morning at 12 noon on the dot Jock would call for sherry or better a gin and tonic—Bang! And nothing would happen until it appeared. And similarly if we were ever still doing something at 6 o'clock. When Albert Sloman came in all of these frivolities disappeared.[24]

By 1985, all members were graduates but with a much more varied academic background. (Only three of them had been at Oxbridge.) There were fewer representatives of particular constituencies and at this point ten commissioners held academic posts, with eight from universities, one from a polytechnic and one from a college of adult education. Two of the academic posts were held by doctors: this was the usual practice throughout the period of dedicated medical awards. The other four were the chairman, an engineer in private practice, the chief education adviser from ODA and the director general of the British Council. With an average age of about fifty-nine, commissioners were slightly younger than their predecessors in 1960; the number of women had doubled from one to two. In terms of academic status there were two vice-chancellors and a polytechnic director with most of the other university members holding chairs. The shadow of the first world war, and of the raj, no longer fell over the commission.

Three had served in the second war, and one on military signals research; with the exception of the ODA representative they had little international experience.[25]

After Walker's ten years as chairman, government came up with a more imaginative appointment when Sir Michael Caine took over in 1987, bringing a completely different kind of international experience. Caine had spent his working life at Booker Brothers, which had extensive interests in Guyana and Africa, and had moved up from being a management trainee to become in turn managing director and chairman. Booker's policies gave it the acceptable face of capitalism, even to the extent that the Guyanese government brought it back to run the sugar industry after independence and nationalisation. "Caine's business acumen, lateral thinking, and total lack of pretension and pomposity made him particularly successful. He had a special bond with Africa and Africans, and was trusted, respected, and liked throughout the continent".[26] By this time the commission's staffing had also changed. Temple retired after his quarter century in the past, in which he was described as the "mother superior and father confessor of the commission".[27] Peter Hetherington, who took over from him after long service also at the ACU, thought Caine's was "a good appointment because he had us on our toes in a way that Michael Walker didn't really. But it was entirely amiable … He asked damn hard questions and once we had learnt that he wanted answers to damn hard questions, he was friendly".[28] He impressed his fellow commissioners but knew little about universities. One of them recalled:

> I remember Michael Caine, the big man that he was, full of charisma and power. But also incredibly remote from the realities of university administration—terribly remote. … I do remember … [that] it always seemed to take twice as long for the paperwork to come back from Oxford and Cambridge as it did from other places. … I remember looking at the woman who at the time was representing the University of Cambridge and he gave a long hard look and said "This will improve won't it?" She just sat there and said "Yes, it will improve" and I knew full well, and she knew full well, actually we had no control over this.[29]

The quiet nineties

The commission's work has always been constrained by its university environment and by national policy towards aid and the Commonwealth. All were changing in the early 1990s.

Higher education was changing. In 1992, polytechnics gained university status so that within a year the United Kingdom had eighty-six universities as compared with the twenty-three in 1959. Their new powers to award degrees and to run their own finances increased their capacity to experiment. While controls remained on the level of fees to be charged for British and European undergraduates, universities could now teach what they liked and charge what they wanted at postgraduate level and to students from outside the European Union. The 1990s were marked by an expansion of master's courses and a flurry of experiments with nonconventional teaching methods including distance learning and the use of the internet. The post-1992 universities saw new methodologies as a means of differentiating themselves and of attracting new groups of students.

At the same time as these changes were taking place in Britain, international demand for higher education, and for study abroad, was rising. All this meant that overseas students were no longer a quota to be rationed as in the late 1970s, or a source of anguished debate as in the 1980s, but an attractive source of income. Differential fees, and the state of the world economy, meant that the number of Commonwealth students in the United Kingdom fell slightly in the 1980s, from 31,000 to 30,000, then rose again to 48,000 by 1997/8.[30] Universities had now overcome their objections to the principle of differential fees: by 1988 when the university grants committee suggested a 7 per cent increase in fees, the committee of vice-chancellors and principals recommended one of 10 per cent.[31] As table 4.1 shows, fees increased steadily and ahead of inflation throughout the period from 1981 to 2001.

While universities were expanding, aid for higher education and training was contracting. The international community held a world conference on education for all at Jomtien in Thailand in 1991 which drew attention to the large numbers of children out of school. Along with its peers among the aid agencies, ODA began to switch its priorities away from training and higher education and towards basic education. Whereas in 1991, 53 per cent of its educational aid went on higher education, and only 18 per cent on primary and nonformal education, by 2000, after the change of government, nearly 80 per cent was going to basic education.[32] As a matter of policy, ODA also moved away from projects and programmes and towards more general support in which recipient countries had a greater say on aid priorities. Within this context it reviewed its training policy in 1992. Until then its technical cooperation and training programme had funded large numbers of students—24,000 in 1990. Following the review, training was treated as a component of other aid activities rather than as a separate activity and the programme was closed down.[33] Expenditure of some £10 million on Commonwealth scholarships looked more exposed when it was no longer seen against a bilateral training budget of £85 million, largely spent in British institutions.

The commission came into the 1990s concerned not with these medium-term changes but with renewed short-term financial crises alongside an increased budget. Forecasts of overspend and underspend followed each other within six months in 1990; once again relations with the British Council deteriorated as they were castigated within the commission. In 1994, the commission found that it had underspent its ODA and diplomatic wing budgets by 3.6 per cent and 9.4 per cent. The British Council explained that its computer system was outdated and inflexible but they were getting a new one that should solve the problem. The foreign office and ODA representatives combined their "considerable concern" with a warning that "this could have a negative impact on the bidding process for the following year's budget". A year later the ODA expenditure was within 0.2 per cent of the budget but the diplomatic wing figure ended up stubbornly 11.6 per cent below the allocation. Only in the late 1990s was a robust model for financial forecasting developed.[34]

Despite its difficulty in spending its money, the commission's budget was increasing. The total number of award holders rose to 979 in 1991/2, with the budget reaching a new peak, in cash terms, in 1993/4, although in real terms in the previous year. It was edging towards new policies. In 1990, it began to relax its restrictions on fieldwork, arguing that it was inconsistent not to fund this where it was relevant to scholars' home countries, an agreed priority. The tenor of the paper on this long-running issue was now quite different and it specifically dismissed as undesirable and unworkable the notion that scholarships should be awarded only when no fieldwork was likely.[35] Commonwealth ministers of education called for a third ten-year review at their 1990 conference; in discussing its response in July 1992, the commission touched on possible differences between the original objectives and current needs and the possibility of looking at new needs or target groups. Split-site PhDs were mentioned. It was suggested that the commission might give more weight to "the needs (though not … upon the merely immediate—perhaps transitory—needs) of scholars' home countries".[36] The commission was, however, still moving cautiously. Less than six months later, and echoing the opinions of his predecessors, "The Chairman expressed doubts that the Commission was qualified to answer questions on the developmental needs of other countries which he considered to be outside its terms of reference".[37] There was a different nuance by the time of its next annual report where the commission explained that it tried "in its selections and placements, to effect a proper balance between excellence and pertinence. Of its own initiative it places no limits upon the subjects in which overseas countries make their nominations, believing that they are the best arbiter of their own need". But "pertinence" was now in the dialogue.[38]

The Commonwealth Secretariat produced its third ten-year review in 1993. It still wanted high academic quality but went on to argue for "achievement of excellence both intellectually and in terms of technical and professional performance". It favoured experiment with short awards, split-site scholarships, and distance learning. As with previous reviews it stressed "the principle of gender equity", wanted to ensure that scholars returned home at the end of their awards, and argued for the continuing collection and sharing of information about the plan.[39] The report seems to have disappointed both ODA and the commission, which spent little time discussing it although, within a decade, it introduced most of its new ideas. The overseas development administration promptly commissioned the British member of the Commonwealth team, Cedric Hassall, to review the British component. This provided a document that Iredale could use, in his last year on the commission and in ODA, to fend off attacks.[40]

The commission spent more time considering the Hassall report than the Commonwealth's, and was encouraged by advice that the minister was prepared to be flexible in considering Hassall's views and the commission's. Hassall had recommended closing down both the academic and the medical awards. He argued that there was no strong reason for separating medicine from other disciplines; the commission found no convincing defence for the separate awards and doctors were now to be considered and funded alongside their peers. The commission was prepared, however, to defend the academic awards in the interest of overseas university development. They survived, on the understanding that they should be concentrated on countries where this remained a significant need.[41]

The existence of the Hassall report led the commission to review its policies, looking at its goals, strategies and purposes, at the balance between different types of award, and at their geographical distribution. Its goal was defined as to create:

> in all countries of the Commonwealth a cadre of professionally well-trained people capable of becoming strategic thinkers and planners in whatever aspect of life they may work after their return home; people who at a high intellectual level contribute to the quality of debate in their home countries about all aspects of national and international life; who can contribute to its wealth, its government and its education and examine critically the private and public purposes which conjoin to these ends.

Additionally it wanted "to maintain and foster a special relationship with Commonwealth partners", to promote good government, democracy, human rights and sustainable development, and to promote a positive view of Britain and recognition of "the UK as a source of value and technology". The commission thought it would be helpful to have fuller guidance from its funding departments.[42]

There were subtle changes in the methods it now proposed to use. It began to express reservations about the relevance of its work throughout the Commonwealth, especially in relation to academic staff awards. It questioned the need for Hong Kong, Kenya, Nigeria and Singapore to rely on British postgraduate awards for its academic staff when these countries now had their own, well-established, postgraduate programmes. In a move away from its historical policy of seeking out the ablest scholars regardless of their location, it now argued that: "There seems little to be gained from bringing junior Indian academic staff to the UK to study for masters or doctoral qualifications when there are many world-class or first division institutions in their own country where they could study".[43] Probably for the first time it agreed allocations for master's and doctorates, with master's awards taking up not less than 20 per cent of the total. It toyed with the idea of moving to four-year doctorates, with a first-year master's course followed by a three-year doctorate.[44]

Following the Hassall review and the commission's reactions to it, government agreed to provide guidance on priorities for both the diplomatic wing and overseas development administration. The diplomatic wing set out its objectives:

1. To work for a situation where the UK continues to attract the maximum possible number of overseas students of high intellectual calibre particularly in the higher education sector.
2. Specifically to identify and offer study or training opportunities in the UK for future leaders, decision makers and opinion formers from around the world. Thereby, to further the UK's long term political, diplomatic, commercial and other interests through the cultivation of influential friends overseas.
3. To work to ensure that the impression of the UK, its people and its institutions, which overseas students take back with them to their own countries, is as positive and long lasting as possible.
4. To do everything possible to ensure the appropriate cultivation and follow up of returned official scholarships students, and to encourage other appropriate UK institutions to do likewise for their students.[45]

The overseas development administration does not appear to have provided its own statement of priorities although, two years later and in the context of budget reductions, it did advise on its geographical policy, setting out in order four loosely defined regions, subsaharan Africa, south Asia, the Caribbean, and others.[46] The commission responded by agreeing a new geographical set of priorities with a shift towards Africa: of ODA-funded awards 45 per cent would now go to Africa, 30 per cent to south Asia and 25 per cent to the rest of the Commonwealth.

Just as the commission was beginning to redefine its policy, its political environment was changing. In the mid-1990s the bilateral aid budget suffered two cuts and, unlike the 1960s and 1980s when the commission had survived cuts in government expenditure, it was no longer immune from them. At the Edinburgh European Council in December 1992 the British government had approved increases in European Commission aid, which came out of the ODA budget. In 1993 the same budget was frozen in cash terms for three years. The effect of these two changes was to be a 16 per cent reduction in aid over three years.[47] The Commission was told that its ODA budget would be reduced for 1996/97 with a warning of further reductions in later years.[48] The foreign office seemed in no mood to increase its budget. The commission lost a friend at court when Iredale retired as chief education adviser at ODA and left the commission. (His successor did not join it so that, from this time, neither ODA nor the British Council were in the anomalous position of at once funding or serving the commission and being represented on it.)

The financial threat was followed by a political one. In 1995 the house of commons foreign affairs committee examined "the future role of the Commonwealth". The commission did not present evidence, beyond providing statistics, even though its funding was the largest British contribution to a Commonwealth programme. The report was not encouraging. The foreign office came back to a theme hinted at in its 1987 *Financial management review*, warning that Britain's future support of the plan could depend on the contributions from other member countries. For its part, the commission was criticised from the Institute of Commonwealth Studies of the University of London as "too much the product of routinisation which is not appraised often enough".[49] (No-one noticed that the commission had been reviewed in 1987 by the FCO and in 1993 by both the Commonwealth, as part of CSFP, and by Hassall on behalf of ODA.)

The commission was, perhaps strangely, quiet as its budget was cut and it was attacked in parliament. It was, at this point, politically weaker than its predecessors. The Commonwealth still had some resonance for Britain although it is difficult to think it took much cabinet or ministerial time. British ministers of education, though bruised at the triennial conferences of ministers of education, still came to them, in contrast with their

Australian colleagues who no longer bothered. (They did not always stay long. In 1990 the British minister flew to Barbados but was summoned to return home on the same plane for a parliamentary vote on dog licenses.) There were not many in Whitehall who would listen to pleas couched in terms of Commonwealth interest. The warning that full-cost fees would deter Commonwealth students had been proved false by their increasing numbers in the 1990s. Their evident capacity to attract funding made it more difficult to justify the unique value of a Commonwealth scheme. Financially, the commission's case had been weakened by its underspending. Politically, it now had neither political grandees who could make its case in clubland, nor even a clutch of vice-chancellors; there was only one at this time. Although the chairman was married to a conservative MP, he was neither a politician, like the first three of his predecessors, nor a former diplomat familiar with the corridors of the FCO, like the last two. The commission's academic expertise had grown but at the expense of its political influence.

New directions

The new labour government of 1997 changed the context within which the commission was working. Overnight ODA was transformed into a separate department for international development (DfID). For the first time since 1979 overseas development was free from the control of the FCO and represented at cabinet level. The department had a powerful secretary of state, Clare Short. She and her successors managed, over ten years, to increase the department's budget and restore a long-lost commitment to raise official aid to 0.7 per cent of gnp. Within six months of coming into office the government issued a white paper on international development, the first for over twenty years. DfID now had clearly articulated priorities: "The first and overriding target is that of reducing by 50 per cent those living in abject poverty by 2015. A complementary target is that of universal primary education by 2015".[50] The white paper was followed by an innocuous-looking International Development Act in 2002, which appeared to do little more than re-enact existing legislation but had a powerful sting in its head with part 1, clause 1, paragraph 1 reading, "The Secretary of State may provide any person or body with development assistance if he is satisfied that the provision of the assistance is likely to contribute to a reduction of poverty." Development assistance is then defined as embracing sustainable development and improving welfare.[51] Aid funds could no longer be used to promote British strategic or economic interests.

The Commission itself was continuing to change, with a new chair in 1996 and a new executive secretary in 1999. By this time the government had accepted recommendations made by a committee on standards in public life, chaired by Lord Nolan, to introduce new procedures for making public appointments. Under the Nolan rules the posts of commissioners and of the chair were advertised. This led to a quite different kind of appointment. Geoffrey Caston succeeded Caine as chair, having submitted an application and been interviewed: an innovation. He had just returned to Britain from a period as vice-chancellor of the University of the South Pacific. Caston had previously spent some time as a civil servant, initially in the colonial office and later in the department of education and science, and some years as registrar of Oxford University. Immediately before going to the South Pacific he had been secretary-general of the committee of vice-chancellors and principals.[52] Thus, for the first time, the commission was chaired by someone with extensive international and academic experience. He brought in as executive secretary an administrator from the National Institute of Economic and Social Research, with a background in university administration at Brunel, John Kirkland, who was charged with improving the commission's external relations.

Both chair and secretary were anxious to establish their credentials with the new government and to set the commission off in new directions. Kirkland described the commission as a body that had been doing just the same things for forty years. (He put this more tactfully on paper claiming that "during the forty years of its existence, the basic aims and operations of CSFP have remained remarkably intact".)[53] But they were hesitant to approach the new secretary of state. She rapidly established a formidable reputation as a minister who would let nothing impede her educational priority of supporting basic education, whose benefits for human welfare were now overwhelmingly well-established. A second world forum on basic education, at Dakar in 2000, at which Short played a prominent role, brought a commitment by Britain and others that shortage of aid funds would not stand in the way of any sensible proposals for expanding primary education. Money for anything else was tight and civil servants were reluctant to discuss secondary education with her, leave alone tertiary; some recommended the commission to keep well away. When the meeting did take place it went surprisingly well. The commission had new ideas and there was consensus that it was time for a review of its activities. At this point it emerged that consultants were among the secretary of state's *bêtes noires* so she was happy with the suggestion that the Commission should undertake its own review.[54]

Caston and Kirkland therefore carried out their own review which was endorsed both by the commission and by the secretary of state. Ahead of the review the commission had in 1998 introduced split-site scholarships to allow developing-country scholars to spend one year in Britain while working on a doctorate in their home-country university.[55] It now made two main changes, one of priorities and one of programmes. The first was to align the commission more closely with DfID policies and priorities. The report argued that "the evidence obtained has confirmed the Commission's views that higher education, and CSFP in particular, has a central role in development policy". It saw valuable synergies between its work and DfID's programmes and stated the commission's belief "that effective development is best served through rigorous selection procedures, which emphasise both capacity to assist in long-term development and the quality of the applicant".[56] With this phrase the commission had, after forty years, reversed its priorities so that academic excellence was no longer, by itself, justification for an award. Both Caston and Kirkland thought that there might be opposition, possibly even resignations, from some commission members but, in the event, there was an easy consensus in favour of it.[57]

A series of programme changes were agreed at the same time. Some 40 per cent of scholarships were to go to master's programmes. The commission would seek fuller information on national, and DfID, priorities in relation to individual countries and would explore new routes for nominations. Over the next few years it accepted as nominating agencies a number of nongovernment organisations working with refugees and members of DfID-funded research consortia. Academic fellowships were to be reduced from twelve months to six, with a new emphasis that they were for updating rather than for research. A new alumni programme of work was set up to develop and maintain contact with former award holders. Two completely new types of award were introduced. It had long been an anomaly that university staff members, but members of no other profession, could come to Britain for professional updating. A new programme of professional fellowships opened the doors to professionals to come and work with an agency in their own area of expertise for up to three months. The commission also agreed to experiment with distance-learning degrees, which had by this time acquired a measure of legitimacy. Following a Canadian precedent it made funding available to universities which were working in partnership with a developing-country university (see chapter 6 below).[58] Table 4.2 shows the numbers reached by these new programmes.

The changes of direction led to an easier relationship with DfID, formal statements about the value of the plan, and a measure of assurance that it could be expected to continue in existence. Budgets from DfID and the

FCO were increased. Commonwealth shared scholarships, in which candidates were nominated and partly funded by a British university, came within the commission's responsibilities. While they had been introduced in 1986, and administered by the ACU, they had until this point been outside the commission's remit.[59]

The commission formalised its procedures for awarding scholarships and explicitly required applicants to relate their proposals to developmental aims. (Scholars from the old Commonwealth, together with those from the Bahamas, Brunei, Cyprus, Malta and Singapore which were no longer eligible for aid funding, had the more nebulous job of demonstrating their leadership qualities.) In 2003, it changed its selection procedures to match its changed policies. Until then, each selection committee took account of the views of its subject advisers and agreed a single score for each candidate on an A to C scale. With adjustment by multiple pluses, minuses and question marks, advisers and committees could lengthen the scale to an estimated, though perhaps apocryphal, ninety-four points. Commissioners and advisers were now required to use an agreed five-point scale in assessing candidates separately on three criteria: their academic strength, the quality of their study plan, and either the developmental relevance of their proposal (for those funded by DfID) or their leadership potential (for FCO).

By the new century the funding model had been tuned so that the commission could generally work within a permitted tolerance of 3 per cent of its budget. Expenditure now began to take on a new shape. Professional fellowships and distance-learning scholarships had lower unit costs than conventional scholarships and fellowships. Professional fellows generally came to Britain for no more than three months while most distance-learning students did not get a stipend or have travel costs. All these changes were reducing the average cost per award. At the same time, universities were now increasing their costs. Within the sciences, bench fees had to be added to the basic fee. The commission agreed in 2007 to set a normal upper limit to fees of £20,000 but found that it had to exceed this for some doctoral courses particularly in the life sciences. It resisted pressure to pay high fees for MBAs by an extreme reluctance to fund them at all. University costs continued to rise above the rate of inflation. Even with increased budgets—which were still lower in real terms than those of the early 1990s—the commission strained to maintain the number of conventional scholars (see table 4.2)

Changes in the character of the commission matched the policy changes. Three commissioners were recruited to fill vacancies in 2000 from an advertisement which specifically sought a developmental back-

Table 4.2: British awards 2002–8

Year ending	Scholars					Fellows		
	Conventional	Split-site	Distance learning	Shared	Total	Conventional	Professional	Total
2003	260	30	84		374	77	23	100
2004	255	32	164		451	74	51	125
2005	265	34	146		445	72	60	132
2006	216	30	138		384	62	56	118
2007	225	22	158		405	63	69	132
2008	215	26	283	140	664	55	63	118
2009	272		123	161	556	61	68	129

Source: CSCAR and ACU database
Note: Split-site awards included with conventional from 2008-9

ground. Caston was succeeded by his deputy, Professor Trudy Harpham, who had joined the commission in 1998 and had become the first deputy chair who was not headhunted to carry out the job of running the selection process. She was then professor of urban development at the London South Bank University and also held a visiting chair at the London School of Hygiene and Tropical Medicine where she had worked for ten years. Most of her research interests were in the developing world. Thus she was the first practising university teacher to become chair of the commission with a quite different background from, for example, Lord Scarbrough. They had grown up fifty miles apart, in Yorkshire and Lincolnshire but with two classes and two generations between them. Harpham's father had left school at the age of eleven to look after the pigs and she had gone on to study at Portsmouth and Keele.[60]

By 2005, with one post vacant, there were five women on the commission. Virtually all of its members now had some development experience; all were holding or had held posts in higher education although two engineers and one specialist on small enterprises had spent much of their careers working in the field. There was only one ex-vice-chancellor and three Oxbridge graduates. They probably knew more about the developing world than any of the previous commissions but lacked the political contacts which some of their predecessors had enjoyed. Whereas the Marshall commission, at this time, had a group of members who also served on the governing boards of other national public bodies, few of the scholarship commission did so. Commission members were a couple of years younger than their predecessors twenty years before. The long shadow of war and empire was almost gone. Only two of the commission were old enough to remember the second world war or to have done national service when they could have been sent to fight in the last imperial conflicts in Aden, Cyprus, Egypt, Kenya or Malaya. (In fact only one had done national service, in the ranks, and had faced nothing more dangerous than confronting rabid badgers in west Germany on which there were routine monthly warnings.) If Ryszard Kapuściński is right that "a person who has lived through a great war is different from someone who has never lived through any war" then this commission no longer shared one defining experience with most of its predecessors. And this commission had grown up after the days when much of the world map could be painted pink.[61]

The commission was attracting new attention from policy makers. In 2004 the house of commons science and technology committee welcomed its new programmes and the allocation of almost half of its awards to science, medicine and technology, and reported:

> We are pleased that the Commonwealth Scholarship Commission continues to recognise the importance of doctorates for development of expertise in scientific subjects, despite the fact that PhDs are significantly more expensive than taught postgraduate courses. We also commend the Commonwealth Scholarship Commission for following a demand–led approach, and for ensuring strong representation of science and technology in the review process for award applications.[62]

Further encouragement came when, following its easier relationship with DfID, the commission was assured of three years funding, from 2008 to 2011, which was to rise from £15.93 million to £17.5 million.[63] Even with increasing university costs this made it possible both to continue its newer programmes and to expand its conventional scholarships.

But the same government spending round which increased DfID's budget reduced that of the FCO. The diplomats had to find savings somewhere and in March 2008 the foreign secretary announced in parliament that he would withdraw funding from Commonwealth scholarships for the industrialised Commonwealth. The Chevening awards, still run directly by the FCO, had their budget reduced but found greater favour in FCO's eyes and were to remain. Ironically the foreign secretary argued that, "The savings we make from this reform will support new priority programmes, principally on climate change", despite the select committee's evidence that Chevening usually made only 5 to 10 per cent of its awards in the sciences.[64] (It may be that these new programmes were not using scholarships at all.) The FCO did not welcome a suggestion from the commission that it could develop proposals for a targeted set of awards in the FCO countries and later argued that Chevening awards offered better value for money: as these generally funded only master's degrees and not doctorates it was possible to finance more potential friends of Britain for the same amount of money.[65]

The commission objected, arguing both that this change moved the scheme away from its Commonwealth-wide remit and that it had an established track record in producing the future leaders and friends whom the foreign office wanted to cultivate. A volume of protest followed including an early-day motion in the house of commons, a debate in the house of lords, a protest signed by two former prime ministers in *The Times*, and an electronic petition—this was the 2000s—on the Downing Street website. The level of protest gave the commission more publicity than it had received for many years and seems to have surprised the FCO. But it was not to be moved. It had, at this time, a one-page list of strategic priorities in which the word "Commonwealth" appeared only in the title of the office. Its views were not, however, shared throughout Whitehall and Kirkland proceeded to negotiate with universities and with their government department, now the department of innovation, universities and skills (DIUS), for a new funding arrangement. In the autumn of 2008 he was able to announce that a group of British universities and DIUS would together fund a reduced number of Commonwealth scholarships at postgraduate level. Their interest and justification was neither Commonwealth cohesion, nor the making of friends to Britain, but the benefit to British universities of attracting the ablest students.[66]

Changing assumptions and policies

The latest twist in the commission's tale demonstrates that scholarships remain in the political as well as the academic world. By the early years of the twenty-first century, Commonwealth scholarships had, for Britain, moved from being a Commonwealth-wide plan, seeking academic excellence wherever it was to be found, towards being part of a developmental aid programme; some commissioners, and some in its parent ministry, always wanted it to be that. Through its new types of awards it was no longer treating experience within Britain as so uniquely valuable that it had to be maximised; some scholars could now graduate without even coming to Britain. Commonwealth higher education had changed at least as dramatically (see chapter 6). Commonwealth Africa, for example, had fourteen universities in 1960, over a hundred in 2000. The pattern of student mobility had changed too. In 2000, 45 per cent of the 178,000 overseas higher-education students in Britain came from Europe and 25 per cent from the Commonwealth whereas, in the early 1960s, 9 per cent had come from Europe and 60 per cent from the Commonwealth. The 600 Commonwealth scholars now represented less than 2 per cent of the Commonwealth total although, with the ending of other programmes, they now formed a much larger proportion of government overseas award holders than they had in the 1960s.[67] Over this period the commission itself had changed, gaining in professionalism, and in the most recent decade displaying a new willingness to argue its case, while, like the Commonwealth itself, probably declining in its influence.

We look next at the parallel changes in other Commonwealth countries.

CHAPTER FIVE

COMMONWEALTH: THE PLAN IN THE NORTH

Just as British politics shaped its contribution to CSFP so the plan as a whole was influenced by the politics of the other member countries and the development of the Commonwealth as an association. The story in the north, and in this chapter, is one of interplay between scholarships and politics, first as the new Commonwealth emerged after decolonisation, then as it developed and changed in the 1970s and 1980s, and more recently as international relations have changed in the post-Soviet world.

For politicians of the 1940s and 1950s the Commonwealth was near and seemed close. Australian and New Zealand forces fought under British command in north Africa. Canadian troops took part in D Day. Indian regiments were deployed from Burma to east Africa and Italy. The African pioneer corps fought, and did the dirty work with picks and shovels, in Africa and Europe. Nehru, on attaining Indian independence, effectively created the modern Commonwealth by bringing India into it. Churchill, with no apparent irony despite his long opposition to Indian self-rule, saw a link between the idea of freedom and the idea of the Commonwealth when in 1950 he defined the British position in the world:

> I feel the existence of three great circles among the free nations and democracies. ... The first circle for us is naturally the British Commonwealth and Empire, with all that that comprises. Then there is also the English-speaking world in which we, Canada and the other British Dominions and the United States play so important a part. And finally there is United Europe. These three majestic circles are co-existent .... Now if you think of the three inter-linked circles you will see that we are the only country which has a great part in every one of them.[1]

Over the next quarter century Britain, and its Commonwealth partners, tried to manoeuvre round the circles. Europe was to change as it moved steadily towards economic and political cooperation or even union. America maintained its economic and cultural dominance as one of two superpowers. The Commonwealth changed and grew in numbers but remained the most difficult to classify. A British cabinet paper drawn up by six Commonwealth countries argued in 1960 that the

> member countries of the Commonwealth constitute a free association of independent sovereign states, all of which have, in varying degrees, the following common characteristics: a certain weight of population; political, financial and economic viability; the ability to play a role in world affairs and to carry weight in world councils; and the capacity for self-defence, not least against local acts of aggression. It is, in short, a relatively small group of relatively large countries.[2]

Much of this was about to change; almost all of it to do so in the next forty years. Cyprus was to set the precedent in terms of population, soon to be followed into the Commonwealth by the small states of the Caribbean after the collapse of the West Indies federation. With neither population nor economic viability remaining as a criterion for independence or Commonwealth membership, it could by 1975 be described as a relatively large group of countries, more than half of them relatively small.

The 1960 definition said little about politics, perhaps because there would be no easy agreement between Ghana and India, then formally non-aligned, and the four old Commonwealth members. For the latter group, the Commonwealth was seen as an actual or potential bulwark against the Soviet bloc. The pace of decolonisation had, at least for Britain, been justified because independence was seen as preferable to communist agitation or domination: officials argued in 1959, for example, that "only nationalists with independence would form 'a strong, indigenous barrier to the penetration of Africa by the Soviet Union and the United Arab Republic'"[3]

The Commonwealth was linked by economics as well as politics. In 1960 all Commonwealth countries, apart from Canada, were members of the sterling area (along with Burma, Iceland, Ireland, Jordan and Libya) so that the value of their currency was determined by decisions in London. When, in the 1960s, Harold Wilson was trying to stave off devaluation, he was held back in part by his concern for the interests of other sterling-area members.[4] Trade continued to bind the Commonwealth even after independence brought a parade of different flags. In the first half of the 1960s three-quarters of the sterling area's exports of manufactures came from Britain.[5] Although Australia had reduced its dependence on the British market, in 1962/3 it sent 19 per cent of its exports to Britain including 82 per cent of its butter, 45 per cent of its cheese and 25 per cent of its mutton and lamb. New Zealand was even more dependent with figures of over 85 per cent for its staples, while Britain was Canada's second largest customer.[6] Canadian exports of wheat to Britain were seen as being economically and therefore politically significant. As Britain began a decade and a half of negotiations with the European Economic Community (EEC) it felt duty bound to consult the Commonwealth. Reginald Maudling, then paymaster general and responsible for European trade negotiations, reassured the House of Commons in 1959 that "We could not contemplate any system of working with Europe which was at the expense of our ties with the Commonwealth", even though, only six months before, he had told the prime minister that any Commonwealth alternative to European free trade was "fanciful".[7]

The Commonwealth and the first scholarships

Scholarship policy was to be shaped by the policies of individual member governments and by the nature of the Commonwealth itself. When the first Commonwealth scholars took up their awards in 1960 they did so within a small, even cohesive, group of countries, predominantly sharing a currency, with tightly linked economies; the economically most powerful members of the group were firmly aligned with America and western Europe, against the Soviet bloc.

Commonwealth universities, which had set up their own association in 1913, were also closely linked. The Commonwealth secretary-general claimed in 1988 that "with common traditions, structures and approaches in teaching and research, Commonwealth universities share ideals and goals as well".[8] With the limited development of postgraduate education in Canada, its universities still recruited teaching staff from Britain as well as the United States. Despite the distance, Australia valued British degrees for its university staff and for many years had recruited university teachers from Britain or sent its potential staff there for their postgraduate degrees.[9] For some this was a matter of scorn at the idea of "setting down an Oxford quadrangle under the gum trees". But for others it was a simple fact of life. One Australian Commonwealth visiting professor reported in 1962 that one of the benefits of his spending a year in Cambridge was that in future he would send his able postgraduate students there as well as to Oxford.[10] Academic links between the industrialised countries of the Commonwealth were part of the regular pattern of academic life. Over the next ten years more than a quarter of all Commonwealth scholars were to move between the industrialised members of the Commonwealth.

While claiming much in common, Canada, Australia and New Zealand had come to the Oxford conference with differing expectations. The Canadian position was the most fully developed, having been worked out in a series of meetings, of academics and civil servants, between the Montreal and Oxford meetings. In a statement of policy drawn up for the conference, the Canadian delegation drew a contrast between technical assistance and the proposed Commonwealth scheme. Technical assistance was primarily concerned with economic development whereas there were also "large groups of people who are not eligible for scholarships under technical assistance programmes, but who would benefit from a period of study abroad". Technical assistance, too, mainly involved the movement of people from more developed to less developed countries. In contrast the plan should be reciprocal. While there would not be "mathematical equality in the degree of reciprocity" the Canadians cited "the benefits which would accrue to Canada, to Canadian universities and to Canadian scholarship through increased first-hand knowledge of Africa and Asia". It would exclude "skilled trades" but would be broader than technical assistance embracing all disciplines and in particular the humanities. They went on to identify that

> in our view, the Plan has a threefold purpose. First it should aim at training men and women of general skills and attitudes who are needed, in the words of the Report of the Montreal Conference, "to serve in all the elaborate and varied processes of a complex society" which are the natural outgrowth of economic development itself. Secondly, we believe that the Plan will help to cement the Commonwealth association as such. There is great diversity within the Commonwealth. The opportunities for cross fertilization are immense. At the same time, we hold many values in common, the most important of which is a common devotion to the ideals of freedom, justice and truth. The Plan should help to preserve and strengthen these ideals. Finally, the Plan should result in a wider sharing of educational facilities. Some Commonwealth countries are in a position to provide a surplus of educational facilities and the Plan should be designed to exploit this surplus in the interests of the Commonwealth as a whole.[11]

Australia and New Zealand had come to Oxford with more reservations. In a meeting with the British at UNESCO in the autumn of 1958 the Australian and New Zealand delegates "made it absolutely clear that they were interested mainly in sending Civil Servants and teachers overseas but would be glad to welcome scholars or Civil servants or teachers".[12] Australia was "not attracted by Rhodes type selection [as] Australians going overseas [were] adequately covered".[13] New Zealand was reported to be "receiving enough fellowships to skim off the cream of first-class students".[14] By the time of the Oxford conference, the Australians were still worried about the possible repercussions of a Commonwealth plan on their Colombo plan activities, of which education and training was "much the most rewarding part". New Zealand thought the proposal was too narrow.[15] These hesitations may have been partially overcome by the inclusion of fellowships within the plan, which could be used principally to benefit the host country, and which were not competing for recent graduates. New Zealand's programme of administrative rewards also responded to its concern for awards to benefit and strengthen the civil service.

Eventually, if reluctantly, all four industrialised countries pledged awards. Reciprocity was assured, at least among the rich countries of the Commonwealth.

Each of them then set up machinery to select and nominate scholarship candidates. In Canada this went to a committee, dominated by senior academics, but also including government representation. Balance of one kind was achieved by having both anglophone and francophone members and of another by including a woman, just like the commission in Britain. George Curtis, who had chaired the relevant committee at Oxford, was in the chair and was to stay there for the next ten years. The National Council of Canadian Universities and Colleges, later to be renamed the Association of Universities and Colleges of Canada (AUCC), was commissioned to administer the plan. Australia and New Zealand set up similar committees, including both university and civil service members. Administration rested with the Commonwealth office of education in Australia and the university grants committee in New Zealand.[16]

The recruitment of scholars presented a number of difficulties. For Australia and New Zealand it was complicated by the difference between their academic year and that in the northern hemisphere. Canada was dismayed to find that it came below Britain in applicants' order of preference. Only six nominees were received from Hong Kong, for example, none of whom proved to be eligible although 146 had been sent to Britain.[17] There were only 100 applicants from Ceylon, far less than for British scholarships, partly because "Wealthy Ceylonese for a century or more have formed the habit of sending their children to the United Kingdom, preferably to Oxford or Cambridge"; they were familiar with ivy league colleges in the United States, but not with Canada.[18] Canada was also surprised to find applications, particularly from south Asia, dominated by scientists and engineers. The Canadian high commissioner in Delhi was dismayed at the number of engineers seeking scholarships within a plan that he understood to be mainly for the humanities and social sciences. One of his Ottawa colleagues apologetically argued that "it is however better to have a highly qualified engineer than a poorly qualified humanities student studying in Canada".[19] Nor was it always easy to find rich-country applicants for outward scholarships: during the plan's first ten years New Zealand was asked to nominate twice as many scholars as the number of awards available to it but had difficulty attracting this number.[20]

The arithmetic of scholarship numbers began to present difficulties as initial assumptions about the length of awards had to change. Most awards were for postgraduate study but about a quarter of Australian awards were at undergraduate level. Early calculations of these numbers were complicated partly because the pledges at Oxford were in terms of the total number of awardees at any one time, while decisions about new awards were made annually, partly because students were taking longer to complete their degrees than anticipated. The Australian undergraduates needed three years. Although there were six vice-chancellors or senior university officials on the Oxford committee—one Australian, three British, two Canadian—all three countries seem to have assumed that scholars could get a doctorate in two years (see also chapter 3). In Canada numbers were constrained by a budgetary ceiling, and by the fact that three-year awards and marriage allowances increased the costs above what the civil servants had anticipated.[21] Despite the difficulties, within five years the number of scholars holding awards in the four rich countries matched their pledges almost perfectly with 99 in Australia, 520 in Britain, 236 in Canada, and 25 in New Zealand. By this time, too, the plan had reached its target of 1,000 people on award in the Commonwealth as a whole.[22]

Most awards were given by industrialised Commonwealth countries to scholars from the developing Commonwealth so that after ten years the four "older Commonwealth countries were sustaining 90 per cent of the scholar beneficiaries, and providing only 28 per cent of them".[23] From the outset, however, exchanges within the old Commonwealth made up a significant proportion of the total; most Commonwealth scholars from these four countries went to one of the other four. In the 1960s, scholars coming from the industrialised Commonwealth made up between 20 and 25 per cent of the total in Britain and Canada and over 35 per cent in Australia and New Zealand. Both these countries reported that overseas experience was particularly valued in their universities, from which the majority of the scholars were drawn.[24] As fellowship programmes got under way, and with the exception of the British academic and medical fellows, they were even more heavily dominated by rich-country exchanges. Australia, Canada and New Zealand hosted 131 fellows of whom all but twenty-five came from the other three rich countries. Benefits flowed both to the host university and to the individual visitor. The Institute of Education in London, for example, commented on the value it had gained from a visit by Clarence Beeby, the former director of education in New Zealand who had been involved in discussions about the plan in 1958 and led the New Zealand delegation to the Oxford conference. He came to Britain in 1967, gave seven lectures at other universities, and spent time working on what was to be his classic book *The quality of education in developing countries*. In his account he stressed the personal value of the fellowship:

> I have always felt some slight sense of guilt that, towards the end of my career, I was occupying a post that might have yielded better returns if it had been given to a younger man, but, this said, I have no doubt whatever that the opportunity to work in London for a year has been of immense value to me professionally and personally, and that any work I may do in the future as a consultant or a writer will be the better for it.[25]

The pattern of these early rich-country exchanges, both of scholars and of fellows, differentiates the plan from aid programmes like the Colombo plan or the developmental activities of the Rockefeller and other foundations. They are consistent with the Oxford conference's concern for Commonwealth cohesion and its expectation that if

> its recommendations are implemented with vigour and determination, all the people of the Commonwealth will reap the benefit and the bonds which bind the Commonwealth together will be strengthened by service given and received. ...
> The Plan ... will play an important part in maintaining and strengthening the common ideals on which the Commonwealth is founded.[26]

The bonds of the Commonwealth

Within five years the Commonwealth's linking bonds were weakening and the association looked less cohesive. By 1965 India and Pakistan were at war with each other and a ceasefire was eventually brokered, not through the Commonwealth, but by the Soviet Union. Singapore was expelled from Malaya. A planned Commonwealth mission to Vietnam was stalled when the authorities in Hanoi were not prepared to meet the junior minister despatched by Britain as the advance guard. Southern Rhodesia, still under white minority rule, made a unilateral declaration of independence (UDI). The British government, which had already ruled out a military response, imposed gentle sanctions, and was castigated for its feebleness by other Commonwealth members. (The sanctions were feebly gentle; one small example deserves its historical footnote. Secondary-school examinations were then run from Britain by the Associated Examining Board and were in progress at the time of UDI. The board's chief executive immediately sought government advice, asking whether he should continue with the examinations, as this was maintaining law and order, or stop them as he would otherwise be consorting with the Queen's enemies in her realm, which was treason. The advice was to continue as normal.[27]) Ghana and Tanzania broke off diplomatic relations with Britain.

British economic policy was also moving away from the Commonwealth. Britain's failure to join the six meant that it was in danger of losing both its standing in Europe and the chance of restoring its relations with the United States which now saw the EEC as the dominant European group. By 1960

> The posture of the British Government had thus changed totally. It had formerly been argued that one of the reasons why membership of the EEC was impossible for the United Kingdom was that it would be injurious to the Commonwealth. Heath was now claiming that membership of the EEC might well be necessary if the United Kingdom were to be able to continue to assist the Commonwealth.[28]

By the time Wilson was attempting another round of negotiations for British entry to the common market, government was no longer moved by the "grave apprehension and concern" that Commonwealth finance ministers had expressed at this prospect in 1961.[29] British diplomats who "had for many years been suspicious, even dismissive, of the six Common Market countries" were "on the verge of a Damascene conversion".[30] Once negotiations were under way the government, which in its 1964 manifesto had claimed that "the first responsibility of a British government is still to the Commonwealth" would not go beyond trying "to negotiate for a period of transition to enable the Commonwealth countries to have the opportunity to adjust themselves to the new circumstances".[31] France vetoed that bid to join Europe, arguing that the British needed first to achieve equilibrium in the balance of payments and abandon the use of sterling as a reserve currency. A sterling devaluation in 1969, and the abandonment of fixed exchange rates in 1971 and 1972, overcame those economic barriers even as de Gaulle's retirement overcame some of the political ones. At the same time, devaluation and floating currencies took the Commonwealth further away from being a single economic and trading bloc. Well before this, British trade with the Commonwealth had fallen to about 30 per cent of the total and "the EEC issue ceased to engage the attention of Commonwealth Governments".[32] The changes left a sense of disillusion, in Australia at least, at the loss of what had been seen as a special relationship with Britain.[33]

Even as the Commonwealth was declining as a political and economic force, it was growing in terms of membership and of institutional structures. Membership went from eleven in 1960 to thirty-one in 1970 and forty-two in 1980. Commonwealth heads of government continued to meet at least every two years. In 1965 an independent Commonwealth secretariat was established which overcame the constitutional anomaly that Britain had, till then, run Commonwealth meetings. With the agreement of the Queen it moved into Marlborough House as its headquarters, alongside the Commonwealth scholarship commission's office. Though the secretariat was initially headed by a cautious and diplomatic Canadian, Arnold Smith, the British remained deeply sceptical; the agreed memorandum on the powers of the secretariat required that it should not "arrogate to itself executive responsibilities". The wording reflected a tension between the idea of a secretariat that would service occasional meetings and one that would meet whatever international demands its member countries put upon it. Those tensions were to increase in the 1970s and 1980s. Arnold Smith was succeeded as Commonwealth secretary-general in 1975 by the rumbustious Sonny Ramphal who had been minister of justice and foreign minister of Guyana. He brought a Caribbean vigour and eloquence to the job along with a commitment to a triple agenda: to make the Commonwealth count in world discussions, to argue the interests of the south in the world terms of trade, and to bring an end to the racist regimes in southern Africa.

Throughout the 1980s Commonwealth policies were dominated by South Africa where Britain was alone in opposing sanctions against the apartheid government. Ramphal's policies, like those of the rest of the Commonwealth, were at odds with the British but he managed to antagonise them on other issues as well. The Canadians felt they had to restrain him from confronting the British foreign secretary in relation to Canadian constitutional change which, by a historical quirk, required parliamentary approval in Britain.[34] More profoundly, British ministers thought Ramphal interfered unhelpfully in relationship to Southern Rhodesia. By this time Britain's senior politicians no longer had a personal concern for the Commonwealth of the kind displayed by Macmillan and Wilson in their premierships. In international affairs Heath's priorities were in Europe. Thatcher, though less sympathetic to Europe, devoted time and energy to her negotiations with the rest of the European Community while building up the warmest relations with the United States, and suffering being in an unpopular minority at meetings of Commonwealth heads of government. She also resented the way British policies were pilloried by countries whose governance she saw as at best questionable.

In contrast with his frosty relations with the British, rumour said that Ramphal got on well with the Queen, and he was fortunate in his relations with Australia and Canada where, perhaps for the last time, there were prime ministers strongly supportive of the Commonwealth. In his short period in office (1972-75) Gough Whitlam had sought to realign Australian policy with a new concern for international affairs and in particular for the Asia Pacific region. Malcolm Fraser, who succeeded him in 1975 retained the emphasis on the region but also set out to play an active role in the Commonwealth so that "for the first time for a long time there was genuine interest in the Australian government in the association".[35] He established good relations with other Commonwealth prime ministers, called the first Commonwealth regional meeting of heads of government in Sydney in 1978, and saw the Commonwealth as giving "an effective channel to promote its foreign policy objectives globally and within its region". At the Lusaka meeting of Commonwealth heads of government in 1979 Fraser was one of the six heads who worked out the eventual Zimbabwe agreement and claimed some credit for the successful outcome.[36] (Fraser's genuine interest in the Commonwealth was demonstrated, again, when he ran for the office of secretary-general on Ramphal's retirement.) In Canada, Pierre Trudeau's enthusiasm for the Commonwealth matched Fraser's. He was in office from 1968 to 1979 and again from 1980 to 1984 and brought an élan to meetings of Commonwealth heads of government meeting—a rare achievement—when he famously slid down the banisters in Marlborough House. His foreign minister described him as an "ardent advocate" whose standing in its affairs meant that "Canada had become the effective leader of the Commonwealth. Thatcher was unpopular, as Trudeau was popular, with Commonwealth leaders".[37]

Aid, students and scholarships

While Ramphal was seeking to establish the Commonwealth's position in international politics he sustained and attended its regular cycles of meetings of functional ministers—including law and health as well as education—which were serviced by the Commonwealth Secretariat, alongside the established meetings of heads of government. The existence of the secretariat did not change the constitutional structure of CSFP which continued to be based on bilateral agreements; the plan went almost placidly on. As early as 1968 ministers were arguing that it had gone past the period of consolidation.[38] But when problems of international student mobility came to the Commonwealth's political attention in the 1980s, they, and the secretariat's response to them, were to affect the climate within which the plan was working.

Though skirmishes about its primary purposes continued (see chapter 2), education ministers in 1974 still defined the plan in terms that would have been recognised in 1959:

> The C.S.F.P.'s essential characteristic is that it is student oriented, and it allows for the highest opportunities to be made available in a variety of fields without the requirement of linking awards to national development plans. The humanities, fine arts, pure sciences and other cultural subjects come within the pool of programmes available to prospective candidates. In this it is unique in concept and operation.[39]

The total number of scholars and fellows on award remained at between 1,000 and 1,250 from the mid-1960s to the late 1970s with exchanges between the rich Commonwealth countries continuing to make up between 20 and 30 per cent of the whole. Canada planned in 1970 to increase the number of its scholarships to Africa and Asia and reduce the proportion going to the old Commonwealth to 18 per cent, although the figure appears in fact to have fallen only in the 1980s.[40] Australia and New Zealand drew between 27 and 44 per cent of their scholars from the old Commonwealth in the 1970s and 1980s; Australia drew 89 per cent of its fellows from the same source while, of the 40 fellows who went to New Zealand only one came from outside Australia, Britain and Canada.

The record is surprisingly sparse as to the objectives of the rich-country awards and neither the commission in Britain nor the committee in Canada seems to have discussed their purpose. The brief for the British delegation to the Commonwealth education conference in 1971 argued that "There is no doubt that the inclusion of the old Commonwealth countries as equal partners enhances the prestige of the scheme".[41] Ministers at that conference approved the first ten-year review of the plan. It noted arguments for giving more attention to "immediate development needs as expressed in the form of man-power requirements" but, while favouring minor modifications, found that "the original philosophical concept of the plan" was not called into question".[42] Changes were to come from outside the plan, not from its own decision-makers or those of the Commonwealth. By the late 1970s they, and the plan more generally, were working in a climate that had become less benign towards student mobility. New administrative structures, a shortage of university places, and changing fee policies all affected the climate.

New structures were put in place in Britain, Australia and Canada at much the same time. Canada converted its external aid office into the Canadian International Development Agency (CIDA) in 1968 which took over responsibility for CSFP a year later. The AUCC remained its administrator. In the light of this change the head of the AUCC awards office decided it was necessary to reiterate that CSFP was not an aid programme but an exchange programme and not to be "confused with other programmes which were designed solely to assist developing countries".[43] Changes were to follow in Australia after Gough Whitlam came into power in 1972. The aid budget was increased and in 1974 it was announced that fifty new awards would be available under CSFP in future years. At the same time Australia announced a new long-term programme for the south Pacific based on the same principles as the Colombo plan. The Whitlam government also established a new aid agency, the Australian Development Assistance Agency (ADAA, later ADAB, AIDAB and then AusAID), which became responsible for CSFP in 1974. A year later responsibility was split so that the federal education authorities became responsible for outward awards and inward rich-country awards while the development agency retained responsibility for inward awards from the developing Commonwealth. From this time, as in Britain where the change took place in the same year, the plan had two separate funding streams.[44] In all three countries, aid departments now provided the greater part of the funding.

Governments and universities were becoming concerned about pressure of numbers in the 1970s. As noted in chapter 4, there were moves to restrict the number of overseas students in Britain during the 1974-79 labour government. In Canada the AUCC passed resolutions of concern about "government policies aimed at limiting the admission of foreign students". Universities themselves felt under pressure: the University of Alberta warned that "we may have to set upper limits on the numbers we are prepared to accept". A hostile television programme claiming that "thousands of Canadians were being kept out of Canadian universities because of foreign students" was evidence of a public backlash.[45] Australia had experimented with limits. Although this did not apply to government-funded students, Australia imposed a limit of 10,000 on private overseas students in 1973. By the end of the 1970s three government departments, concerned with immigration, foreign affairs, and education had conflicting views on the issue: immigration thought the policy was being abused by students seeking back-door entry to the country; foreign affairs valued them for its own policy reasons; education valued their presence but wanted entry to be controlled in order to avoid displacing Australian students.

One response to these pressures was to increase fees to students. In Canada, where these were determined by provinces, Alberta and Ontario had introduced differential fees for foreign students by 1976 to be followed by Quebec in 1978 and the Maritimes in 1979. Fees were steadily increased. By 1983 all but four Canadian provinces were charging differential fees. In Ontario, which received over half the total number of foreign students, fees were increased by 40 per cent over the previous year, so that they met about two-thirds of the full cost of study.[46] Australia introduced an overseas student charge in 1979, at a rate well below the full cost but progressively increased the figure so that by 1988 it met 55 per cent of the average full cost of a higher education place. By 1990, while four Canadian provinces still had no differential and the others charged less than full-cost fees, both Australia and New Zealand had moved to a policy of charging full-cost fees to all overseas students.[47]

The level of student fees was to remain on the Commonwealth's political agenda throughout the 1980s. The sudden move by the British government from partial subsidy to full-cost fees in 1980 led the Association of Commonwealth Universities, in company with Commonwealth high commissioners, to ask for the issue of student fees to go to the education ministers' meeting planned for Colombo in 1980. They argued that the introduction of full-cost fees

> had implications wide enough to bring it into the arena of Commonwealth debate. Among the factors which gave it the Commonwealth dimension were: the abruptness of the introduction of full cost fees without consultation; the impact of the policy on the development plans of Commonwealth countries who traditionally had access to higher education in developed countries; the expectation that such access would continue; and the value of educational exchange, interchange of scholars and ideas for maintaining and developing Commonwealth links.[48]

Canadian records suggest that this was "the dominant topic" at the conference.[49] Ministers eventually recommended that countries should consider fixing fees at reasonable levels; their discussions led to the establishment of a Commonwealth Standing Committee on Student Mobility. Clashes on fee policy were to get noisier even as the industrialised Commonwealth countries were quietly falling in line with British policy and as the plan proved more resilient than a general belief in Commonwealth educational preference.

Commonwealth ministers of education met again in Nicosia in 1984, by which time the committee on student mobility had met three times, producing a report each time, and the second ten-year review of the plan had been completed. In Britain, the Pym package meant that the plan was rescued from the cutbacks which full-cost fees would otherwise have required; news of this reached Canada together with information that British awards to Canada would increase.[50] The external affairs department had previously advised the prime minister that Canada should not decrease its awards under the plan and that it would give "serious consideration" to increasing them for students in countries "where facilities are not available for undergraduate or graduate programs and training is directly related to development needs".[51] Despite reservations by the Canadian committee, pressures grew for Canada to increase its awards. The president of the University of New Brunswick persuaded the AUCC to call for a significant increase, of perhaps 33 per cent in the number of scholarships; Ramphal wrote to governments seeking pledges at Cyprus to increase their awards.[52] By the time of the conference Canada had agreed to increase its awards from 300 to 500, beginning in 1985/86, with an increase in the budget from Cdn$4.4 to $7.4 million.[53] While the British and Canadian positions were now clear, policies in Australia and New Zealand remained uncertain. New Zealand had a new government while Australia was faced by two reports, both commissioned by government, with opposing recommendations on foreign students. The Goldring report thought full-cost fees would discourage students from coming to Australia while the Jackson report favoured full-cost fees, offset by expanded scholarship programmes.

The Nicosia conference proved to be acrimonious or in Ramphal's words marked by "frank and informative dialogue" and "spirited exchanges".[54] It was clear that Britain was unwilling to move on the principle of full-cost fees and the British got flak for that, rather than credit for increasing the funding for the plan over and above what was necessary to compensate for the increased fees. Perhaps from a silent recognition that they were to get nowhere on the fee issue, certainly from a belief in the plan as a demonstration of a working Commonwealth institution, Ramphal and the secretariat worked to get increased pledges of awards to go alongside the 150 announced by Britain in 1983 and Canada's 200. There was an expectation that the number of award holders would rise above 1,650 in 1985. Pledges were made, though not always later translated into reality, by thirteen countries of which five (Bahamas, Guyana, Kenya, Papua New Guinea and Zimbabwe) were to offer awards for the first time.[55] (I have mixed feelings, as a member of the secretariat at the time, about getting a pledge of five awards from the Zimbabwean minister of education, in the small hours of one conference morning.) Australia and New Zealand subsequently confirmed that they would maintain their awards at the same level.

The immediate consequence was to increase the number of awards. By the time of the next conference in 1987 ministers were able to "express satisfaction" that the Nicosia targets had been reached.[56] Britain and Australia were helped in meeting their targets by abandoning two small but costly fellowship programmes in 1980 and 1986. But the increases took place in a political climate that had changed not only for higher education but for the Commonwealth as a whole.

The post-Soviet world

The world's geopolitical plates shifted in the late 1980s with the collapse of the Soviet Union, the crumbling of apartheid, and the end of military regimes across Latin America. The ending of the cold war closed down the argument that the Commonwealth merited support as an extra bulwark for the west. Increasingly international politics were shaped by regional interests rather than the struggle between two power blocs, leave alone the increasingly amorphous Commonwealth. South Africa was no longer a dividing or defining political issue while, after Ramphal's retirement, there were few speeches from Marlborough House on the terms of trade. Under his successors' more emollient regimes, the Commonwealth Secretariat was willing to play a quieter role, with a new emphasis, pressed on it by the industrialised countries, on the good governance whose absence Thatcher had deplored.

The Commonwealth was less important to its rich members. In Canada, Brian Mulroney, while supporting collaborative programmes offered by the Commonwealth and its French-speaking counterpart *la francophonie*, devoted major political efforts to the creation of a North American Free Trade Area. In Britain relations with its European partners and with the new post-Soviet Europe dominated political dialogue. It is difficult to identify any politician after Fraser and Trudeau prepared to invest moral capital in the Commonwealth. (Perhaps Mulroney is an exception; he increased funding for Commonwealth scholarships in 1984, argued against cutting it ten years later, and provided funding and a headquarters for a new agency, the Commonwealth of Learning in 1987. But his autobiography's only references to the Commonwealth are about meetings of heads of government and his struggles with Margaret Thatcher.[57])

Fraser's interest in Commonwealth affairs had run against the grain of late twentieth-century Australian politics, in which relations with America and with Asia were increasingly dominant. Gareth Evans, foreign minister in the early 1990s, traced the change back to the second world war when Australia was "rescued not by the Imperial British but by the republican Americans".[58] Australia's shift towards Asia continued to gather momentum in the 1990s. Its trade and aid matched its foreign policy. In the early

1990s exports to east Asian markets rose from 50 to more than 60 per cent of the total in five years. Indonesia remained consistently in second place in Australia's bilateral aid expenditure, after its former colony Papua New Guinea. Trade with Singapore and Hong Kong and aid to Bangladesh reflected Australia's regional concerns rather than the Commonwealth legacy.[59]

International educational policy, and political decisions about its funding, responded to these broader changes. In Canada the plan remained for some years uncomfortably within CIDA although reservations were expressed internally about the policy of giving a proportion of awards to the industrialised Commonwealth as "*il nous serait difficile de continuer à justifier cela sous L'Aide Publique au Développement*".[60] A 1986 ministerial task force recommended ending all CIDA scholarship programmes and, while this was not implemented, responsibility for the plan moved to the external relations branch of external affairs. This may have been a more congenial home but scholarships had to compete for support with the priority task of encouraging Canadian studies. (This was also the first priority of the academic liaison office in the Canadian high commission in London.[61]) The budget holder for the plan in the department of external affairs saw the difficulty that

> political support at the ministerial level was sagging in respect of scholarship programmes generally and in respect of the Commonwealth programme specifically—too elitist was an allegation frequently heard, along with the idea that with thousands of foreign students coming to Canada annually on their own funds, why do we need to spend money to bring what can only be called a drop in the bucket of additional students.[62]

Despite support from the prime minister, who had been in office in 1984 when the programme was increased in size, pressure on funding meant that the plan was reduced by one third for the year 1993/4.[63] Uncertainty about its future may have increased as responsibility for its administration went in the mid-1990s from the AUCC to the Canadian Bureau for International Education (CBIE), and then to the International Council for Canadian Studies. It was to return to CBIE again in 2005. In 1997 Canada followed Australia and Britain in abandoning its fellowship programmes, which tended to have higher unit costs than scholarship programmes. The total number of scholars coming to Canada in the 1990s was down on the figure for the 1980s, with 832 scholars as against 1,094, but the proportion of rich-country scholars increased slightly, from 14 to 16 per cent. The 117 scholars who came to Canada in the 1990s from Britain, Australia and Canada were matched by 358 who travelled in the other direction.

The plan ran into difficulties in both Australia and New Zealand in the late 1980s and the 1990s. The visiting professorship scheme to Australia had been discontinued as "no longer operating effectively"; professors were by now not short of opportunities to travel.[64] Meanwhile policy on overseas students was being clarified and articulated. The government took up the recommendations of the Jackson report and from 1985 introduced an overseas student policy that established a quota of subsidised students but required others to pay full-cost fees. Australia at the same time adopted a related policy on the export of education services designed to recruit more fee-paying students. Although this can be seen as a move from aid to trade, Australia also increased the subsidies to international students, with their total rising from about 3,500 in 1983 to nearly 6,000 in 1995.[65] To put CSFP in context, Australia appears to have funded a total of fifty-six Commonwealth scholarships in the three years from 1990 to 1993. New Zealand also moved to a full-cost fee policy for all overseas students, though government funding was in place to meet these fees for development and exchange programmes, which included CSFP. Both countries demonstrated their reluctance to look at fees in a specifically Commonwealth context by declining to attend a meeting called by the Commonwealth secretariat to discuss a "fair and favourable fee regime" in 1992.[66]

Commonwealth education ministers met again in 1994 and agreed to increase CSFP awards to 2000 by the year 2000 and Australia announced that it would increase its allocation when circumstances permitted. That decision was, however, overtaken by a move to rationalise and merge scholarship programmes. From 1996 AusAID announced that there would be a single type of scholarship, the Australian Development Scholarship, for developing countries while applicants from industrialised countries would be eligible for a new International Postgraduate Research Scholarship. Australian vice-chancellors failed in an attempt to get government to change this decision. Canada responded by withdrawing awards to Australia in 1998 but Britain continued to provide them. For their part, Australian universities were able to continue a shadow of the plan by offering a small number of one-off awards—ten in the three years from 2001 to 2004—for specific master's courses.[67]

New Zealand followed suit and withdrew government support from Commonwealth scholarships in 1998. Here, however, the vice-chancellors' committee agreed to continue to fund scholarships. This gave a new lease of life to the plan so that, in the three years from 2003 to 2006, New Zealand made fifty-seven new awards, with the number rising each year.

In Canada the plan survived the 1990s without challenges of this kind. Canada always saw the plan's reciprocity as something that distinguished it from aid programmes and marked it out as a Commonwealth activity with a consequent rationale for rich-country exchanges. But by 2002 it was being judged by new criteria. The Canadian foreign affairs department commissioned an evaluation of the plan in order to see how far it was "still relevant to the overall context of Canadian foreign policy objectives" and was cost effective. The authors of the review looked at its costs and noted, as something to set against them, that scholars brought an average of Cdn$15,000 each to spend in Canada, reducing the net cost to the taxpayer. They found that the plan was working cost-effectively and successful in recruiting students of academic merit but

> were unable to determine whether the programs are achieving their objectives in terms of development assistance to home countries of the selected scholars, disseminating Canadian cultural values, promoting Canadian systems of higher education, assisting Canadian diplomatic efforts by creating a network of "friends to Canada", and other strategic objectives.

In short, the aims had changed, the Commonwealth was not mentioned among them, and the case for continuing the plan was not proven.[68]

In 2006 a new government came into office on a cost-cutting platform; in June 2006 the treasury board, which oversees all government expenditure, announced that it would limit its funding for scholarships to programmes ending one year later and could not guarantee funds beyond that date. The scholarship commission in Britain was told to halt the recruitment of scholars to travel to Canada for the academic year beginning in 2007, although it was assured that British scholars on doctorates in Canada would be able to complete their three years. Fulbright awards were treated in the same way. Press publicity was negative and both political and university pressure was put on government to reverse its decision. By December 2006 the decision had been reversed and funding guaranteed until 2011. Awards would continue; for the first two years at least they were to be at postdoctoral level rather than for higher degrees.[69] The reversal of policy suggests that the idea of the Commonwealth still had just enough resonance to preserve the plan in Canada in a way that it had not in Australia.

Two years later, as discussed in chapter 4, Britain was the next to abandon its support for the plan, although in this case the move was specifically against north-north exchanges. They were rescued, not in the interest of Commonwealth cohesion, but because a flow of able students into British universities was seen as a benefit to them. Academic self-interest for the north and development for the south were now more powerful levers than appeals to Commonwealth interests.

The Commonwealth and its scholarships

The Commonwealth is frequently described as an irrelevance of negligible political significance. A powerful case can be made out. In 1995 a British House of Commons select committee looked but found "little formal evidence" of Commonwealth influence on national policies. In his evidence to the committee, the head of political studies at the School of Oriental and African Studies compared it unfavourably with *la francophonie*, still pursuing its *mission civilatrice* through close links with African politicians and at a considerable financial cost. In contrast he argued that "The Commonwealth does not have any of these features. That is why I say it is an aimless, purposeless organisation. It does not have the ties that bind".[70] And yet, despite the sceptics, prime ministers still attend biennial meetings, ministers of education turn up every three years, and so on. Britain continued to attend even when being castigated at each meeting.

Perhaps the scholarship plan can stand as a metaphor for the Commonwealth. In scale, it is now dwarfed by the total flow of international students and indeed by regional scholarship programmes. It is justified, when it is, in terms quite different from those used by its founding fathers. It often fits awkwardly with national priorities. The political costs in closing it down can be set against the fact that it does not demand huge resources. Its purposes have quietly changed even while lipservice is paid to its original principles.

At the same time the plan has an almost symbiotic relation with other Commonwealth activities. Triennial meetings of Commonwealth ministers provide an opportunity for them to acclaim it as embodying values which no-one would want to dispute. The prospect of attending a meeting empty-handed may have restrained ministers wanting to walk away from the plan.

CHAPTER SIX

UNIVERSITIES: EXPANSION IN THE SOUTH

As the first Commonwealth scholars set out in 1960 their minds were not on Commonwealth cohesion but on the practical values of a scholarship. Woodville Marshall, a young history graduate of the University of the West Indies, took his scholarship because it funded the extra years he needed in Cambridge for a PhD and did so on more generous terms than anything else available in Barbados.[1] From the viewpoint of governments the scholarships had prestige, with the names of scholars recorded in the press.[2] But they were only one of many sources of funding for study abroad as the rich countries of the north competed to support higher education in the south. Over the next twenty years, while Nigeria made use of 537 Commonwealth scholarships, her universities also attracted support from the Carnegie Corporation, the Ford, Nuffield and Rockefeller Foundations, UNESCO, the Netherlands, the United States and both east and west Germany.[3] Pakistan used a variety of different channels, along with the plan, to help increase capacity in the sciences within its universities. The pattern was repeated across the Commonwealth.

The developing Commonwealth's use of the plan was generally a function of government policy, university preference, and individual choice. For the most part awarding countries eschewed specific policies in terms of particular academic disciplines and seldom targeted their awards on particular institutions. While there was a scholarship and fellowship plan, there was no plan in the sense of a set of agreed and detailed objectives. The lack of a plan in the second sense makes for difficulties in assessing CSFP's outcomes or its effects. For all that, it makes sense to look at impact within the universities of the south: selection on grounds of academic merit ensured that current and future academic staff always made up a high proportion of the plan's scholars and fellows. In this chapter their achievements are explored in the context of the development of higher education over the last half century.

In the early 1960s, as argued in chapter 2, higher education was still small. In 1961 the French and English-speaking countries of subsaharan Africa had 15,000 students at university within the subcontinent and 11,000 studying overseas.[4] A year later Malawi, then Nyasaland, was said to have only twenty-two African graduates of whom twelve were in gaol.[5] In 1963 the federal University of East Africa had only 1,229 undergraduates with "hardly a score of indigenous academic staff members" to serve the needs of Kenya, Tanzania and Uganda. Only in 1965 was northern Nigeria, with a population of 50 million, to get a university. The ten-year review of the scholarship plan found in 1972 that "the old Commonwealth has university facilities fifty times as available to its citizens as those enjoyed by the citizens of some of the new African countries". In Asia, Malaysia had a single university; in Sri Lanka there were three, with two of them founded only in 1959. The distribution of universities within India before partition meant that, at independence, Pakistan had one university in East Pakistan—later Bangladesh—and two in West Pakistan, one of them only three-months old.[6]

Hong Kong and India were already different. For its population of three million, Hong Kong had one university with 1,200 students in 1959 to be joined by a second with the establishment of the Chinese University of Hong Kong in 1963. (Sir Frederick Lugard founded the first in 1912 when he was governor during an unwelcome break from ruling Nigeria where he left an imperial tradition but no universities.) The proportion of the age group in higher education was to rise to 5 per cent in 1985, 13 per cent in 1991 and 19 per cent in 1997.[7] At independence India had less than thirty universities; within fifteen years the number had risen to forty-five with 1,500 colleges and over a million students for a population of some 430 million; over the next twenty-five years universities grew to 149 with 3.5 million enrolments. Indian universities pursued a policy of expansion, in response to public demand, itself partly fuelled by the government of India's policy of requiring a degree for entry to the civil service. While the quality of Indian higher education has been consistently criticised, especially within the colleges whose students made up a significant proportion of the total, governments have "accepted the hard reality of the inevitable expansion of higher education".[8] The large base of, albeit mediocre, undergraduate-level teaching has allowed India's major universities and institutes to run flourishing departments and provide good postgraduate education to large numbers of students. Indian experience contrasts sharply with that of African countries with similar gnp per capita.

As the plan was getting under way, universities throughout the Commonwealth were facing two principal kinds of demand: to produce the trained people who would staff the civil service, and to produce enough potential academics for their own future. Broader interests of the economy came after these. Governments differed in the priority they gave to each.

University development and the role of the plan

In many countries, government demands took priority for the first ten or fifteen years of the plan. This coincided with the early years of independence for much of the Commonwealth. Manpower planning held intellectual sway at this time, encouraging the view that governments could and should control the size and shape of higher education in the interests of specific job markets. Scholarships were one means to that end. In Malaysia, for example, it was reported in the mid-1970s that "public education, particularly higher education, has been geared to train civil servants and professionals for the public and private sector to meet the expanding demand and, wherever possible, to replace expatriates". This policy fed through into Malaysia's use of the plan: the first ten-year review reported in 1972 that, following national development policies, Malaysian civil servants were at an advantage in applying for scholarships. The same review found that 55 per cent of former scholars from Sri Lanka (then Ceylon) were in professional jobs, almost entirely in the public service, against 37 per cent in universities.[9] Small states saw the plan in the same light. In 1971 Montserrat reported that all returning scholars had senior positions in the civil service while in Dominica returning scholars "invariably accept appointments with the government"; the two former scholars who had left government, one for commerce and one for the University of the West Indies, had done so after two years in its service.[10]

East Africa followed a similar path. As Tanzania, Uganda and Kenya gained independence in 1961, 1962 and 1963, their first priority was to localise the civil service which they succeeded in completing within ten years. The proportion of Tanzanian citizens in middle-grade and senior posts, for example, went from 26 per cent in 1961 to 94 per cent in 1972. To help with this process Tanganyika, along with Kenya, was among the countries pressing for the scheme to provide more undergraduate awards at the 1962 ministers' conference when these were still seen as a priority. Within ten years that pressure had eased so that, by 1975, Uganda reported it was satisfying demand for undergraduate degrees locally and had more than enough applications to put forward for postgraduate awards. National priorities meant that their nominations were in scientific, commercial and technical subjects with none in the liberal arts.[11]

The sixth education ministers' conference in 1974 was able to sum up experience across the Commonwealth:

> Developing countries increasingly see the Plan as one more instrument available to them for the training of their higher level manpower. As against the initial few years where the academic excellence and potential of

the students to benefit from the awards were the predominant factors in the selection of the candidate, now the nomination of personnel can also be made against a projected spectrum of manpower requirements, indicated in national development plans.[12]

Universities were not far behind governments in wanting to use the plan for their own purposes. At the 1964 conference of education ministers, "the most persistent theme running through the discussions was the need for the developing countries of the Commonwealth to become masters of their own educational progress". The vice-chancellor of the University of Kerala, who addressed the conference on CSFP, was more specific:

> In countries with no local tradition of university education, the aim should be to enable a sufficient number of young people to receive higher education in the United Kingdom or other advanced Commonwealth countries, so that they may then assist in the task of setting up or developing institutions in their own countries.[13]

One response to this demand was the launch of the British academic staff awards which came at an opportune moment for some of the Commonwealth's new universities. Gajaraj Dhanarajan, for example, was then a young entomologist on the staff of the new Universiti Sains Malaysia. His vice-chancellor encouraged him to travel to Aston University in Britain to do a doctorate both in his own interest and that of staff development. The only constraint, apart from uprooting his family, was the availability in Birmingham of the termites he needed for his research, overcome by importing them from the south of France.[14] By 1972 the ten-year review found that the plan had "made an essential contribution to university facilities in many countries and in some cases has become almost part of the system—the only valid complaint being that it provides insufficient numbers and on this ground at all has not made an outstanding contribution". Some countries, such as Singapore, had embraced a deliberate policy of using the plan for university development. Hong Kong, in contrast, did not regard the scholarships "primarily as a source of aid. They are open scholarships for which there is a keen competition among candidates ... with outstanding academic qualifications". The University of the West Indies, then the one university in its region, was described by the review as valuing "overseas experience, as distinct from erudition" because of its belief that "staff members should have some academic experience outside of the West Indies". British delegates attending the ministerial conference in 1974 concluded that while the plan was "basically subserving the needs of a country as a whole, it was often regarded as serving the university interest more than any other".[15]

University development did not move at an even pace. In east and central Africa university staff had been localised more slowly than the civil service. In both Tanzania and Zambia government had "implicitly decided that the University should have relatively low priority in localization and so has often deprived it of its outstanding staff members". The three colleges comprising the University of East Africa were still quite small, with local staff in a minority at two of the three; by the mid-1970s they held 30 per cent of posts at Dar es Salaam, 45 per cent at Nairobi and 70 per cent at Makerere. The university was benefiting from a targeted staff-development programme of the Rockefeller foundation which provided 163 scholarships for east Africans to do higher degrees between 1963 and 1970.[16] Over the same period 236 Commonwealth scholarships were provided to the three countries. Although Commonwealth scholarship agencies did not take part in the donors' conferences that were seeking to shape higher education in east Africa, the programme's concentration on postgraduate awards suggest that, even allowing for the demands from governments, Commonwealth scholars may have been of a number to make a significant difference to university development in east Africa. One Ugandan scholar, who came to Britain slightly later, in the 1980s, saw the plan as "undoubtedly the biggest sponsor of Makerere university academic staff development programme every year".[17]

Many universities expanded rapidly in the 1970s. In Nigeria this process was fuelled by the flow of oil revenues. It assumed that the future of many Commonwealth scholars would lie in university teaching, while it recognised that the numbers involved, for a country of its size, meant their contribution, though valuable, could only be small.[18] By the time of the second ten-year review in 1982, university needs looked even more important for the plan as developing-country universities were increasingly developing their postgraduate work. The review foresaw that,

> One of the main tasks of the eighties will be to assist universities and other leading tertiary institutions in developing countries of the Commonwealth to build their own capacity for post-graduate study and research. The Commonwealth Scholarship and Fellowship Plan has an important contribution to make.[19]

The review also noted the growth of centres for advanced study and research and recommended that awarding countries might target awards on such centres. These might be of various kinds including conventional scholarships and fellowships, third-country awards, support for field work and link arrangements with centres with shared research and teaching interests.[20] The idea of concentrating or targeting awards, which was a mainstay of foundation scholarship policy at the time, went against the twenty-year conception of the plan as driven by individual academic excellence and does not seem to have led to any significant change of practice by the main awarding countries.

Educational expansion was checked in the 1980s as the world economy turned down. Public expenditure on education in the developing world as a whole fell, in real terms, between 1980 and 1985 and even by 1990 had not reached the level achieved ten years before.[21] Where they were able to influence government policy, as they could in much of subsaharan Africa, the World Bank institutions imposed policies of structural adjustment. Government expenditure was cut while, at the same time, many of the international aid agencies were switching their attention, rhetoric and funding from tertiary to basic education. Meanwhile, as primary and secondary education had expanded, so the number of potential entrants to higher education was growing. Universities were required to admit more students even while their income was frozen or reduced. African universities in particular had to run hard to remain in the same place. The third ten-year review commented sadly:

> An evaluation of the effectiveness of CSFP cannot be divorced from consideration of the overall economic and financial environment within which it has had to operate. Since the last review, serious economic difficulties have bedevilled both Commonwealth developed and developing countries. Slow economic growth and recession in the developed countries, and even more negative growth trends combined with structural adjustment in the developing countries, have been constraining factors in increasing the resilience of the Plan.[22]

Despite the difficulties, there is evidence that, by the mid-1980s, the plan was having an impact on university development, though this may have been easier to discern in Asia than in Africa. Temple reported to the commission on a visit he made in 1984 to Malaysia, Singapore and Sri Lanka. He carried with him a list of the 220 Malaysians who had held awards and in each of the, now five, universities, "learned much through meeting some of the 104 former award holders already identified from the Commonwealth Universities Yearbook as being staff members. ... Many of the academics were heads of departments or otherwise leading members of their universities".[23] At this time the Canadian programme seems to have been particularly fruitful in training future academic staff. Over half of scholars recruited in the 1980s, whom it was possible to trace, went on to take up academic posts, including future vice-chancellors in Kenya, Nigeria, Sri Lanka and Swaziland. As one index of academic productivity Lendela Ndlovu went back to supervise some sixty-seven research animal science students in Zimbabwe.[24] Appropriately enough, Cisco Magagula, who studied educational administration at the Ontario Institute for Studies in Education was to write, nearly twenty years later and from his standpoint as vice-chancellor of the University of Swaziland, about the significance of crossborder education for Africa.[25]

By the 1990s the beleaguered African universities were attracting two lines of criticism: that their costs were too high in comparison with those of other levels of education and that they continued to be teaching an elite at a time when other parts of the world were moving towards mass higher education. In an attempt to relieve their funding problems university presidents, at a meeting of the Association of African Universities, resolved in 2001 to support the introduction of tuition fees, where enrolment had previously been free. Cost sharing and cost recovery were becoming part of normal practice.[26] Private-sector universities were accepted or welcomed as a means of widening enrolment. Meanwhile some of the international funding agencies, which had effectively abandoned support for African higher education by the 1980s, began to move back in support of a number of targeted institutions. Makerere, for example, benefited from an agreement in 2000 by the Carnegie, Ford, Rockefeller and MacArthur foundations to set up a five-year $100 million programme for African universities.[27] Despite these measures the numbers in higher education remained sadly low; in the ten years from 1990 the tertiary level gross enrolment ratio in subsaharan Africa crept up only from 1.6 per cent to 2.5 per cent.

While Africa was suffering, these were the years of the Asian miracle and university enrolments in southeast, and to a lesser extent south Asia, tell a different story. The Singapore government saw itself as being cautious on university expansion in the 1970s and 1980s but, already by 1980 had 5 per cent of the age group in university and a further 8 per cent on tertiary-level diploma courses. University enrolments increased almost fourfold from 9,000 in 1980 to 35,800 in 2000, with a target of getting 25 per cent of the age group into universities by 2010. The policy aim was "to identify potential niches for Singapore within the global economy and then to marshal resources within the higher education system toward the filling of these niches". Gender balance changed along with this expansion, with female enrolments going from 23 per cent in 1960 to 44 per cent in 1980 and 50 per cent in 2000. Expansion in Hong Kong was at least as dramatic: it had 7 per cent of the age cohort in higher education by 1987 with a further 3.4 per cent on other tertiary courses; by 1994/5 18 per cent were studying at university level. Expansion had been driven both by the expansion of upper-secondary education in the 1970s and 1980s and by changes in the Hong Kong economy; the move from the manufacture of textiles and plastics to higher-value products and services increased the demand for higher education. With eleven public and fifteen private universities Malaysia had by 2002 outstripped both Hong Kong and Singapore. Public university enrolments increased tenfold in twenty years with student numbers going from 20,200 students to 201,300 between 1980 and 2000. Government policy was then to increase the participation rate to 25 per cent in 2005 and 30 per cent in 2010. Unsurprisingly academic staff were seen as being underqualified; in 2000 only 22 per cent of public university staff had PhDs while there had been concerns about low research productivity.[28]

All three of these countries have joined the ranks of middle and high-income countries. For them, the natural comparators are the enrolment ratios in the industrialised countries of the OECD. But India has set itself on a similar road with some 6 to 7 per cent of the age cohort at university. The Indian Association of Universities made the point in arguing that this was low in comparison to OECD member figures of 50 per cent with "20 per cent considered essential to sustained economic development".[29] The scale of this expansion means that the scholarship plan could not have played a major role in providing postgraduate degrees for the new ranks of academics. Malaya (as it was), for example, was given fifty-four scholarships in the plan's first five years—a significant number in relation to the 103 local staff of the two branches of the University of Malaya in Kuala Lumpur and Singapore in 1960. The recent average of less than ten awards a year is insignificant now that the academic profession in the two countries has grown to more than 20,000.

It is more difficult to gauge the significance of Commonwealth scholarships and fellowships for universities in its second quarter century than in its first: the universities were bigger, there were more of them, and the tacit decision by awarding countries not to concentrate their awards mean that effects are dispersed. But, across the whole period of the plan's existence, the record shows that a significant proportion of alumni have made their careers within higher education. A British survey of alumni in 2000 suggested from partial data that some 64 per cent of alumni from developing countries were working in higher education. It concluded:

> The dominance of higher education is not particularly surprising. For developing countries, the Commission reserves 40 per cent of its resources for new awards each year for those currently working in this sector, with the specific intention that they should return to their previous employment.

> In addition to this it is likely that a proportion of those winning General Scholarships will enter higher education, particularly given the limited employment prospects in many recipient countries. The figures could, therefore, be seen as confirming that the scheme is meeting one of its key objectives.[30]

It went on to note that

> In many developing countries universities are seen as the main source of new and radical ideas, or challenges to government and it is also the case that senior staff are often closely involved in government. The survey reveals ample evidence for this, with staff whose main employment was listed as academic also holding public office on a variety of Commissions and Enquiries, as well as NGOs and voluntary bodies ...
> Those award holders who do remain in higher education have a strong record in rising to senior positions within their institutions ... [so] that a substantial number have reached senior managerial positions (defined to include Vice-Chancellor, Pro-Vice-Chancellor, Vice-Principal, Dean and Head of Department), and that the strong majority reach at least senior academic positions (including Professors, Readers and Senior Lecturers).[31]

Reflecting the policies of its main funder, a later evaluation by the scholarship commission concentrated heavily on the contribution alumni were making to development, and had little to say about universities. It found, however, that over 60 per cent of respondents were working in education, and of these 97 per cent in higher education. From the earliest years of the scheme it quoted the example of an Indian water engineer, Professor Omkar Wakhlu, who did a doctorate in fluid mechanics at the University of Birmingham and went home to train more than 2,000 engineers in a twelve-year academic career. Emeritus Professor Anoja Wickramasinghe, who graduated in the 1980s, had built on her academic career to promote forest ecology and local capacity through community organisations in five districts of Sri Lanka. From the 2000s it quoted as examples a split-site scholar from Nigeria and an academic fellow from India who had gone home to work within and beyond their universities on curriculum development and on the extraction of oil from apricot stones. Their universities were not ivory towers.[32]

As the Commonwealth's university systems have grown, so CSFP's effects have inevitably become more scattered. The Commonwealth review committee in 1993 recommended targeted awards "to accommodate national human resource development needs and the strengthening of higher education institutions" to be agreed between nominating and awarding countries, but the main awarding countries did not pick up the idea.[33] Commonwealth education ministers met in 1994 but the conference report makes no reference to this recommendation. Almost as a separate development both the Canadian and the British agencies launched distance-learning programmes, discussed below, which concentrated on cohorts of students, studying through partnerships between northern and southern universities. Both announced that one of their concerns was capacity building in the south although progress towards it proved more difficult to gauge. In 2003 the commission in Britain announced a new programme of institutional capacity grants in which awards would be promised to selected institutions over a period of years.[34] It proved difficult to mesh these with the commission's regular programme of awards and, in the first five years, only three grants had been agreed.

Three case studies

The detailed record of the plan in the Caribbean, in India, and in distance learning makes it possible to look in more detail at its role in the south, and at the part it has played in university development.

University of the West Indies—Barbados

Barbados is one of the most densely populated countries in the world where, after emancipation, there were few opportunities to work except on the sugar plantations. A plantation economy, dependent on the export of a single crop, dominated the country well into the twentieth century. A glass ceiling existed beyond which even the most affluent and well-educated black Barbadians could not pass. One consequence was a high priority given to education by black politicians, who had a measure of power from 1944.[35] By 1962 education had been made free in all secondary schools and on independence in 1966 all children were reported as attending primary or secondary school. (This section is based mainly on Stafford, *Caribbean*, and material not separately referenced is drawn from there.)

The University of the West Indies was established as a university college in 1948 with its first campus in Jamaica; a second campus was created on the site of the Imperial College of Tropical Agriculture in Trinidad and a third in Barbados where teaching started in 1963 with 118 students. With these small numbers, Barbados was among the countries stressing the demand for undergraduate degrees up to the late 1960s.[36] As the university expanded, that demand fell away but there remained a need for scholarships for higher degrees, that would enable beneficiaries to teach at tertiary level. While other scholarships were available in Barbados, few of these supported postgraduate study. From the 1970s the government saw the plan very much as a mechanism for strengthening the university. In doing so it was helped by the bias towards small states exercised by the awarding countries; by 2006 Barbados, with a population of less than 300,000 had received 215 scholarships as contrasted with the 204 that had gone to Malawi with a population of over 13 million. By early in the present century at least sixty staff members had benefited from the plan, nearly a quarter of the total number of awardees. An analysis of the campus staff in 1995/96, shown in table 6.1, demonstrates the way the university and government had used the plan.

Table 6.1 Plan alumni at Barbados campus

	Principal/ pro-vice-chancellor	Deans and heads of department	Other teaching staff
Administration	2 of 2		
Faculties			
Arts/general studies		2 of 5	7 of 22
Education			3 of 7
Law		2 of 3	2 of c10
Medicine and surgery		1 of 3	about a quarter
Science and technology		1 of 6	2 of 40
Social science		2 of 5	7 of c28

With the exception of the sciences, where the university has continued to rely heavily on staff from outside Barbados or the region, the plan alumni are spread across the faculties. Commonwealth scholars and fellows have, however, had a particular impact in certain departments.

In its early years Barbados used the plan to train medical faculty at the Queen Elizabeth Hospital which served as a teaching hospital for the university, with fifteen awards over twenty years. At this time the University of the West Indies policy was to train general practitioners, regarded as the primary medical need in the region. Specialist training had to be obtained beyond the region and ambitious young doctors successfully sought Commonwealth awards. As the number of such doctors came to exceed the supply of scholarships, an increasing number of them identified funding to study elsewhere, particularly in the United States. Large numbers stayed there, leading the university to change its policy and develop an active postgraduate programme. Fewer doctors have since applied for, or gained, Commonwealth scholarships.

Perhaps by example as much as by planning Commonwealth alumni are clustered in at least two other departments. Woodville Marshall returned to Barbados after his doctorate in Cambridge and academic posts in Nigeria and at the Jamaican campus of the university. Once there he shaped the history department away from the eurocentric roots of the university college, retiring as emeritus professor in 2000. Sir Keith Hunte went to McGill university in Canada in 1961 on a Commonwealth scholarship, wanted to study some aspect of Caribbean history but discovered that this was impossible with the supervision available and opted for a study of the role of the Roman Catholic Church in Canadian schooling, a subject he was able to compare to that of the Anglican Church in the Caribbean. Hunte subsequently became deputy principal and then principal of the campus. His successor, Sir Hilary Beckles, was yet another historian who returned to Britain, where he had done his first degree, as an academic staff fellow in 1986. While other historians have followed in their path, the percentage of history department staff who have received awards has declined in recent years as the university has been able to expand its own postgraduate teaching. By 1995, for example, the department had five PhD students, eight working on taught master's and eight working on MPhils and was well placed to develop its own staff.

The school of education has also benefited from a steady flow of Commonwealth scholars. It has played a role in developing an appropriate curriculum for the Caribbean in Barbados and the eastern Caribbean and in supporting the training of primary school teachers. Among its alumni Rudolph Goodridge did an MEd at Leeds in 1964/5. returned to Barbados to work as a community education officer and then was seconded to develop a university-based inservice diploma. He was followed by Desmond Clarke who travelled to Britain twice, initially to do a diploma course at Manchester in 1969 and then, nearly ten years later, to follow it up with a master's in reading studies at Lancaster. He then lectured in teacher education as well as working on a UNESCO/UWI project on language teaching. Specialist qualifications were obtained in the 1970s by Workeley Brathwaite in science education at Chelsea College and by Gerry Rose in mathematics education at Keele. They, and others, went on to apply their skills within the Barbados and eastern Caribbean education systems as well as at the university.

Commonwealth alumni are not limited to these faculties but also appear, for example, in faculty lists for languages, law, the social sciences and the physical sciences. Their numbers suggest that, in a small country and on a small campus, deliberate policy coupled with personal influence has allowed the plan to have a significant bearing on university development. Without any general policy on the part of the main awarding countries towards institutional development, or the targeting of scholarships, Barbados and the University of the West Indies have in practice benefited from a Commonwealth-wide generosity towards small states in the allocation of awards.

India

As the largest Commonwealth country India has always been a major player in the plan. At the time of the 1959 conference it already had a central government mechanism in place which was administering about 1,000 overseas scholarships and fellowships a year.[37] Since then, it has given over 1,000 awards and received over 3,700. In 1960 some fifty-four scholars set off from India while one fellow—a specialist in ancient Indian history and culture—went in the same year to New Zealand.

India has maintained its central system for administering awards, although responsibility is now shared between the university grants committee, for nominations from universities, and the ministry of human resource development for others. Awards given by India are administered by the Indian Council for Cultural Relations. (This section is based mainly on Jodhka and Raina, *India*, and material not separately referenced is generally drawn from there.) Its policy appears to have been one of careful even-handedness, possibly at the price of bureaucratic rigidity. It has not, for example, favoured centrally funded universities over state funded, even though the former tend to be academically stronger. And, despite the complexities of operating from a capital city in a huge country, it has tried to avoid regional bias in its selections. In 1998, for example, the chairman of the UGC expressed his dissatisfaction with the panel on medicine that consisted entirely of experts from New Delhi and directed his office to make sure that in future "they come from all corners of India" and that none of the current panel should be reappointed.

It seems that most Indian scholars and fellows have returned home to university posts. Any attempt to assess the impact of the plan on India is complicated by the scale of the country and by the decisions, by the governments of India and of the awarding countries, not to concentrate awards in particular institutions or on particular subjects. India originally used scholarships mainly to support science and technology. Of 151 Indians who took up Canadian scholarships in the 1960s, for example, fifty-three were in engineering and twenty-two in the physical sciences.[38] More recently India has followed a deliberate policy of nominating scholars across the range of disciplines.

Jodhka carried out a small survey and series of interviews of plan alumni, for whom contact details were available. While the sample was not representative, the variety of responses make it possible to identify a number of different outcomes from studying abroad on a scholarship or fellowship. He found that while only 32 per cent of respondents reported an increase in salary as a result of studying abroad, 75 per cent saw it as having a positive or very positive effect on their career. Positive indicators included invitations to national or international seminars, improved opportunities for contact with other academics nationally and internationally, and international research grants. Some gained promotions, though these did not come automatically. Madhu Raka, chair of the mathematics department at Punjab University put it

> It positively influenced my promotion as reader and then as professor. I was awarded the INSA Young Scientist Award for the research work that I started at Cambridge University during this fellowship.

Some saw the awards as bringing professional benefits without immediate benefits in terms of career mobility. One former scholar reported:

> There was no scheme of promotions in our universities then (1972). I was appointed Reader, through an open selection, fourteen years after my PhD (from the University of Warwick). This was partly because there were very few positions and partly because there were a large number of candidates with similar qualifications. I must add however, that the situation was probably different in many other subjects. Also, even in the short term, probably there could have been a difference if I had moved to some other university.

In contrast some award holders faced hostility on their return and saw their new qualifications as generating a sense of insecurity among colleagues. Another scholar reported:

> In the short run the impact may have been negative ... [with] acts such as the increments being denied for PhD for a long time, bungling with seniority of the cadre and the accruing benefits. After some struggle many of these issues have been settled. At present (medium term) there has been neither significant gain nor loss, but in the long run I am optimistic that the benefits of PhD will eventually accrue as there are few people in the field with equivalent qualifications.

Others respondents, particularly in smaller universities and research institutes, reported a sense of frustration that they could not readily use the skills they had acquired abroad in teaching or research. One scholar, for example, went from a state agricultural university to do a PhD in biochemistry at Edinburgh University (1993-6). She found a ten to fifteen year technological and knowledge gap between the two universities (although this would probably not have been the case if she had come from a leading research institute). At least as serious, her teaching load left her few opportunities to maintain the networks and pursue the research which she had developed in Edinburgh. A colleague who followed her a year later reported similar experiences since returning home. Neither was in a position to publish internationally and neither travelled outside India after their award. In contrast with these stories—and Jodhka reports that they have not been uncommon from state universities—Pandurangappa, who went to Oxford from the department of chemistry at Bangalore University, a state university, was able on his return to attract research funding in the area of gas sciences, to develop a new course, and to publish consistently. Also in Bangalore, at a state agricultural university, P. Narayanaswami was able to introduce a research programme in tissue culture, which he had studied at Imperial College, London, and to launch into publishing in internationally refereed journals.

Academics working in major universities or research institutions are at an advantage and many report on the positive benefits they have gained from their awards in relation to their own discipline. Professor Eadala Saibaba Reddy of JLN Technological University, Hyderabad, set up a new centre for research in geo-environmental engineering at his own university. India has made considerable use of the plan for advanced training in medicine, through both scholarships and fellowships and this, too, is reflected in accounts by scholars. A. V. Lakshmanan, on returning to his university, was able to "set-up a doctoral programme in Medical Physics in 1975, which at that time was the first of its kind in India". He went on to initiate an MSc programmes taking fifteen to twenty students a year and commented that "The institution benefited greatly from my training in the UK".

Partha Basu, a head of department at the National Cancer Institute, Kolkata, similarly attributes the success of a new programme initiated by the government of India to his training abroad as a Commonwealth Scholar:

> The major focus of my CSFP training was to learn about the community based cervical screening programme. After I came back from UK I was given the charge of running the community based cancer control programmes of our institute. Through this programme supported by Government of India I could organize cervical and breast cancer screening for

thousands of women in rural areas of our state. ... The new cervical screening test I worked to develop and validate is now being used widely in India and many other low-resource countries. That is a big personal satisfaction for me. I initiated the School for Cervical Cancer Prevention with assistance from my thesis supervisor and WHO that is recognized as a training centre for doctors from all over India and neighbouring countries.

Anil V. Kulkarn, a scientist at the ISRO Ahmedabad, realised on his return from Canada after studying glaciology as a Commonwealth fellow that he

was one of the few academically qualified glaciologists in the country and this subject had great importance for Indian society. Over a period of last twenty years, I could make major contributions to developing our understanding of Himalayan glaciers, wrote a large number of scientific papers in international and national journals and trained a team of scientists to study Himalayan glaciers .... I think, without the Commonwealth fellowship and an academic understanding developed at a Canadian university, it would have been very difficult to develop glaciology programme.

Returning scholars were also able to mobilise the networks they had developed while abroad. C. V. Kantharia, from KEM hospital in Mumbai, for example, explained that with the help of doctors he worked with as a scholar they set up "a specialised department of gastrointestinal surgery in their hospital in India, which is the first of its kind in western Maharashtra". His overseas colleagues also helped establish a liver transplant programmes at his hospital. Former scholars and fellows also report on being able to arrange for their overseas supervisors to conduct specialist workshops in India and on consulting their overseas supervisors on difficult clinical cases.

Scholars and fellows working in Britain were impressed with the greater resources available but also influenced by differences in work practices. S. Shivashankaran, a paediatric cardiologist in Kerala, spent a year at Guy's Hospital in London and was impressed by the focused work culture, the approach to patients, and the collegiality that he found among the doctors. He explained that:

My approach to problems changed a lot. In the short term, my specific output as a trained person in paediatric cardiology gave me a special identity. In the medium term, contrary to my training in India, where I learned to find fault with all my colleagues, system and juniors, I learned the art of identifying the problem and solving it in a manner suited to the place and to encourage people to get the best out of them. In the long term I could refine myself into a good team leader and an academician, who has state of the art knowledge in his field of specialization.

Another doctor, Sanjay Behari of the postgraduate Institute of Medical Sciences, Lucknow, reported in similar terms:

> Since this fellowship enabled me to work in a new country, I gained in many aspects and resolved many of my preconceived and false perceptions (that inevitably form with a superficial knowledge of another country). I learnt the importance of establishing protocols which need to be systematized for an efficient working of my own department. I learnt what it means to work in a team where people with different backgrounds work towards a common goal to achieve amazing results. I learnt to adjust to a new set of rules and mannerisms which I hope has made me more open and perceptive towards different ideas and opinions. Finally, I understood that working and staying in different countries is not difficult since people everywhere have the same aspirations and apprehensions.

The effects of overseas study may be amplified if a group of academics from the same institution develop a shared culture and encourage others to follow in their path. Despite the plan's awards being open throughout India, a number of universities and institutes obtained awards early in the history of the plan which allowed the award holders to set a pattern for subsequent generations of scholars and fellows. (Jodhka identifies these institutions as including Sree Chitra Tirunal in Kerala, the state agricultural universities in Thrisur and the University of Agricultural Sciences, Bangalore, Jadhavpur University, Kolkata, and Punjab Agriculture University, Ludhiana.) Informal networks of fellows appear to have developed in a number of cities within particular disciplines. While these networks cannot guarantee awards, they provide a means for publicising scholarships and fellowships, and encouraging academic staff to apply, and reapply if unsuccessful. In this way, for example, scientists from the Sree Chitra Tirunal Institute for Medical Sciences in Kerala report on following in each other's footsteps.

It is more difficult to trace the plan's influence on higher education in India than in Barbados. The total of 3,500 award holders has to be set against the 500,000 teachers now working in tertiary education. Even in 1960 the first fifty award holders were drawn from universities that already had over 50,000 staff members. The deliberate policy of the government of India against concentrating the awards on particular institutions, which was entirely in accord with the original principles of the plan, compounds the difficulty. The qualitative evidence suggests that award holders from some smaller universities encountered major difficulties in applying what they had learned abroad, either for their own benefit or for that of their institutions. But this looks like the experience of a minority. Where the host environment in India has been favourable, universities and their staff have been able to draw major benefits from the able scholars and fellows who had been on award. India has continued to value awards in other parts of the Commonwealth, and has continued to send able scholars to the universities of the north. In 2007, for example, the scholarship commission reported on four doctorates awarded by British universities in agronomy, soil science, biotechnology, and English literature along with four master's degrees in the sciences and five in the social sciences. With two awards in biotechnology and one in nanoscale science and technology the plan was continuing to provide specialist courses relevant to higher education in India where particular Commonwealth universities had a comparative advantage.[39]

Distance learning

Both Canada and Britain have experimented with programmes of distance learning which have had a twofold objective: to benefit individual students and to contribute to institutional development through partnerships between metropolitan and overseas universities. Similar considerations affected the Canadian committee and the British commission in making this move. Both were concerned that the scholarship plan was seen as being elitist and wanted to present something that countered that view to—new—ministers to whom they were reporting. Distance learning was seen in Canada as a way of involving universities that had previously hosted few Commonwealth scholars; while this was not set as an objective in Britain, several of the major players there proved to be post-1992 universities with a similar record. Distance-learning programmes also offered a response to the charge that the plan contributed to brain drain: these scholars would stay at home.[40] The economics of distance learning meant that it might be possible to produce graduates at reduced unit costs.

Canada came first. It launched a "Canada Caribbean Distance education scholarship programme" in 1998 designed to enable students in four Caribbean countries to follow distance-education courses offered by Canadian universities. The scheme was administered by the Commonwealth of Learning, one of whose functions was to promote Commonwealth cooperation in distance learning. It differed from most previous activity under the plan in using distance-education methods and in being at undergraduate level. It had different aims from the established ones of academic excellence in that it was intended to relate to the local job market and to "help the marketing of higher education by highlighting the advances it has made in the use of information and communication technologies to strengthen distance education".[41] Sixty-seven students from Dominica,

Jamaica, St Lucia and St Vincent followed courses in teacher education from Memorial university in Newfoundland, information technology from Athabasca University in Alberta, and tourism management from Mount St Vincent University in Nova Scotia. The courses used the internet both for the delivery of materials and for student support. Each course included a short face-to-face session within Canada. The graduation rate was reported as being 87 per cent.[42]

The programme was seen as contributing successfully to the development of skills within the Caribbean. In terms of capacity building within the region its effects are less clear: the University of the West Indies was hardly involved in the scheme and did not feel that the region had any sense of ownership of the project. The three disciplines were normal subjects at the university but it was reported that the Canadians wanted to structure them as joint UWI-Canadian degrees; the university was not prepared to do this and it appeared to a local observer that cooperation had been "virtually non-existent".[43] Despite claims of success from the funding department, it seems to have been a one-off and Canada has not repeated, leave alone institutionalised the project. Nor does the record suggest that this was a clear and simple method of promoting institutional development.

The Commonwealth scholarship commission picked up the idea of the Canadian scheme in its review of activities in 2000. It argued that distance learning "could play an important role in increasing access to new skills in country". It went on to ask whether the aim of the programme was "to strengthen the human capacity of the individual award holders or ... to help build up the academic capacity of institutions in the developing countries" and answered with the statement that the "Commission strongly feels that any provision for distance learning under the CSFP should have the latter objective". It was expected that the overseas partner would play a major role in supporting students locally. Proposals would therefore be sought from British universities that were working with an overseas partner.[44] As in Canada the commission was breaking new ground in setting institutional development, in defined subject areas, as a priority above the historical aim of attracting individual, able, applicants.

The first cohort of students was recruited in 2003; further cohorts were recruited in each succeeding year. By 2008 the commission was funding 973 students in this way on twenty-nine programmes at twenty-one institutions. Despite its original commitment to partnerships, in 2007 it began to fund a smaller number of scholarships without any partnership arrangement. All were for master's level programmes, although in some cases students had the option to leave the programme with a certificate or diploma if they did not complete the master's. A small number of programmes tried to have the best of both worlds by bringing scholars to Britain for one term while requiring them to study at a distance in their own country for most of the course. Distance-learning students generally take longer to complete their degrees than conventional full-time students so that graduates were produced more slowly. After five years, it was possible to forecast that graduation rates were likely to average around 60 per cent; a small number of programmes had been dramatically more successful than this with completion rates of 100 per cent.[45]

The commission did not spell out what it expected of partnerships or require British universities to explain how they were expected to develop. Although the Caston report noted that "the interest of many UK institutions lies in the development of courses that can be *sold* to students in developing countries" it did not articulate its working assumption that, with time, overseas universities would be able to take over more and more of the running of the programmes themselves.[46] In the event institutional development took one of three forms. First, a number of partnerships concentrated on capacity building and staff development within the academic discipline of the course being offered. Thus a course run by the University of Sunderland with Jomo Kenyatta University of Agriculture and Technology saw its cooperation in terms of staff development at the Kenyan partner. Chainama College of Health Sciences in Zambia used its link with Leeds Metropolitan University as a means of raising capacity among its own staff. Second, in at least one case in which the University of London worked with the University of Pretoria in agricultural development, the partnership built on and developed academic cooperation in the writing of teaching materials. Third, some universities interpreted their partnerships as a way of building up capacity in the techniques of distance learning and student support; this was one of the aims of an aquaculture programme offered by the University of Stirling in partnership with the Bangladesh University of Agriculture and Technology.

In practice, while the scheme was beginning to produce graduates at a distance, and do so cost-effectively, there was less evidence of direct institutional development. By 2008 four partnerships out of the ten funded between 2002 and 2005 had come to an end. While British universities were required to report annually on their progress to the scholarship commission, four out of ten reports made no reference to institutional development in their 2008 reports. All were silent about any transfer of responsibility, or about a date at which the overseas partner would be able to run the programme without, or even with reduced, British support.

The evidence suggests that an indirect approach to university development, of funding good doctoral students, sending them home and waiting a decade or two, has proved resilient and successful. The Canadian and British distance-learning programmes demonstrated that well-run schemes, in which scholars did not have to worry about how to pay for their courses, could produce graduates. But in neither case did the experience suggest that institutional collaboration in distance learning was a short cut to institutional development within universities. Both programmes may be seen as having had more success in their subsidiary aim of offering an alternative route to qualifications needed in local job markets.

Conclusion

The plan did not set out to train university staff, although it was a reasonable assumption that a fair proportion of its alumni would go back to work in universities. It is likely that the proportions doing so have increased since the early years when governments were hungry for graduates to work in the civil service. The decision not to set university development as a priority means that the effects of the plan have been diffuse, and therefore more difficult to assess. Where scholars and fellows have been concentrated in particular departments, as at the University of the West Indies, or at particular universities, it has often been the result of local networks and informal contacts rather than of deliberate policy. The attempts by Britain and Canada to concentrate some of their awards in the interest of institutional development have had limited success.

Chance, luck and serendipity have played their part, along with sound judgment, in determining who should get a scholarship. Bias has also sometimes been a factor, and we come back to this in the next chapter. There is a danger of moving into counterfactual speculation in asking about the effect on higher education of providing scholarships or fellowships to particular individuals: without an award their careers might have languished, or they might have done something totally different, or found another route to a postgraduate degree. Two individuals, both from countries that left and rejoined the Commonwealth, illustrate the kind of effect on themselves and on higher education that they attribute to their scholarships. They demonstrate too, that at different times, awarding bodies were restrained neither by explosive potential nor by a politically charged background. Noor Butt was, in 2008, chairman of the Pakistan Science Foundation after a long career in physics and nuclear engineering at a range of Pakistan institutions. He credits a key part of his success to his PhD at Birmingham in 1965 and to the mentors he met there and the networks that have sustained him since.[47] Thirty years later Saleem Badat became one of the first scholars from South Africa after it rejoined the Commonwealth. With a doctorate in southern African studies from the University of York, he returned to South Africa to become in turn director of the education policy unit at the University of the Western Cape, chief executive of the government's council for higher education, and vice-chancellor of Rhodes University. He commented on the chance of getting his scholarship.

> It would be interesting for someone to take out my CV and see if I would get it [a scholarship] now. My [political] engagement was well known and my results were decent, but some would be asking "should we be bothering with this candidate?" Perhaps they did take that chance on me. I might not have finished [my PhD]. Had I not finished, I would not have applied for the directorship vacated by Harold Wolpe and would not have been head-hunted by the council for higher education and so on. That was a risk.[48]

We look next at the experience of scholars, selected as good risks, while they were learning abroad.

CHAPTER SEVEN

EXPERIENCE: THE SCHOLARS' AND FELLOWS' STORY

The managers of the CSFP had a sense of what they wanted, with a tilt towards renaissance man in the first decade and development woman in the fifth. The successful 25,000 were those who could match their individual hopes to national and international aspirations. Their stories of how they did so—who they were, how fairly they were chosen, where they went, what they wanted to study, and what it was like to do so—come next.

Who were the scholars and fellows?

The scholarship plan began with the Commonwealth-wide bang its founders expected. Britain, Canada and Australia made the largest number of awards but in the first twenty years nearly 750 scholars, or 9 per cent of the total, travelled to universities in the south. Total numbers, shown in table 7.1, rose rapidly and remained fairly stable until the 1980s. They then declined in the 1990s, for the reasons discussed in chapters 4 to 5, with the total number of new awards falling from about 4,700 in the 1980s to 3,800 in the 1990s. Australia's awards fell to 20 per cent of their previous level while awards offered by developing countries fell to 2 per cent of the total in the 1990s. (Fuller figures are in the appendix.)

Since the plan's inception nearly 60 per cent of all scholars have travelled from south Asia and Africa to the industrialised Commonwealth countries. The numbers, and the balance between the two continents, reflect both population and educational demand. Britain and Canada increased their awards to Africa, partly at the expense of south Asia (see chapters 4 and 5) so that Africa's 24 per cent of new awards in the 1960s rose to 32 per cent in the 1990s. The numbers are also a function of the Commonwealth's composition and politics. Small states make up more than half of its membership and, as noted in relation to Barbados (chapter 6), they have tended to receive scholarships that reflect their independent status rather than their population. Some 1,820 awards went to scholars

Table 7.1 Numbers of fellows and scholars

By nominating region	Africa	Caribbean	E and SE Asia	Pacific	Mediterranean	Old Common-wealth	South Asia[a]	Others / not specified
1960s	981	346	329	80	82	1,234	1,226	22
1970s	1,201	363	435	142	118	1,279	1,577	0
1980s	1,882	533	443	157	174	1,325	1,656	0
1990s	1,514	534	221	72	125	923	1,471	170
2000-05	1,190	211	72	39	33	374	797	0
Total	6,768	1,987	1,500	490	532	5,135	6,727	192
By hosting region								
1960s	80	5	51		2	3,914	248	
1970s	64	10	43		1	4,719	278	
1980s	33	18	48		1	5,844	226	
1990s	24	14	38		0	4,737	217	
2000-05	3	11	63		0	2,501	138	
Total	204	58	243		4	21,715	1,107	

Source: CSFPAR to 1996; "ACU Submission, 14, 15, 16 CEM", ACU database
Note: a. includes Aden.

from the Caribbean, 500 to the South Pacific and 490 to the Mediterranean with the largest number going to Malta, for much of the period the only one of the three territories (Malta, Cyprus and Gibraltar) with a university.

Smaller numbers travelled to, or within the south. India in particular, with its consistent programme of awards, attracted scholars both from Africa, which sent nearly half of the total number of scholars in the plan's first thirty years, and from the industrialised countries of the Commonwealth with over 20 per cent. In the 2000s about half of all Indian awards have gone to Africa. One quarter of those awarded scholarships by African universities came from within the continent but they were outnumbered by those from the industrialised Commonwealth who made up just over half of the total.

The industrialised countries have generally offered scholarships throughout the Commonwealth, with less evidence of regional preference than might be expected. Canada has consistently offered between 12 and

18 per cent of awards to the Caribbean, lying only a few hours of flight to the south: cricket in Ontario depends heavily on Caribbean immigration. But its awards have also been available throughout the Commonwealth with much larger numbers coming from Africa and Asia. These continents also provided scholars to Australia and New Zealand, surpassing the numbers from the Pacific, which were at a modest 13 and 7 per cent respectively.

Most rich-country scholars stayed within the rich countries (see chapter 5). While debates rumbled on about the extent to which the plan was one of academic exchange or of aid, a steady proportion of awards were for movements between them. Australia, Britain, Canada and New Zealand are among the six largest beneficiaries of scholarship awards, alongside India and Nigeria.

Wandering scholars have always been young and young scholars have dominated the plan from the beginning. They have got older over the years, as shown in table 7.2: while 48 per cent of scholars were 25 or younger in the first two years of the plan; by the late 1990s only 12 per cent were twenty-four or younger. The third ten-year review noted the steady rise in scholars' age, could not fully explain it, but attributed it partly to the reduction in the number of undergraduate awards, partly to an increasing number of awards to scholars in employment (presumably in contrast with scholars who took an award immediately after completing a first degree), and partly to the increasing proportion of women.[1] Scholars from the industrialised Commonwealth and the Mediterranean were the youngest with an average age of twenty-four. They were followed by students from Asia and the Caribbean at twenty-eight to twenty-nine and then by the Pacific at over thirty-two. High national enrolment ratios make for younger scholars.

The proportion of women awarded scholarships has increased by fits and starts, as shown in table 7.3. The figures reflect differences between regions and programmes as well as changes over time. In the plan's first ten years, women took up a steady 10 to 12 per cent of awards. Hong Kong and Singapore sent twice this proportion, but Ghana and Nigeria only half.[2] By the 1980s women were taking 25 per cent of awards and reached 29 per cent by 1990/91. (Ghana achieved parity in the awards it made that year, providing scholarships to one man and one woman.[3]) There were marked regional differences. The most dramatic changes have been in Africa where the proportion of women, among scholars coming to Britain, rose from 3 per cent in the 1960s (17 scholars in all) to 41 per cent in the 2000s. The south Asian figures remained below 10 per cent for twenty years but then rose ten percentage points in each decade, reaching

Table 7.2 Ages of scholars

Percentage of all scholars

Year	Under 26	26–28	over 28	
1960/62	48	23	29	
1974/5	32	28	40	
1990/1	16	15	69	
	20–24	25–29	30–39	40 and over
2000/1[a]	19	34	39	8
2005/6[b]	12	33	40	15

Source: Rev 1, 43; Thompson, *Statistical briefing paper*; "ACU Submission 15 CEM", 6; "ACU Submission 16 CEM", 11
Notes: a. Excluding scholars in Australia and India; partial figures for New Zealand; b. 4 scholars below the age of 20 are included in the 20–24 column for 2003–6.

Table 7.3 Percentage of female scholarship award holders by nominating region

	1960/1[a]	1970/1	1980/1	1990/1	2000/1[b]
Africa	10	4	11	25	31
Caribbean and Atlantic	11	22	33	40	56
East and Southeast Asia	21	21	24	32	32
Mediterranean	0	4	23	24	43
Old Commonwealth	13	21	38	38	59
Pacific	17	3	9	19	60
South Asia	11	8	13	24	31

Source: CSFPAR; "ACU Submission 14 CEM"
Note: a. Data on four scholars missing from 1960/1; b. Including fellows

41 per cent in the 2000s. By the 1990s over half of the scholars coming to Britain from the Caribbean and Canada were women, to be joined by Australia and New Zealand in the 2000s; in the new century men made up only 36 per cent of the Canadian scholars. The latest figures confirm these trends. By 2007, while women made up only 43 per cent of scholars travelling from Africa and south Asia to Britain, the figures for the Caribbean had risen to 50 per cent and for the industrialised countries to 56 per cent.[4] These trends are similar to those for overseas postgraduate students com-

ing to Britain. The Robbins report found that only 19 per cent of those studying in 1961 were women; this figure rose to 38 per cent in 1996 and 45 per cent in 2005.[5] Figures for scholars hosted by Australia, Canada and New Zealand show a similar pattern though with considerable fluctuations from time to time. In Australia, for example, the proportion of women awarded scholarships rose from around 35 per cent to between 46 and 55 per cent between 1982 and 1986 before falling back again.[6]

Individual programmes have had their own gender bias. While it was running, the British programme of medical awards was dominated by male Indian doctors to the extent that it held down the proportion of women Commonwealth scholars in Britain. Women were under-represented in the CASS programme, for academic staff members mainly in Africa and Asia, because of the gender balance within their own universities. The distance-learning programme introduced in Britain in 2002 was unexpectedly dominated by men: one of the largest programmes turned out to be on agricultural development in southern Africa where the academic discipline is still dominated by men while women do much of the work in the fields.

Men have remained the majority of scholars. The plan slowly evolved its own policies, usually following changes in its host societies rather than leading them. In 1972, the first ten-year review noted that "the sex of scholars has not been the subject of any concerted policy of awarding countries or of nominating countries".[7] Just over ten years later, at their triennial conference, Commonwealth ministers were reported to have "sat in baffled silence as Dorothy Armstrong, director of Canada's [department of foreign affairs] Commonwealth Division, insisted that 200 new Commonwealth scholarships must be offered equally to men and women. They shrugged, finally, and agreed".[8] Another ten years on, the Commonwealth review team found that, where it had the data, 33 per cent of awards went to women although they made up only 25 per cent of applications. The 25 per cent figure was "disturbingly low" but the team did not respond to voices—mine at least—within the Commonwealth Secretariat arguing that countries should be required to make balanced lists of recommendations. The report went on to uphold "the principle of gender equity" and suggested changes to age limits and measures on childcare to help women applicants.[9]

Fellows were always older than scholars; as established academics they may have been wiser; certainly more of them were male, recruited from university staff, still dominated by men in much of the Commonwealth. Numbers could only go up from the early days of the plan when, in the first two years, there appear to have been no women among the eleven men. While the nature of the fellowships has changed, from the most distinguished academics at the beginning to those in mid-career under the later British academic fellows' programme, over forty years later the proportion had risen only to 36 per cent for the period 2003 to 2006.[10]

Were they chosen fairly?

The selection of scholars and fellows has been at least a two-stage process, involving a nominating agency in the applicant's home country and an awarding agency in the host country. There have therefore been risks of bias, and opportunities to guard against it, at both stages and in both countries. Some nominating agencies, which have usually been ministries of education, set up advisory panels to help them; some interviewed candidates, a job that required many days of interviewing applicants in their hundreds in India. The processes for specialist programmes and for fellowships were sometimes different. Overseas universities were responsible for nominating CASS scholars to Britain, while British universities played a part in selecting distinguished academics as fellows in the plan's first twenty years and, more recently, in selecting distance-learning and split-site scholars.

It is difficult to assess how far the process was transparent and unbiased. British legislation recognised the need for this in banning ministerial directions about any particular candidate. It went without saying that eminent commissioners would be unbiased, or at least see themselves as such within appropriate limits: the first chairman "would not be very anxious to have an active left-winger on the Commission".[11] In Canada, government ensured that there were members from both anglophone and francophone universities on the committee. The Canadian committee also cold-shouldered candidates informally nominated by members of parliament.[12] Bias was seldom discussed. The three ten-year reviews appear to have taken it for granted that process was above board in both nominating and awarding countries; it does not appear as a topic of discussion in the, inevitably bland, reports of education ministers' conferences; the financial management review of the scholarship commission in 1987 did not ask about it.

Despite this quietness, allegations of political, ethnic or individual bias have been made throughout the lifetime of the plan. Politics and ethnicity could go together. To take an extreme example, one South African scholar from 1960 made the point that selection under the apartheid regime was inherently unfair.[13] The British high commissioner reported at the time that although South Africa might let "some non-Europeans accept scholarships, say, in England or Canada, they would certainly not let them go to

India or Ghana" and it seems unlikely that any were nominated.[14] In an early selection round, the Canadians thought that nominations from Ceylon demonstrated ethnic discrimination.[15] In 1967, the Biafran war in Nigeria brought accusations of bias but the Commonwealth relations office warned the commission off:

> despite indications that the nominating authority in Nigeria was exercising discrimination on grounds of racial origin rather than those of residence in the rebel areas, the Commission would be unwise to accept nominations from any authority other than that set up under the Plan by the recognised government of Nigeria. It was decided with great regret to accept the advice of the Commonwealth Office.[16]

In two cases—Cyprus and Zimbabwe or Southern Rhodesia—Britain set up exceptional arrangements to bypass local nominating agencies in the absence of a legitimate government. In Zimbabwe this was necessary as the regime was illegal (see chapter 3) while in Cyprus, after the country was invaded and partitioned, a decision was taken that scholarships should still be available to Turkish Cypriots from the northern part of the country, necessitating ad-hoc structures. At the time of the education ministers' conference in Cyprus in 1984, Temple made his way quietly across the UN line in order to make contact with colleagues dealing with scholarships in the occupied zone. He avoided explaining this to the ACU secretary-general, whose family were Greek Cypriots from a village in the occupied north of the island.[17]

Accusations and reports of malpractice on an individual rather than a political basis were more difficult to address and the evidence here is mainly anecdotal. Potential scholars needed first to get hold of an application form and there have been repeated complaints, down the years, about the practical difficulties in doing so. Ministries of education were suspected of harbouring them jealously and making them available only to those in favour, or with easy access to officials.

There have been occasional and more specific reports of bias. After the independence of Bangladesh, the British Council repeatedly told the commission of its suspicions about the process of selection. The war had led to "extreme disruption" in the universities that were reported to be marked by cheating, spurious qualifications, and too many first-class degrees. The British Council continued to criticise the process, and the commission to discuss it, even while the Bangladesh university grants committee was seeking increased help from the commission in building up its universities.[18] Complaints of bias also came from India. The scale of the Indian programmes led the British medical awards administrator to visit India from time to time. On a visit in 1976, Indian medical departments criticised the procedure for selecting senior medical fellows, which made use of recommendations from Britain. He reported that the fellowships went to "part-time professors with substantial practices of their own and [who] are generally more interested in their own professional development than in education". On his advice the policy was changed. His successor visited India ten years later and found a different concern, this time about practice within India, where medical schools outside Delhi complained of bias in favour of the medical schools there and of the, highly regarded, Postgraduate Institute of Medical Education and Research at Chandigarh.[19]

These scattered reports did not lead to major changes of practice by the commission in Britain. In his report, however, Hassall identified problems that he discussed in relation to academic scholars and fellows:

> The fact that candidates are already members of university staff establishes some preliminary selection but it also invites the criticism that there is undue potential for bias and conservatism in the selection process, overseas. This is not a trivial problem. Almost all the F/Ss [fellows and scholars] from developing countries, whom I interviewed, drew my attention to difficulties in dealing with bias and nepotism in their home countries. My interviews in poor countries, confirmed that this view was widespread.[20]

In its response the commission was wary of the term "nepotism" and argued that, where it existed, it was picked up by the secretariat and the selection committee. The ACU secretary-general said that they "experienced fewer problems with nominating Vice-Chancellors who were, as a group, individually known to the ACU", almost suggesting that Hassall was aiming at the wrong target.[21] The commission accepted the evidence that there was sometimes bias in selections but argued at their next meeting that its policy on quotas was a safeguard; while there were broad quotas by region there was no specific quota for any one country:

> The lack of a quota system allows for the standards set by the Commission to be maintained by affording the possibility of offering awards in a range from all of a country's nominees to none. This control over the selection process has meant that nominating agencies have, in general, placed the best candidates they have forward for CSFP awards. It has helped to keep the effects of nepotism to a minimum. Only people suitably qualified actually receive awards.[22]

The commission has continued to argue that its quota policy is a valuable safeguard. Countries are invited to nominate a specified number of candidates that, within any one region, broadly reflects the size of the population. In 2008, the commission drew attention to marked disparities between neighbouring countries in the proportion of successful applicants, for which bias in the selection procedure offered one plausible explanation.[23]

Concerns, even expectations, about bias remained. In Pakistan most of the people interviewed by Raza "showed concern about this issue and felt that they had been selected *despite* the nepotism in the system". In India (see chapter 6) the two nominating agencies had well-established procedures for resisting letters from ministers; from his research Jodhka considered that the system was robust and generally even-handed, though bias was sometimes expected. In South Africa, some recent scholars thought that the system might have been biased against them because they did not come from a previously disadvantaged background.[24]

Countries offering awards tried to put in place measures against bias or favouritism and in more recent years began to talk about it. In its 2002 report the scholarship commission reported on new ways of applying for awards under the heading "openness and transparency". It was widening the range of organisations able to make nominations. Refugee agencies, and later research consortia funded by DfID, were now able to nominate candidates alongside the existing nominating agencies, usually government ministries. Professional fellowships and distance-learning scholarships introduced new routes to nomination. The commission also developed a website on behalf of the plan as a whole which not only provided information about the plan, country by country, but also included application forms for awards.[25]

Bias, even corruption, is hard to trace. Perhaps the warning, "Treason doth never prosper: what's the reason? Why if doth prosper none dare call it treason", can apply to bias when evidence comes from its beneficiaries.[26] We can identify measures that have been taken against bias, and cite the relatively small number of cases where it has been identified. It is difficult to take the analysis further. The evidence of success on the part of the plan's alumni confirms that the selection methods did find the academically able; it cannot tell us whether there were yet more able people excluded for one bad reason or another.

Where did they want to go?

Most scholars wanted to study in the industrialised world, generally preferring Britain to Australia, Canada or New Zealand and followed a conventional pecking order in their choice of university.

Within these countries, their preference for particular universities was often at odds with a policy of distributing scholars as widely as was reasonable. In some cases governments reinforced their scholars' wishes: in the second year of the plan's existence Pakistan reported that it wanted more of its scholars to go to Oxford or Cambridge which was not what the British had in mind.[27] Even before the Oxford conference the Commonwealth relations office had tried to persuade the Pakistan minister of education that "accommodation and training at some of the 'red-brick' universities was reaching a very high standard" and might have the edge over "the less attractive rooms or less specialised training" at Oxford or Cambridge.[28] In 1971, the British commission saw scholars' preferences as "a problem by no means confined to the developing parts of the Commonwealth. Indeed, almost the opposite is true; it can be more difficult to persuade a candidate from the 'old' Commonwealth than one from the 'new' that a Scholarship at, say, a provincial (once called 'Redbrick') university would be just as beneficial as, if not more so than, one at Oxbridge or London, in his particular subject".[29] But the problem continued, sometimes baffling members of the commission: one commissioner, with a chair at Liverpool and degrees from both Oxford and Cambridge,

> expressed his astonishment at the suggestion that for some scholars from New Zealand the supposedly general and cultural attractions of study at either Oxford or Cambridge held greater sway than the possibility of an award at other advanced centres of excellence in UK; he was profoundly sceptical of references to the "total cultural experience" of study at Oxford and Cambridge.[30]

The problem was not limited to Britain and persisted into the 2000s. William Lawton, drawing on his experience as academic relations officer in the Canadian high commission, complained about "the lopsidedness of the preferences indicated by the British applicants for where they wanted to go to Canada. You could look at thirty applications and there would be one for east of Montreal. It was a great chagrin for me because I never saw one for Memorial [in Newfoundland] ... You'd get about 90 per cent for about five universities".[31]

Distance-learning students of the British or Canadian programmes did not have the luxury or the complications of choice as they were recruited in cohorts by the hosting university. Many did not travel at all. While a period of residence at the Canadian host university was built into their scheme, Britain did not follow that precedent, although it did not rule it out. In the event only two of the twenty-nine courses funded in the first five years of the scheme had a British residential component. Commonwealth integration and first-hand experience of studying in Britain were no longer priorities.

Much smaller numbers studied in the developing Commonwealth. The Oxford conference hoped to have about 170 awards out of 1,000 from the south and the British, at least, were disappointed that these figures did not build up as planned. The house of commons, perhaps a touch impatient as this was only 1962, were given the figures:[32]

	Pledged	taken up
India	100	22
Pakistan	30	2
Malaya	12	3
Ghana	10	0
Central African Federation	10	3
Ceylon	6	2

One scholar in Nigeria and two in Hong Kong should have been on the list but would not change the overall picture. The figures continued to tell this story and India has remained the only developing country with numbers of scholars regularly in double figures. It had an average of 39 scholars holding awards in the 1960s which rose to 58 and 71 in the 1970s and 1980s, falling back to 48 in the 1990s but rising again in the early years of the present century when India continued to make a regular quota of awards. Within Asia, Malaysia and Pakistan offered scholarships in the early years; Malaysia usually hosted between two and ten scholars until the mid-1980s and since 2000 has offered some six to ten new scholarships a year. Hong Kong hosted an average of seven scholars at any one time until it ceased to be a colony in 1997. Much smaller numbers went to Africa where in the early years awards were offered by Ghana and by east Africa, then with a federal university. Numbers declined as African universities themselves suffered in the 1980s and 1990s. Nigeria has offered scholarships with numbers fluctuating from two to twenty-two; South Africa came, went, and returned as a scholarship provider.

These figures disappointed administrators from the beginning. Despite early references to agricultural schools in New Zealand and to the potential for studying tropical medicine and the life sciences in Africa and Asia, the plan's fourth annual report referred to "the difficulty of attracting strong fields of applicants for awards offered by less developed Commonwealth countries"; the third ministers' conference in 1964 took up the theme that "full advantage had not so far been taken of the awards offered by some of the developing countries".[33] Ten years later, at their meeting in Jamaica, ministers again argued that "more needs to be done to publicize the offerings of developing countries so that nominating countries can be better informed of their potential" and wanted to encourage "a more general interchange at both scholarship and fellowship levels in *all* parts of the Commonwealth". The rhetoric continued but practice did not change. The Commonwealth Fund for Technical Cooperation announced at the education ministers' conferences in 1974 and 1977 that it was prepared to top up awards by developing countries.[34] But the offer appears never to have been taken up. By 1991/2 only 63 awards were made by developing countries, with only 13 scholars, less than 1 per cent of the total, travelling from the north to the south. [35]

The scholarship plan reflects broader trends in student mobility: in 1998 Britain and Canada had 25,000 and nearly 30,000 students respectively travelling abroad, of whom only twenty-six and thirty were in India; even Malaysia with over 49,000 abroad had only thirty-seven in India. The larger numbers in India (461 from Bangladesh, 639 from Kenya, 398 from Mauritius and 368 from Sri Lanka) can be explained partly in terms of historical ethnic ties and the Indian diaspora.[36] But even these numbers are small in relation to the size of the Indian system of higher education and of international student mobility generally.

Developing-country awards were always more popular in the south than in the north, in a ratio of about two to one in the first three decades of the plan. There were some changes within that period. India, for example, which recruited scholars from throughout the Commonwealth, gradually hosted a decreasing number of scholars from Britain and an increasing number from Africa, which made up over a third of the total by the 1980s, a proportion that has since risen. In the 2000s it usually made about thirty awards a year so that it was usually hosting some fifty-five scholars. They came from three of its neighbours, Bangladesh, the Maldives and Sri Lanka, from eight African and two Caribbean countries, and from Britain, Canada and New Zealand.[37]

It is difficult to avoid the conclusion that, despite the original hopes of reciprocal Commonwealth exchange, the plan was generally seen more as a way of getting access to the wealth of northern universities. Politics and finance provide part of the explanation but prestige and practicality were also at work. Jamaica, for example, reported in 1991 that it had advertised awards available in India but had got no responses. Two years later it had to decline a Nigerian award citing a lack of communications, the low level of emoluments, uncertainty about which body would be responsible for paying them and the unstable political climate.[38]

What did they want to study?

The plan was always intended to be primarily for postgraduate awards but, from the outset, undergraduate awards were available, mainly for countries without a university or limited access to one. Between 1960 and 1985, there were usually between thirty-five and fifty undergraduate awards each year across the Commonwealth as a whole. The industrialised countries were always reluctant to expand the number of these awards (see chapter 2). As universities developed in the south, and it became easier to nominate talented postgraduates, so the demand for undergraduate awards fell away. There is, however, still some demand and just over a third of awards made by India between 2003 and 2008 were at undergraduate level.[39] In Britain the commission fixed an undergraduate quota of five awards a year from 1996, to be made available only to Maldives, the Seychelles, the Falkland Islands, St Helena and, for one year only, Anguilla.[40] The quota was treated as an upper limit rather than a target and in the five years from 2002 to 2007 Britain had only four graduates at first-degree level, two from the Seychelles, one from the Maldives and one from the Gambia.

Most scholars sought a master's degree or a doctorate. For many years neither Britain nor Canada had a clear policy about the balance between the two. In the first twenty years there were usually twice as many British awards for research degrees as for taught master's, with about thirty-five to sixty taught awards as contrasted with eighty to 140 for research degrees. British policies began to shift towards master's programmes (see chapters 3 and 4). By 2000, some two-thirds of awardees came to Britain for a year or less although expenditure on doctorates took up 80 per cent of the general scholarship budget. The quota for doctorates from industrialised countries was set at one third on the basis of guidance from the FCO rather than a formally stated policy. In Canada the policy was described as "a bit fuzzy". The academics on the committee wanted to fund doctoral students with the aim of helping university development in the south. Master's awards were in a minority with a proportion of them offered to scholars who might in due course do a doctorate but were not up to it at the time.[41]

Over the years the length of awards has tended to shorten. Despite pressure from scholars who said it was unrealistic to complete a doctoral programme in less than four years, and from universities wanting four-year awards and fees, awarding countries have generally kept these awards down to three years. Britain cut its fellowship awards from twelve months to six in 2001. Its new professional fellowships were for periods of less than six months. The introduction of split-site degrees by Britain in 1996 meant that these scholars came to Britain for one year, spending most of their time in their home country.

Scholarships and fellowships were intended to be available in any subject. In practice, the proportions offered in different subject areas have been a function of individual choice, of demand on the part of nominating countries, and of policy on the part of awarding countries. Some of the consequences have been fortuitous rather than planned. Engineers and lawyers are among the largest professional groups funded by the British, for example, without this ever having been an explicit policy. Summary figures are in table 7.4.

The first ten years of the plan displayed a clear trend: using very broad categories 60 per cent of developing-country scholars were in science and technology, with 40 per cent in the arts, while the proportions were reversed for scholars from the industrial countries.[42] The trend has continued, with the plan usually attracting relatively more scientists and technologists from the south, which provided most of the scholars, and more in the arts and social sciences from the north. Canada has consistently provided between 42 and 50 per cent of its awards to scientists and technologists in each decade.

Within that general picture, there have been major changes over the plan's history. The British figures, for example, show a marked decline in pure science, from 30 per cent of the total in the 1960s down to 18 per cent. This may reflect recent British developmental policies and a consequent favouring of the applied over the pure. Figures for the arts or humanities have steadily declined, and for the social sciences increased, within the major awarding countries. In the plan as a whole, while there were nearly two arts scholars in 1960 for each social scientist, by 1980 the ratio was 3:2 while by 1985 social scientists were in a majority. In Britain numbers in the arts fell from 22 per cent in the first ten years to 11 per cent in the 2000s; the Canadian figures have fallen from 9 per cent of the total to 6 per cent. In 2005, with a new commitment to developmental aims, Britain awarded 128 scholarships in the social sciences and only seventeen in the arts, with all but three of those coming from the industrialised Commonwealth.[43]

In some cases these proportions reflect national policies. India explained in the plan's second annual report that it nominated scientists or technologists in a ratio of 70:30 to those in the humanities, arguing that "though considerable emphasis has been placed on the development of scientific and technical education in India in recent years, the Government of India is keen not to underrate the importance of subject fields under the Humanities and Social Sciences".[44] Similarly Pakistan's national policies for scientific development led it to nominate a high proportion of scientists in the plan's first decade. British figures show that science and technology remained a priority for south Asia, with between 49 and 76 per cent of scholars in these areas, until a drop in the 2000s brought these down to between 31 and 39 per cent.

Awards held within developing-country universities have shown a different pattern. Up to the early 1990s nearly half of the scholars from the south, travelling within the south, received awards in science, technology and medicine. They benefited from specialist courses that were not available within their own countries. Pakistan, for example, responded to pleas at the 1962 education ministers' conference to widen the plan by offering awards on three-year vocational courses such as radio repair, metallurgy and refrigeration technology. Scholars were recruited from Sri Lanka and east Africa to follow courses in automobile and refrigeration engineering at Karachi Polytechnic.[45] India offered awards in areas that were not available elsewhere, which included medical awards of particular relevance to small states with no medical school. Other awards were more specialised: in 1971, India provided awards to six Nigerian hockey coaches. It has continued this pattern so that, in the 2000s it offered scholarships in genetics and plant breeding as well as forestry and computer science.[46] Offers of technical courses were not always taken up; there was little enthusiasm from Britain—though there might have been in other parts of the Commonwealth—for forestry courses in Cyprus in the 1960s which the commission thought British universities could do better.[47] Southern travellers were not confined to the sciences—scholars of Buddhism went from India to Sri Lanka and scientists made up just under 40 per cent of the most recent Indian awards —but until recently they dominated the picture. Indian courses in management have grown in popularity and made up nearly a quarter of the total awards between 2003 and 2008.

Scholars travelling from the north to the south were different, with numbers dominated by the humanities. In the period up to 1990, 55 per cent of these northern scholars went to study the arts: philosophy and the fine arts make a rare appearance in their lists. Historians made up a surprising 15 per cent of scholars travelling from the old Commonwealth to the new in the 1960s and 1970s. Janice Jiggins, for example, went from Britain to Sri Lanka to do a doctorate in history, an experience she described as "excellent—active scholarship, lively, well planned seminar series, sustained inter-university contacts with centres of excellence outside Ceylon, numerous overseas scholars resident and passing through".[48] Scholars in the humanities were not alone, and anthropologists, geographers and medical specialists also travelled from north to south, following

Table 7.4 Subject areas of scholars coming to Britain

		Arts	Social sciences	Agriculture, veterinary studies	Medicine, dentistry, health	Science	Technology	Unknown/other
Africa	1960s	91	122	28	49	116	64	18
	1970s	85	146	53	45	157	115	1
	1980s	60	244	74	79	178	182	6
	1990s	83	247	64	107	136	168	3
	2000–7	44	329	68	111	112	142	3
Caribbean and Atlantic	1960s	17	54	9	9	19	25	10
	1970s	18	62	9	8	27	38	1
	1980s	12	75	20	10	16	49	7
	1990s	17	123	13	25	20	54	8
	2000–7	5	79	2	10	9	24	2
South Asia	1960s	93	76	16	48	196	157	7
	1970s	37	63	33	18	230	169	3
	1980s	67	135	96	42	247	169	4
	1990s	54	179	62	65	170	178	0
	2000–7	17	111	36	43	66	93	0
East and South East Asia	1960s	29	29	7	17	54	29	5
	1970s	17	45	7	11	39	36	2
	1980s	23	58	9	14	30	47	0
	1990s	6	40	3	7	15	24	3
	2000–7	2	10	0	3	6	14	0
Mediterranean	1960s	6	8	5	2	6	16	4
	1970s	8	18	1	4	16	26	1
	1980s	4	36	0	4	13	32	0
	1990s	6	26	2	8	5	23	0
	2000–7	7	8	0	2	2	3	0
Old Commonwealth	1960s	208	111	8	9	143	52	16
	1970s	187	179	1	5	153	51	2
	1980s	252	223	5	12	151	64	5
	1990s	220	221	5	18	133	42	0
	2000–7	115	219	1	18	52	21	1

	1960s	0	4	0	1	0	0	0
Pacific	1970s	2	11	1	0	5	3	0
	1980s	2	22	1	2	6	7	1
	1990s	2	24	3	5	3	3	0
	2000–7	2	11	1	0	3	0	0

Source: ACU database (January 2007)

their professional interests, but were in a minority.

The academic interests of the larger number of scholars who travelled between the industrial countries form a different pattern. Social scientists already made up 49 per cent of Canadians travelling abroad in the 1960s and scholars in the arts a further 18 per cent. In the following decades the numbers within these two areas rose to between 70 and 80 per cent of the total. The minority of scientists often wanted to work in a particular laboratory, or a particular environment: New Zealand, for example, attracted marine scientists. Larger, and increasing proportions, were attracted by perceived strengths and opportunities in the arts and social sciences with classicists, for example, travelling in the opposite direction, film schools in Canada recruiting internationally, and British university libraries acting as magnets.

What was it really like?

Academic visitors travel hopefully, buoyed up by their own and their sponsors' expectations. The hopes were shared by the plan's founding fathers who wanted scholars to benefit by gaining an understanding of a different culture as well as by successfully following their own disciplines. Reality came after they arrived when they had to match their academic, financial and social expectations against the practicality of living in a different country.

Academic expectations

As scholarships and fellowships have always been competitive, both award holders and their host universities had high expectations.

Some of the expectations, particularly of those coming to Britain, arose from an imagined view of its culture. Kamau Brathwaite in the Caribbean—discussed in chapter 6—pointed out the absurdity of children in the tropics being asked to write poems about the snow. In Uganda the poet Okot p'Bitek was as scathing about learning by heart poems "about the beauty of snow in the winter, although [the child's] experience is confined to the destructive power of hailstones" leaving the learner a lost victim of the school system "unable to dance the dance or play the music of his own people".[49] But some relished the colonial, or even post-colonial, curriculum. In Sierra Leone, Julius Sandy had spent afternoons in the primary school listening to stories about England, Oxford and Cambridge; all the texts were by English writers which gave him "the urge to go to Britain one day and study at a British university". Similarly Sanghamita Misra wanted to do a doctorate in Britain having "grown up [in India] with huge amounts of English literature. I read Hardy and Austen and everything else. I grew up with all of that".[50]

More often scholars were attracted by the strength of a particular institution or department. Scientists and technologists had precise demands. In 1965 Cham Tao Soon went from Singapore to Cambridge to do a doctorate in fluid mechanics because of the strength of the department there. Permanand Mohan went from Trinidad to the University of Saskatchewan in the 1980s to study computer science in a way that was impossible in his own country at the time. It was not only scientists: Richard Campbell came to Britain from Australia to do a doctorate in 1966 as there were "more philosophers to the square inch in Oxford than at any other university in the world".[51] Many other scholars have been less precise in their expectations, putting their desire for a higher degree from a rich-country university ahead of specific academic interests. The proportion of scholars who had a clear vision of the institution in which they wanted to work can be expected to have increased over time as awarding bodies have made their expectations clearer, and the existence of the internet has made it easier to find out about a department's particular strengths.

Over the years many of scholars' and fellows' expectations have been met. In Britain the commission surveyed 165 scholars in the first cohort and found that 65 per cent of them praised the experience and 64 were satisfied. The twenty-nine complaints were mainly not about their academic experience but about practical issues such as accommodation, limits on overseas travel and the marriage allowance. Supervisors were also positive with comments that ranged from: "Progress is satisfactory if one has regard to the point from which she started, less if one thinks of where she has to reach", up to, "One of the most brilliant research students I have ever had the privilege to supervise".[52] Most comments were at the upper end of that spectrum; they recur in reports of the plan down the years. Supervisors' reports have repeatedly used phrases such as "outstanding", "top of the class", or "one of the best we have had". A Sri Lankan academic fellow at Leeds "made almost a quantum leap in the development of the original idea" in inorganic chemistry on which he had been working.[53]

Later reports refer to an engineering scholar from Cyprus who was "an excellent student from every point of view" and won the best student of the year prize from the Institution of Electrical Engineers, and a doctoral scholar at Nottingham whose supervisor saw him as "the most organised student I have ever known. He completed within the three year period—indeed I had to make him stop out of sympathy for his external examiner".[54]

A minority of scholars found their academic experience disappointing. One consistent complaint has been that three years is not long enough to do a doctorate. A New Zealand pharmacologist remembered his time in Britain like this:

> It was hard work. ... Three years is quite tight to come fresh from abroad and be expected to do a PhD and have it written up, completed, and examined in three years. So I think my abiding memory was how tight it was in the end and knowing that I had a February deadline to finish and you had all these obstacles like the Christmas period—all these little blocks.[55]

Other scholars were disappointed by their introduction to study in the north. In Britain the commission noticed in 1967 that scholars' reports often described graduate work as initially challenging and frustrating, with some later coming to value the independence that was expected of them.[56] Sir Michael Berridge remembered his first days as a graduate student coming from Southern Rhodesia in the 1960s as

> every bit as hard as I thought it was going to be, to be honest ... Well, the other two [postgraduates in his department] were Cambridge graduates and they knew their way around the department—they had experiments going, they had results on his desk within a few weeks and I was still looking around for apparatus and not really knowing what I was doing. I learnt very quickly.[57]

Ancient universities sometimes wanted to demonstrate their superiority. One Canadian student told the scholarship commission in 1967

> I will never forget almost the first words my tutor (not meaning to be unkind) said to me on my first day in College, when I arrived feeling very homesick and certainly unsure. She said, "Now that you are at Cambridge, you know, you're going to have to start to think". I could scarcely forget the words and they seem to my symptomatic of an attitude which eventually may make the foreign student himself feel he wants to conceal his "inferior" undergraduate background.[58]

In its early years there was a steady flow of criticism to the commission of the quality of teaching, particularly at doctoral level in the humanities. Scholars from the industrialised countries were more vociferous than those from the south. A doctoral student of English found himself in Edinburgh "totally unprepared for the kind of solitary and independent pursuit that research is". From Oxford there came a recommendation, from a scholar leading a "mole-like existence" to dissuade others from going there to begin research in English literature: "There is little actual teaching, apart from obligatory classes in bibliography and the apparatus of scholarly writing. As a result, the graduate finds himself in splendid isolation in the Bodleian for most of the day and in his (usually grim) bed-sitter for the night".[59] In contrast there were repeated comments by scholars who welcomed the freedom offered to doctoral students in Britain where, in contrast with north America, they were free of course requirements. Some relished the prospect when "They basically said 'Hello young man. Now go away and write a book'".[60]

Some academic problems are inherent in research. Practical difficulties have most often been reported by life scientists. In 1980, a scholar from Papua New Guinea found that red spider mites had been introduced into the growth room where he was trying to simulate a natural environment and eaten all the leaves on the plants he was cultivating. Nor was he allowed to use nematicides to get rid of them. Meanwhile a vet working on embryonic and foetal mortality needed a supplementary grant in order to buy a few extra pregnant cows.[61] In 2008 the commission was concerned at the practicality, and the customs' officer's reaction, of a west African scholar who wanted to fly into Britain with his collection of varied stool samples.[62]

As far as it goes, the evidence suggests these criticisms have become less common since the 1970s among scholars coming to Britain. Universities have more postgraduate students and many have increased the amount of support they offer to them.

Finance

Did scholars and fellows have enough to live on? The evidence is mixed and a flippant answer is that they complained more at the time than they do in their reminiscences. In Britain, regional conferences of scholars were held for many years at which there were complaints about the level of stipends, although the commission's early policies on marriage allowances and field work were criticised more severely. But from the 1960s to the 1980s there is some evidence that scholars in both Britain and Canada thought they were adequately, even sometimes generously, paid. A number of scholars reported quite comfortable circumstances, which allowed them to buy a car and travel extensively throughout the British countryside.[63] In the 1960s one scholar found at the end that there was a slight surplus from his stipends that helped him pay for his fare to a postdoctoral job in the United States.[64] In 1981, one Zimbabwean scholar received enough through her stipends to support a mortgage. She decided to buy a flat instead of rent one with the intention of selling it when her course was completed.[65] Almost all those surveyed in the eastern Caribbean reported that they had sufficient funds while on award with few complaints. Other scholarships available in the region were less well-funded.[66]

Scholarships in Canada were also seen as generous. A British doctoral student in Canada in the 1970s reported that the scholarship provided all the support he needed for his PhD and that "not only did I get a monthly stipend, but I could also access travel funding for research and conferences. Unlike my colleagues in graduate school, I never had to worry about financial support".[67] Another scholar wrote to the commission from Alberta in the late 1980s noting that the Cdn$900 per month stipend was generous enough for her to "enjoy University life, and to go on weekend trips with friends to the Rockies and to various other part of Alberta. I also had enough to travel through British Columbia to the West Coast and Vancouver for a few weeks in the summer of 1987".[68] In the early 1990s, in another report, the "scholarship was really good because it was a lot of money ... I was best off of all the years of my graduate education that year".[69]

Stipends were less generous for married scholars and those with dependants, which presented particular difficulties in Britain for scholars with families (see chapter 4). Terms were more generous for fellows, with travel grants as well as allowances for their families, although this led to a long-running tussle about Australian fellows' liability to tax at home on emoluments received in Britain. Eventually their stipend was regarded as being tax-free but lecture fees were to be declared and taxed.[70]

The value of stipends was affected by deliberate policy, by inflation, and by changes in comparative costs, especially of accommodation. Table 7.5 shows how the basic British stipend fell in real terms in the 1960s and then, as the country struggled with rapid inflation in the mid-1970s, fell even more dramatically. A partial recovery in the 1980s and 1990s left the 2006 figure very close to that of 1971. These raw figures conceal a more complicated story. A comparative study in 1985 showed that accommodation costs took up a similar proportion of the stipend, between 21 and 29 per cent of the total, alike in Britain, Canada and New Zealand. Only in

Table 7.5 British scholarship monthly stipends

	Personal stipend		Marriage stipend		Children's stipend[a]	
	Current ££	Constant 2008££	Current ££	Constant 2008££	Current ££	Constant 2008££
1960	52	888	17	288	0	0
1965	57	819	23	326	5	72
1970	68	788	27	313	6	70
1975	110	691	44	277	9	57
1980	219	704	110	353	14	45
1985	320	727	149	338	20	45
1990	386	658	193	329	25	43
1995[b]	493	710	247	356	33	50
2000[b]	580	732	290	366	38	48
2005[b]	689	771	200	224	144	161

Source: CSCM various dates; 1996 *Prospectus*; 2000 and 2005 *Handbook*
Notes: a. Stipend listed for first child; b. Extra London stipend not included in total.

Hong Kong were things quite different: scholars there needed to spend 69 per cent of their stipend on accommodation, leading the University of Hong Kong to complain on scholars' behalf.[71] Over the next twenty years, however, British property prices and rents increased more rapidly than inflation. By 1994, government found evidence of hardship among overseas students and the rates were adjusted. In 2003, a further review was carried out, prompted by significant increases in research council grants, designed to attract young people into research. The new review found that overseas students' hardship had eased, partly, it was suggested, because of a relaxation of rules on students' working during vacations. Incentives were not seen as necessary for them and their stipends could fall below the research council levels. A new formula was adopted which took as a working principle that some 40 per cent of the stipend would have to go on rent. Children's allowances went up, marriage allowances went down.[72] While there were major differences between rents in different parts of the country, and between different types of accommodation, the inescapable conclusion is that, at least in Britain, scholars' disposable income, over and above their rent, had declined.

Many of the scholars who travelled to developing countries had a leaner time. Their stipends were generally based on the allowances paid to nationals and seen, at least by scholars from the north, as inadequate. Fixed exchange rates and the levels of inflation reached in the 1970s exacerbated the problem. Both Britain and Canada paid supplements to their scholars studying abroad and were under steady pressure to maintain and increase them. Although British supplements were then between 100 and 200 per cent of the local stipend in India, the British Council urged in 1967 that they should be increased so that scholars could lead a European lifestyle.[73] In contrast with Niven's experience in the 1960s, described in chapter 2, by the 1980s a telex from the Canadian high commission in Ghana was warning that the local stipend "could purchase four beers or provide four bananas per day per month. Even if current terms are increased by 300 per cent sum will be totally inadequate to provide living standard accustomed to Canadian students".[74] In Britain the commission responded to foreign office questions about the overseas supplements that were paid to scholars in India, Pakistan, Sri Lanka and Sierra Leone, by explaining that this had always been part of the scheme, that Canada supplemented all scholars going to developing countries, and that Nigeria supplemented its nationals who were going to India.[75] The policy was to continue, with foreign office not development funds.

Policymakers seem to have assumed that scholars should be neither affluent nor impoverished. The impact of inflation, and the hard cases that make bad law—usually women, those with large families, and those hosted by developing countries—meant that some were impoverished. Accidental generosity rather than policy left some affluent.

Society

At two extremes scholars' time abroad was life-changing but unsurprising. Some got married, and may have lived happily ever after; others got so depressed that their period of study was delayed or cut short. The latter group was smaller than the former but the data are not good enough to calculate either a marriage or a depression rate.

Between those extremes, scholars who came to the north reacted with excitement but also with dismay to their environment. South London presented its difficulties to two—and probably more—of them. One Nigerian biologist commented in 1966 on "the deserted and chilly Clapham Common through which I passed early each morning and the hard crust of ice, crushing beneath my worn shoes and perhaps with luck, a few cold stricken birds gaping hungrily at me. I learnt something from their endurance and attempt to survive".[76] He might have been joined a couple of years later by a physicist who complained that "taking a person from a country such as New Zealand with almost a surfeit of natural beauty, and sending them to a place such as Battersea is bound to have a profoundly disturbing and depressing psychological effect".[77] Forty years later a Zimbabwean student found that her "circadian clock was disrupted when early nights and late mornings came in winter and also when the reverse happened in summer. I learnt to use a watch more rather than depend mostly on the sun and daybreak and sunset".[78]

Scholars and fellows needed to make greater adjustments in response to assumptions within their host societies, to social differences, and to race prejudice. Visitors to Britain and Canada were surprised at the level of ignorance they found. It was not just individual. A Nigerian scholar found in 1965 that the BBC's

> documentaries on Africa have consistently shown huts, jungles and witch-doctors (whatever that means) relieved by squalid localities and beasts as if these are the only features one finds in that continent. Nobody challenges the right of viewers to be treated to the bizarre. But must this be at the expense of the African? If British viewers have a right to see the worst aspect of African life, they also have a corresponding right to see the other side, the best side. ... Apart from the danger of driving a permanent wedge between the "whites" and the "coloureds", apart from weakening Commonwealth ties, the BBC's policy of presenting only huts and jungles might also possibly succeed in hardening the view that Imperialism was an unmitigated evil.[79]

On the other side of the Atlantic a Camerounian scholar was asked with surprise by an airport customs official where he had learned English. Once settled he recalled

> going to church ... Do you know the dresses that we wear, the long flowing robes? When I got in there, people started running out. I didn't know what they were running out for. They went out to bring cameras to take pictures of a man in, according to them, bed sheets. I went with a fellow student who was a Canadian and he was really mad. So I told him don't worry, I would pose for them.[80]

The Australian picture may have been brighter. One Indian academic reported in the 1970s that he had experienced less discrimination in Canberra on grounds of race than he had in three and a half years in Delhi "for reasons of religion, language, and caste".[81] In the United Kingdom, too, the absence of prejudice was sometimes noticed and welcomed. Mothusi Mashologu had studied at Fort Hare in South Africa and found in 1960 that

> Going to Northern Ireland from Basutoland [now Lesotho] was a uniquely liberating experience for me after excursions to South Africa and Rhodesia with their then constraining racial polices. It was the first time that I was able to move around freely outside my own country. In Belfast I had easy access to libraries, theatres, concerts and cultural events that I had never experienced before ... I rarely felt homesick because Northern Ireland became my second home. I even began to enjoy the pastimes of my Irish friends such as going to listen to the quaint oratory of the Reverend Ian Paisley at his Belfast church. Little did we know then that more than thirty years later he would assume office as First Minister of Northern Ireland.[82]

Other scholars were aware of potential prejudice but found themselves untroubled by it. A Sri Lankan doctoral student in London had "not come across an instance of a person discriminating against me by virtue of my colour".[83] Another, while recognising racial prejudice as an element of British society, claimed that universities were different: "a coloured person living in England is bound to feel sooner or later, that he or she is unwanted and looked down upon by a large section of the English population ... however, it is a great relief for us to see that the universities with all their affiliated institutions are totally free from all such racial prejudice".[84] Similarly a Ugandan lawyer found "the usual racial slurs" as his wife was white but argued from his experience of three universities that "they were minimal, really, because we lived in the university communities".[85]

From the 1960s to the 1980s, however, a proportion of scholars did report prejudice. The Montreal conference took place at the time of race riots in Britain in both Notting Hill and Nottingham. Racial discrimination was legal in Britain, even accepted as normal. University accommodation officers would ask potential landlords if they would be willing to accept a non-white student.[86] It was still socially acceptable for Duncan Sandys, a former conservative secretary of state for Commonwealth relations, to talk in 1967 about "turning off the tap" of immigration and claim that "the breeding of millions of half-caste children would merely produce a generation of misfits and create increased tensions". (He had hosted a reception for Commonwealth scholars at Lancaster House in 1961 but was doubtless assured they would all go home.)[87] The first British race relations act came in 1965 and did not embrace employment or, crucial for many scholars, housing, both of which had to await revising legislation.

In Britain, housing caused the greatest difficulties. A student from Northern Rhodesia (Zambia) referred to "the trouble we experience in finding suitable accommodation, and the inconvenience of being asked, very politely, to quit one's digs for very minor excuses".[88] An Indian doctoral scholar in London in 1963 found "the amount and character of colour prejudice existing among the native people proved rather inconvenient for me. This prejudice compelled me to live in uncomfortable accommodation, because being coloured I was refused better flats sometimes openly, and sometimes in a roundabout way". [89] In Belfast, while his Mosotho colleague felt comfortable, a Nigerian scholar found that: "It is impossible to describe the difficulty experienced by strangers—especially so-called 'coloured' people—in finding suitable living accommodation in this country".[90] Prejudice extended beyond accommodation. A scholar from Kenya in Glasgow in the late 1970s said that "I have had, like many of my friends, the nasty experience of being turned away from pubs and discos, with the words 'Sorry, no admission', 'Members only', or 'The management reserves the right of admission'".[91] In the early 1980s, another Kenyan reported an outright refusal by a fish and chip shop to serve him.[92]

Reports of this kind gradually declined. Further legislation extended the ambit of race relations law in Britain so that it covered employment and housing. Prejudice might remain but legal prejudice no longer could. The scholars of the last twenty years have, in this area at least, had an easier time of it than those of the first twenty years.

Scholars in the south

The minority of scholars who travelled within the south, or from the north to the south, had a different set of stories to tell.

They travelled partly because of opportunities that were not available at home, partly to pursue a specialist interest, partly because of the lure of travel itself. The lack of local opportunities meant that, in 1961, when India first offered awards, six of its twenty-two scholarships went to Mauritius, which at that time had no university, with four in the arts, one in social science and one in physics.[93] Fifteen years later the strength of the Indian higher education system attracted thirty-seven students of whom seven, from Fiji, Guyana, Kenya, Malaysia and Mauritius, were to study medicine. Specialist interest has attracted scholars both within the south and from the north. Scholars in the fine arts went to India from, for example, Kenya, Mauritius and Uganda and from Sri Lanka to study ayurvedic medicine. One British scholar went to Malaysia in 1968 to study "the largest of the gibbons—the siamang. ... Gibbons are the most appealing of the apes, of the primates. I was set on going to study it and they only occurred in Malaysia and Sumatra. The British connections in Malaysia made that the obvious place to go".[94] Another went to Nigeria because, as an undergraduate, he had found Wole Soyinka "one of five people in the world at that time who were writing anything that I found significant and interesting".[95]

For a few, particularly from the north, it was an immediate disaster. In the mid-1980s one British scholar, following a common pattern of going to India to study art, found that he was not expected when he arrived in Baroda. After three days he was sent on by train to Delhi, where he was unimpressed with the course that was on offer, and with a suggestion that he might move on to Benares. By this time he was disgruntled, suffering from dysentery and not wanting to go anywhere except home, where the British Council sent him after his two-week stay in India.[96] Another scholar went, and as quickly returned from Sri Lanka with apparent misunderstandings on both sides. The scholar expected a desk—which lecturers in the department also lacked—and found the library inadequate; his supervisor was surprised that the scholar lacked expected language skills and would have to work through translations. Complications over stipends and accommodation compounded the problem and he too returned home.[97] But these accounts, of which there have been a modest trickle down the years, are an exception. Far more scholars report of problems of bureaucracy, stipends, and accommodation, and of the time spent solving them, but saw these as a time-wasting interruption rather than a reason to go home.

Local, national or international politics sometimes added a frisson of interest, sometimes got in the way. One British scholar at the University of Ibadan in Nigeria commented on the vibrant political life on campus in the 1970s, and the part played by radical local and overseas students.[98] Another found work at her Nigerian university, in one of the dark periods of military rule, obstructed by allegations and counter-allegations that divided the campus into two warring factions; she needed to keep on good terms with both and suggested that the capacity to do that was more important than the ability to cope with difficult living conditions.[99] Two scholars came home from Pakistan in 1965, intending this to be a short visit before they returned for the last three months of their award, only to be prevented from returning by the outbreak of war between India and Pakistan.[100] Again, these are the exceptions: wars and rumours of wars bore more heavily on scholars from the south who had good reason not to go home after their award to countries that include Bangladesh, as it fought for its independence from Pakistan, Zimbabwe during the Smith regime, or Uganda under Amin.

Far more scholars found both the experience of living and working in a foreign university a rewarding one, as well as bringing long-term benefits (discussed in chapter 8). A British nutritionist who did a master's degree at Baroda in India recognised that at times the university "fell short of our standards but I feel that perhaps the best part of my education ... was living within another culture and learning to accept or tolerate and live within its limitations". She "found it a bit of a shock to return to England". A contemporary of hers, studying fine arts in Baroda, struggled for two months to find accommodation, complained of librarians who were more concerned to prevent theft than to make books available, and found herself working with poor equipment and materials. But she described the experience as "incredibly stimulating and rewarding".[101] A social anthropologist in Sierra Leone found the university campus isolating, partly because it was closed for three months, nearly ran out of money but managed to get his stipend increased, and duly and appropriately moved inland. In his village he met the people he had not managed to in the capital. Following his anthropological principles he appropriately ate and drank with them, observed birth, marriage and death so that: "Not only did I learn a great deal but the people of [the village] learnt a great deal about me, my family and country. During my stay my father visited us briefly. The people I knew received him with great honour and affection but not as a stranger but as the father of a friend".[102] Jiggins, again, summed up the value of these southern awards in terms echoed by others: "It gave me also opportunities to immerse myself in another society that students rarely get these days—three month research trips are just not the same kind of research experience and insight as longer term residence offers".[103]

Study abroad has not always meant privation but this has sometimes been a focus of research. One of the last Commonwealth scholars doing a master's degree in Hong Kong found it difficult to capture her experience but described it as "A kaleidoscope of sights, sounds, smells, tastes and interpretations which, it is no exaggeration to say, will stay with me for a lifetime; so too I hope will the friendships established in Hong Kong." In her research she explored the way a population "moulds a place out of concrete blocks" and looked at the conflict between affordability in the older low-rise building and "the desperate need for larger living spaces". Her modest conclusion was to appreciate her two years there and to argue that even twenty or two hundred would not be enough fully to appreciate and understand the culture.[104]

Scholarships in the south were never as popular as those in the north and the founding fathers would have been disappointed about the extent to which they have fallen away. Their value is testified by the stories of the anthropologists, artists and scientists who went to the south because of their disciplinary interest. But, to put these in proportion, much larger numbers of scholars travelled within the south: India's contribution to technology, medicine, and the social sciences in Africa and Asia, which we touch on again in the next chapter, is a different kind of Commonwealth story but at least as important.

Success rates

How good were the scholars? The evidence on graduation rates, which should provide an objective measure, is surprisingly patchy. None of the three reviews of the plan report on it. The sixth education ministers' conference were told in 1974 that the "success rate has been very high".[105] As the Canadian minister was preparing to go to the education ministers' conference in 1984 she was told that the success rate was 99 per cent.[106] There is slightly fuller information on awards held in Britain. A report to the commission in 1985 found that of the 216 scholars in the 1979 cohort 174 (83 per cent) had obtained a degree or diploma; some seventeen were yet to complete and eleven had not been working for a qualification; only seventeen (8 per cent) had been recalled or for some other reason had not graduated as they had intended. These figures are broadly consistent with a rather more detailed set four years later for the 1984 cohort:[107]

	Registered	Passed		Still registered	
	No.	No.	%	No.	%
Doctorates	196	137	70	47	24
Master's	75	71	95		
Medical qualifications	6	5	83		
Diploma		6	100		
Undergraduate	6	6	100		

By dint of convention or generosity on the part of universities, or of capacity and hard work on the part of students, British master's courses have high success rates, with most students completing within the allotted time. Commonwealth scholars fit that pattern. A later survey found graduation rates between 2000 and 2005 of between 96 and 100 per cent for taught master's courses and 80 to 100 per cent for research master's.

Lower rates were found in both Britain and Canada for distance-learning students with the graduation rate for the postgraduate students in the British programme forecast at 60 per cent (see chapter 6). Many doctoral students, however, took more than the three years for which they were funded. A series of studies looked at graduation rates over four years, a convenient measure also used by the British research councils, though one that begs the question of how the fourth year is to be funded. The figures, summarised in table 7.6, show that completion rates have varied but that the four-year rate appears to have fallen. Whereas the figures for the mid-1990s cohorts were reported to be broadly comparable to those of the research councils, by the time of the 2008 study they had generally fallen behind. (Research council completion rates, particularly in the social sciences, had been criticised and had themselves risen.) There were particular problems in the arts and social sciences where commission four-year rates of 53 and 58 per cent compared with research council figures of 79 and 80 per cent.[108]

If we can extrapolate from the British figures then the plan has achieved acceptable success rates in terms of the qualifications gained by its scholars. Success in earning doctorates compares unfavourably, as one would expect, with that for master's degrees. Students in the humanities and social sciences have consistently faced more difficulty in completing on time that scientists and technologists.

Table 7.6 Scholars' doctoral success rates in Britain

Year of Cohort	Four-year graduation Percentage	Estimated eventual graduation percentage
1979	76	n/a
1984	56	In range 70 to 94
1993	60 social science; 67 medicine; 73 arts; 80 agriculture; 84 science; 85 technology; 100 vet	
1994	79	n/a
1995	73	n/a
2002	71	In range 84 to 97

Conclusion

For the great majority of scholars the process of learning abroad appears to have been a rewarding one, both socially and in terms of getting a degree. The plan fulfilled its purpose, seen from an individual perspective, in enabling young people to get a higher degree. There have been changes in those selected to do so, as a consequence partly of deliberate decisions by awarding authorities, partly of social and intellectual change, and partly by accident. More scholars are now women, a result both of policy and of changes in education systems internationally. Scholars are now generally older, though it is not clear why. Fewer pure scientists are being selected for awards and there has been a tendency to reduce the proportion working for a doctoral degree. In a major change, fewer scholars now have the opportunity to experience higher education in a developing country.

CHAPTER EIGHT

IMPACT: WHAT THEY DID NEXT

Scholars and fellows were always expected to go home and be successful. This chapter therefore addresses three questions: Did they go home? What did they do? Was the money on their awards well spent?

Return rates

It was of the essence of the plan that scholars should go home at the end of their award. One British administrator relentlessly urged a PhD student who had still not finished after ten years, and was by then a British passport holder working full-time in England, to take her ticket and go home even though both knew she was coming back a week later.[1] Administrators and those monitoring the plan have always been concerned about this. At the second Commonwealth education conference in 1962 "some countries feared that difficulties might be encountered in persuading scholars" to go home.[2] Ministers of education repeatedly came back to the issue. At the ninth conference in 1984, for example, they argued that tracer studies "would serve many useful purposes including that of contributing to the formulation of policies to ensure that award holders returned home after completion of their studies".[3] The British looked at return rates for the first two annual cohorts, again in time for the Canberra ministers' conference in 1971, and at intervals down to an evaluation exercise in 2008.

In practice it has always proved difficult to establish robust figures for returning scholars. (Fellows were generally in established posts to which they were assumed, indeed likely, to return after a year or less away.) Some available figures are in table 8.1.

While the figures demand reading with some caution because of low response rates, administrators, and even external reviewers, have tended to treat them with Panglossian respect. The third ten-year review, for example, claimed that the issue of brain drain had been exhaustively examined in the 1989 tracer study although its response rates included figures as low as 9 per cent for India, 13 per cent for Bangladesh and zero for Pakistan which was at that point outside the Commonwealth; Africa was not much

8.1 Estimates of proportion of scholars returning home after award

Date	Country of award	Home country of scholar	Scholars returning	Nature of dataset
1964[a]	Britain	Any	281/402 (70%) graduated and returned home; 75/402 deferring return (19%)	All 1960 and 1961 scholars coming to Britain
1972[b]	Australia	Any	24% working abroad at date of survey, though 40% had at some period	Survey of alumni (no response rate quoted)
1972[b]	Any	Britain	34% abroad at end of 10 year period	Not stated
1977[c]	Britain	Any	630/734 (86%) of those completing between 1973 and 1976 returned home	All scholars coming to Britain
1989[d]	Any	Developing countries	Over 80% returned home for first job after award	Tracer study with overall response rate of 30%
1989[e]	Any	Industrialised countries	63% returned home for first job after award	Tracer study with response rate for these countries of 50%
1993[f]	Any	Any	Thought to be higher than for other development assistance scholarship programmes	Not stated

2000[g]	Any	Developing countries	95% employed within home country	Survey of 5,800 alumni with 23% response rate
2000[g]	Any	Industrialised countries	77% employed within home country	do.
2007[h]	Britain	Uganda	85% residing in Uganda	134 traced alumni from total of 405
2008[i]	Britain	Developing countries	96% of "shared scholarships scheme" returned home	Survey of 536 scholars 2002-5
2008[j]	Britain	Any	88% working in home country	Survey of 5,673 alumni with 39% response rate

Source: a. CSCAR 5; b. Rev 1, 36–7; c. "Analysis of scholars who have failed to return", CSCM 26.4.1977; d. Tracer study, 16–17; e. Ibid., table 44; f. Rev 3, 20; g. Caston report; h. Unwin and Humphreys, *Uganda*, 13; i. Paper CSC 2008/11, CSCM, 1.7.2008; j. Day, *Evaluating the impact*, 17

better with a 19 per cent rate.[4] The British survey in 2000 had only a 23 per cent response rate. The 2008 survey was slightly more robust, with a response rate of 39 per cent and evidence that the survey respondents matched the population in terms of region, gender, scheme, area of study and year of award.[5] But both have the weakness that they could survey only CSFP alumni of whom the ACU held details.

With those cautions, the figures are consistent in suggesting that probably at least three-quarters of developing-country scholars returned home after their awards. There is, inevitably, better evidence on scholars' first moves (did they go home?) than on their later careers (did they stay there?) so that we cannot infer from this anything about the proportion whose whole working life was spent in one country. As noted in chapter 2, rich-country scholars have been more likely to stay in their country of study than those from the developing Commonwealth. Their home countries criticised the practice from time to time but did not try to impose sanctions to deter it.

Some scholars stayed in the north because they were good academics whom universities wanted to catch and keep regardless of any national policy. As early as 1964 the secretary-general of the ACU wrote to the commission with concern about six cases in which Commonwealth scholars had been appointed to university posts in Britain, and thought that there could well be more. Two, from India and Sri Lanka, had got the agreement of their governments while two Australians and two Canadians did not need to. As their numbers included one future professor of philosophy, one of law, one of mathematics, and one of theology the universities and the commission had got their selections right in terms of academic promise, even if not in terms of commitment to their home country.[6] The rapid expansion of British universities in the 1960s meant that there was a heavy demand for good academics. Some scholars were reluctant to return home simply because there were no jobs for them. By the 1970s the British commission noticed that the "shrinkage in opportunities for employment as university lecturers, due to a halting of university expansion, may lead a few Scholars, not excluding those from developed countries, to accept a teaching or research post in a country other than their own".[7]

Circumstances well beyond the control of those awarding scholarships, affected the return rate. One was the practice of bonding students to return, adopted from the outset by India and Singapore, for example, among others. Despite their expressed concern that scholars should go home, the British were in two minds about this. The brief for the British delegation to the second Commonwealth education conference in 1962 wanted the delegation to express misgivings about the practice. It argued that bonds "tend to affect adversely the purposes for which CSFP was established, since they may deter some of the best potential Scholars from applying and thus limit the field of applicants".[8] The first ten-year review—which followed Logan's example of switching into Latin from time to time—warned, too that "when *animus revertendi* disappears, the value of enforced recall for duty in the homeland is problematical". The same review noted that scale could affect return rate: small countries like St Kitts and Belize (then British Honduras) had few job opportunities for alumni. The report also pointed out that "marriage during tenure of scholarships must be an appreciable cause for non-return; although there is no data on the particular point: nevertheless Canadian enquiries showed that 14 per cent of previously unmarried scholars married during their scholarship tenure, the rate for men being similar to that for women".[9] Politics played its part too and sometimes made it unsafe, undesirable or unwise for scholars to return home. Just as Zimbabwean scholars were not expected to go home while the illegal regime was in power so, at the break-up of Pakistan, and the war with India, scholars were allowed to remain in Britain at the end of their award.

While inclination, employment, obligation, marriage, and politics, or any combination of them, affected individual decisions about where to work, several types of career path can be identified. Some scholars went home, some stayed behind, some followed internationally mobile careers.

Many of the scholars who returned home and stayed there, did so with a stated commitment to their work, just as the founding fathers had intended. (There were not always ready opportunities to travel; a survey of Commonwealth alumni in India found that one in four had never travelled outside India after returning home.)[10] An Indian scholar, G. C. Bahr, for example, returned to India in the early 1970s after doing a PhD at Southampton on lasers, then a recently developed technology, recognising that with emigration he could "have far been enriched academically and financially" but wanted to pave "the path of high-tech training in my home country". Nearly forty years later Julius Sandy took his PhD in public policy home to a senior government post as "I never for once entertained the idea of staying in the UK or anywhere outside Sierra Leone".[11] Others, whose countries have also emerged from conflict or transformation, tell the same story. Recent scholars who have returned to South Africa reported:

> I went to Cambridge to get a multinational view of business to build great South African companies. I returned home to get on with this project.
>
> I always knew that I would come back. ... I did not take up opportunities [in the UK] and it was a very deliberate choice on my part. ... The other thing is that, constitutionally, our society is such an exciting place, and to be able to inform that process and be part of it ... I just wanted to be part of that.
>
> I am passionate about starting an industry in industrial/commodity biotech in Africa. I would miss the sun too much in Europe. My career focuses on finding process solutions specifically for the southern African situation, considering the unique infrastructure, climate and culture conditions.[12]

Culture, climate and family as well as career and commitment have all influenced scholars' desire to return home, to large countries and small. Recent scholars have explained why. Ravi Rathi wanted to return to India "as per a matter of rule but that was trivial. The real reason was—I think it's a question of cultural identity. So this is where I wanted to be ... You know the rules of the game you know." After doing a master's degree in educational management in London, Edgar Howell did "not for one single moment" consider staying in Britain rather than returning to the Turks and Caicos. Xolile Guma, who had come from Swaziland and was to return to the new South Africa, referred to his commitment to return and the needs of southern Africa and went on:

> And thirdly I was particularly concerned about the children not becoming totally alienated in the event of having to return to some place in southern Africa. At the time we didn't know if we would be able to come home to South Africa. Nonetheless I didn't want my children to grow up outside the continent.[13]

At the other end of the career spectrum are scholars who stayed permanently in their host country. Of these, the academics who had worried the ACU in 1964, are an important subset. Sir Michael Berridge can stand as an example. His father was a storekeeper and his mother a clerk; a scholarship in the plan's first year brought him from Southern Rhodesia to do a PhD in Cambridge. He remained there for most of his academic career where he worked on cell signalling in a career crowned with honours that include the Shaw prize, fellowships of the Royal Society and of Trinity College, positions as emeritus fellow at the Babraham Institute, a biomedical research institute sponsored by the Biotechnology and Biological Sciences Research Council, and as a Cambridge honorary professor. Returning to Zimbabwe was never a realistic option.[14] The distinction of his career illustrates a point made by the chair of the selection committee in South Africa:

> We think that there is a global university to which we all contribute. Some [scholars] might not come home immediately ... whatever is right for the academic discipline. I think a large number come home in the longer run. Maybe not the next year. If you are a world-class structural biologist, your appropriate next move will be Harvard. ... We are sufficiently internationalist that it doesn't matter where they go intellectually. We would not have modern physics if Marie Curie did not move to Paris.[15]

Canada thought that scholars should go home, even though it had seen the plan as helping to build up postgraduate study within Canadian universities. But a significant proportion of Commonwealth scholars stayed to work in Canada. A government amnesty in the early 1970s meant that those who had stayed were given landed immigrant status. The Canadian committee did not approve but could do nothing about it.[16] And some of these moved south across the border. Levi traced 269 scholars who had come to Canada in the 1980s and found that, while over 60 per cent were working in their home countries, of those still in north America, 28 were in Canada and 32 in the United States.[17] Limited job opportunities, more often cited as a problem in the developing world, drove some of them in this direction. Laura Gibson returned to Canada with a Cambridge doctorate in engineering but after two years at the University of British Columbia in the early 1980s found that, with the local economy depressed, job prospects were poor—but there was an opening at MIT.[18]

International mobility is of the essence of contemporary academic and professional life. Alongside the scholars who returned and stayed home, and those who stayed in their host country, a group of wandering teachers and administrators form a new category. Cuddalore Krishnamurti, who had a scholarship at the University of Alberta in the 1960s, returned to India but found a "lack of opportunity ... to impart my knowledge to those who needed it most" and returned to Canada for a long career at the University of British Columbia.[19] Other former scholars have mixed national and international experience. From the 1960s, Mothusi Mashologu, who had enjoyed the lack of prejudice in Northern Ireland (see chapter 7), moved into government service, spent time in the Lesotho mission to the United Nations and moved to a second, international, career with the Red Cross in Zimbabwe and Geneva. This kind of international mobility has taken a number of scholars to work for the UN and its agencies. A generation after Mashologu, Shamba Phiri was the youngest child of twelve whose parents were subsistence farmers. With a degree from the University of Zambia she worked as a schoolteacher and for the ministry of education before going in 1992 to do an MA at the Institute of Education in London. She was homesick in her year there and intended to go home to a job in curriculum development but later moved to the UN, spending time working on gender in Liberia, on a school-feeding programme in Malawi and on peace keeping in Croatia and Eastern Timor.[20]

Some alumni followed a variant of that kind of international mobility by going home for some years and then emigrating, quite often to their country of study. Ayal Jayatilaka used his Cambridge engineering doctorate to teach in Sri Lanka for ten years before returning to Britain to set up a business. Another engineer, Hung Wan Chung got his PhD in the minimum two years and returned to Hong Kong in 1965; he held academic posts there for more than twenty years and then emigrated to take up an Australian university post. Migration of this kind has been influenced by the economics and politics of scholars' home country as well as by opportunity in the north. Professor Ademola Afonja had a mixed career teaching engineering and working on the development of the Nigerian iron and steel industry, with all the frustrations of both jobs during Nigeria's periods of military rule, until he eventually retired, leaving the country to move to America. Alumni from industrialised as well as developing countries have migrated in mid-career in this way. Ross Cranston returned to Australia with an Oxford doctorate in law but was attracted back to the larger world of academic law in England when he was appointed to a chair in 1986, from which he moved into British politics, served as solicitor general from 1998 to 2001, and after leaving parliament became a high court judge.[21]

With their concern for Commonwealth cohesion the creators of the plan might have applauded careers that moved within the Commonwealth in that way. They might have given even more applause to the many who spent the greater part of their career in their home country and it is appropriate to explore the effects of those careers on their home society.

Lives and achievements

The scholarship plan, and student mobility generally, have been assessed on different criteria at different times. The debates of the 1980s, on the impact of differential fees on international students, concentrated on the value to the Commonwealth of the exchange of scholars and of the long-term benefit to the economy of the country hosting them as a result of their future influence. In 2008, responses to the FCO withdrawal of funds were couched in terms of benefits to British universities and of the development of leaders. Meanwhile, as noted in chapter 4, the scholarship commission's evaluation report in the same year was dominated by the development agenda, almost to the point of downplaying the commission's impact on the universities where most of its alumni went to work. The evaluation was funded by DfID; no funds were available from FCO to look at the impact of awards assessed against their criteria.[22]

In gauging impact, against a range of criteria, it is worth looking at the record in a cross section of disciplines. Science, technology and medicine have been a high priority for many countries. The original assumption was that some scholars and fellows would become national, implicitly, political leaders. There was also a consensus that awards should be available in all subject areas including the humanities and fine arts. To illustrate the variety of outcomes we look in turn at scientists, politicians, and poets along with their peers in the humanities.

Science and technology

Governments and scholars alike have seen awards in science and engineering as a way of tapping intellectual resources that are often available only in strong universities within the industrialised world. India and Pakistan from the outset interpreted the plan as a means of strengthening science and engineering in their national interest (see chapter 6). In the plan's first phase, before it left the Commonwealth in 1972, some 77 per cent of scholars and fellows from Pakistan were in science, technology and medicine.[23] Individual scholars, from industrialised and developing countries, were attracted by excellence. Rachael Padman explained the specific attraction of Cambridge, where she did a doctorate in radio astronomy: "Australia has some very good universities. You're not going to leave your good university in Australia or Canada and come here to a lesser place just for the sake of going to Britain".[24]

A high proportion of scientists have come from, and returned to, academic posts so that the impact of their work can be gauged by their own research and by the building up of their departments and of new teams of researchers. Martin Green, an Australian pioneer in solar cell development, studied at McMaster University in Canada where he "was steered into photovoltaics, where I am now well known internationally and where I have spawned a new generation of researchers who have had a major impact on the industry".[25] Two Pakistani scholars illustrate the use they made in transferring skills. Dr Iqbal Khan went as a medical fellow to study anaesthesia in Britain where he was, at the same time, introduced to a new, and for him unfamiliar, approach to patient care; he was able to transfer skills in both areas as an assistant professor at the Pakistan Institute of Medical Sciences. Dr Gul M. Khan, a senior academic in pharmacology, studied the transdermal delivery of pharmaceuticals at Strathclyde University, one of the two foremost institutions in this area. After returning home, where he was one of four people in the country with skills in the area, he began supervising PhD students and, following contacts made on his fellowship in Britain was able to establish a university link between his university and Bradford, the other institution with relevant interests.[26]

International cooperation of this kind, and the generation of publications, are further markers of academic effectiveness. All of the university teachers surveyed in Pakistan, who had held academic fellowships, valued the time and opportunity to develop publications. On average, fellows reported that one to two papers came directly from their fellowship; many of these were developed with international collaborators.[27]

Many scientists and engineers in the developing Commonwealth combined their academic work with the practical application of their skills in industry and in their own environment. Scholars from Uganda, Bangladesh and Trinidad illustrate the point. Jackson Mwakali was the first known Ugandan with a doctorate in structural engineering when he returned from the University of Surrey in 1992. He established postgraduate programmes at Makerere, and became head of department there, but also became heavily involved in research and consultancy, advised the Uganda Investment Authority and National Investment Management Authority and chaired the Uganda Engineers Registration Board.[28] A Bangladeshi engineer, Kazi Ahmed, used his 1994 British doctorate in hydrology in his post at the University of Dhaka but was also involved in two research projects of major national importance: one was to develop policy for protecting shallow groundwater from contamination and the other on the sustainable use of water from the deep aquifer. These fed into the long-term water management plan for the city of Dhaka.[29] A split-site PhD scholar from Trinidad and Tobago who had studied in Britain went on to create an aquaculture unit with funding from the University of the West Indies. He explained

> With the closure of a major portion of the Agriculture sector in Trinidad, over 10,000 people were out of jobs. I assisted the government in retraining and retooling some of these workers into the field of Aquaculture. I assisted in developing a course and assessment package for the government. This has led to the training of over 300 people in aquaculture.[30]

The applicability of some scientific and technological awards brought problems for award holders and for awarding countries, concerned about their relevance to scholars' home countries. A biomedical scientist from India, for example, spoke with high praise of the training he had got at the University of Calgary but reported that "when I returned to my parent institution in India I fell prey to the bureaucracy and was given no facility or funds to conduct my research". Despite a financial penalty he left to take up a position in the United States. Awarding countries expressed particular concern about science in relation to small states. In the mid-1960s the Canadian authorities, for example, were concerned about the nomination of scholars from Mauritius who were "unable [to] obtain suitable or any employment in homeland at end of awards ... failure of Mauritians to return serves to defeat purpose of plan".[31] In some countries there is a vicious circle here. Science education in St Lucia, for example, has always been limited and the restricted opportunities for scientists at home mean that they have tended to emigrate. St Lucia has nominated few scholars in the sciences and the shortage of good science teachers looks likely to continue.[32] Politics as well as the job market can have a bearing on the awards available to scientists. Despite the principle that scholarships could be held in any disciplines, Canada imposed a ban on Indian students who wanted to study nuclear engineering there. This followed India's successful nuclear test, although it was said to have used material indirectly supplied by Canada.[33]

Politics and government

One of the early expectations for the plan, at least in the eyes of the Canadians and the British, was to attract potential leaders. Within the Canadian department of external affairs, it was argued in 1958 that it could provide "opportunities for the training of those who in twenty-five year's time will be carrying the responsibility for decision-making in Government, in business and industry, in labour movements, and in the armed forces".[34] This matched the British hope, reported in the same period, of attracting "potential leaders" (see chapter 2). For many years, however, this did not lead to any specific policy, at least for the commission in Britain. Over the period 1982 to 1995 two serving commissioners confirm that academic strength was the sole criterion used for selection.[35] Only in 1995 was the FCO's concern for "for future leaders, decision makers and opinion formers from around the world" turned into specific guidance; despite the terminology it applied only to the industrialised countries (see chapter 4). Evidence on political leadership therefore tells us principally about the long-term effects of a particular group of alumni who were predominantly selected on academic grounds.

Few study leadership as an academic discipline so that we cannot follow the careers of a group of trained leaders as we can with scientists, though there may be a tendency for politicians to have a background as lawyers. Nor can there be a simple equation to suggest the proportion of scholars, selected on a basis of academic merit, who might be expected to gain political influence. Some scholars reacted against the concept of leadership, preferring the CSFP emphasis on academic attainment. One New Zealand historian who went to Cambridge commented that, "I was averse to, and definitely didn't apply for a Rhodes. You had to have a history of being a leading sportsman (which I actually had), but also being Christian, a really good person, and a leader of men (which I wasn't) so the very idea of a Rhodes slightly dismayed me".[36] Alumni of diverse backgrounds have achieved political power and influence in various ways: in politics and the public service, within the international agencies, and through journalism. The data suggest that a modest proportion of alumni made successful careers in politics and that those who did so were often in small states. Levi's survey of some 1,000 scholars and fellow who came from or studied in Canada found only about thirty with a political career. Jodhka's survey of the plan in India made no reference to politicians.[37] Of course there are exceptions which include Ross Cranston (see above) and Michael Cullen who returned to a university post in New Zealand in 1971 after doing his doctorate in history in Edinburgh, entered parliament ten years later and became deputy prime minister in 2002.[38] In both Australia and Canada former scholars have played a political role at state or provincial level. Louis Bernard, for example, who came to study law in London in the second year of the plan's existence, went on to run for leadership of the Parti Québecois in 2005.[39] At federal level in Australia, two former scholars, Michael Tate and George Brandis who had done law at Oxford became ministers in labor and liberal administrations respectively. But few alumni seem to have accompanied them on to the national political stage in either Australia or Canada.

Lawyers dominate the account of politicians who became potential leaders and are prominent in the lists of those who have worked in or close to government. In 2008, the scholarship commission published a list of alumni from industrialised countries who had come to Britain, gained influence, and were therefore of relevance to the FCO's interest in the plan (see chapter 4). While the list was incomplete, it included nine judges with four of them from Australia.[40] Many of the politicians' careers whom it has been possible to trace have followed a similar pattern. They have tended to return home, usually with a higher degree in law, often from a prominent university in Britain or Canada, spent some time in an academic post, and then moved into politics. An Oxford or McGill gown replaces the baton in their knapsack. Joe Borg, for example, came to Britain from Malta to do an LLM at the University of Wales–Aberystwyth in 1987. He held academic posts at the University of Malta, entered parliament and served as foreign minister before being appointed as a European commissioner where, appropriately, he held the portfolio for fisheries and maritime affairs.[41]

Overseas study may be a necessary route to promotion. Jacqueline Cornelius "believes it unlikely that she would have been appointed one of the youngest female judges ever in Barbados by the still fairly pale skinned legal establishment without them respecting that not only did she hold the qualifications she does but also that they were achieved at Cambridge on a Commonwealth scholarship".[42]

A number of alumni have become ministers in Africa. (With the exception of the Maldives, they do not appear in the alumni records for south Asia.) Christopher Ameyaw-Akumfi was unusual as being a politician with a scientific background. He followed an academic career within Ghanaian universities, in which he succeeded both in continuing to produce publications in zoology as well as working on the administration of higher education, before serving as minister of transport and as minister of education in Ghana.[43] Another scientist, Juma Kapuya who did a doctorate in plant physiology at the University of Wales, left his academic post and become minister of defence in Tanzania in 2006 and minister of labour, youth and sports development in 2008.[44] More often African ministers, as in other parts of the Commonwealth, had studied law. This was the case, for example, with Hasan Bubacar Jallow, attorney general and minister of justice in the Gambia (1984–94) and of Kalombo Mwansa who worked at the University of Zambia before entering politics and serving from 2002, in turn, as minister of foreign affairs, home affairs and mines and mineral development.[45] The career of another lawyer, George Kenyaihamba, illustrates some of the complexities of African politics. He left his post at Makerere University in the early 1970s to do a doctorate in law at Warwick University and stayed out of Uganda for some of its darkest days, holding academic posts in Britain. He chaired the constitutional committee of the Moshi conference of Ugandan exiles that helped to remove Idi Amin from power in 1979. After returning home he entered parliament and, unusually, served both as a cabinet minister, when he was for five years attorney general, and as a judge, becoming justice of the supreme court in 1997. In that capacity he went on to develop international refugee law and served for two years on the African court on human and people's rights, a term that was then not renewed amid some controversy and suggestions of difficult relations between judge and government.[46]

Small states are different; just as they have received a disproportionate number of scholarships in relation to their population, so they appear to have produced a disproportionate number of politicians. In St Lucia, with no university campus, there was no natural opportunity within the island for able people to pursue an academic career and the plan has done well in producing politicians. Kenny Anthony did a doctorate in law at Birmingham (1985–8) and spent some years in the faculty of law at the University of the West Indies before returning to St Lucia where he became prime minister from 1997-2006; on the opposite benches, Nicholas Frederick later became attorney general and minister of justice. At first sight he seemed to buck the lawyerly trend as he used his Commonwealth scholarship to study education in Canada. But later in his career, having served as permanent secretary in the ministry of education, he changed careers, did a law degree in England, and moved into politics. The country's governor-general Dame Pearlette Louisey was a Commonwealth scholar at Laval University in Canada (1973–5). Her career took her from childhood in an all-female household of agricultural workers by means of a series of scholarships—the first at the age of thirteen—to a career in education, until she moved from being principal of the island's tertiary college to her post as the Queen's representative.[47]

Canada has a strong record in producing small-state politicians. In the 1980s, for example, at least five future ministers were studying in Canada: from the Caribbean Clyde Mascoll, who studied finance at Queen's University was to lead his party into the Barbados election in 2003 and then cross the floor of the house three years later to take up a ministerial post, Walter Francois became minister of planning in St Lucia and Len Ligenga minister of economic planning in Malawi.[48] The careers of two of their near contemporaries illustrate the turbulent political life of their own countries. Ratu Madraiwiwi had a Commonwealth scholarship from Fiji to Australia in 1976, where he did his first degree in law at Adelaide, followed a decade later by another to Canada where he did a master's degree in air and space law at McGill. He was appointed a judge of the high court but resigned in protest against the 2000 coup and returned to his private legal practice and work as a human rights commissioner. In 2005, he returned to government as vice-president after his predecessor had been convicted of treason, in relation to the 2000 coup. Madraiwiwi is reported to have used his leadership skills when, as acting president, he brokered a truce in 2006 between the prime minister and military commander.[49] Meanwhile in the Maldives, Mohamed Munavvar did a master's in law at Dalhousie University (1990–3) and returned home to become attorney general. He spent ten years in the post but was then jailed in 2004, apparently for his associations with a pro-democracy movement, but released some months later.[50]

Borg's post as a European commissioner and Kenyaihamba's record in international law demonstrate in different ways how political influence can extend beyond national boundaries. International influence is not the prerogative of politicians. The scholarship commission's survey of alumni in 2008 found that 24 per cent of alumni reported some involvement in international affairs, sometimes through bilateral or multilateral international agencies. A Canadian scholar who did an MPhil in Britain in the 1960s went on to a career with the Canadian International Development Agency where, he explained:

> As a planning officer ... and field representative ... for Botswana, Lesotho, Swaziland, Kenya and Uganda, I had a major influence on the design and implementation of Canadian development assistance projects in those countries in a wide range of sectors, including health, education, environment, agriculture, job creation and poverty reduction.

He went on to shape Canadian aid policy in southern Africa and, having moved to the foreign affairs department, governance and technical assistance policies for the Commonwealth with a particular focus on three states at odds with the Commonwealth, Fiji, Pakistan and Zimbabwe.[51]

With characteristic prescience Thomas Jefferson believed "that banking establishments are more dangerous than standing armies".[52] The records show few soldiers but there have been a number of influential, if not dangerous, bankers. A small clutch of future Canadian bankers came to Britain to do economics. Charles Freedman led the way in 1963, graduating with a first in politics, philosophy and economics at Oxford, returning to advance to a position as deputy governor of the Bank of Canada. He was followed two years later by William White who did a PhD at Manchester: his career also took him to a deputy governorship (1984–95) and on to the Bank of International Settlements. Twenty-five years later Mark Carney took his economics doctorate from Oxford first to Goldman Sachs and later, again, to the Bank of Canada of which he became governor. Jonathan Ostry, who became deputy head of research at the International Monetary Fund (IMF), did a first degree at Queen's University, was supported by the scholarship commission in Britain to do politics, philosophy and economics at Oxford followed by an MSc at the London School of Economics, and went on to do a doctorate in Chicago. He says that his time at Oxford and LSE "opened doors" and provided the educational background that was " essential for the work that I have done over the past 20 years at the IMF".[53]

The developing-country bankers have had more varied careers. Akbar Ali Khan did his economics doctorate at Queen's University in Canada and followed a career in government service in Bangladesh, retiring as finance secretary. He then served for five years as an executive director of the World Bank.[54] Xolile Guma was born in South Africa but did his first degree at the (then) University of Botswana and Swaziland followed by a master's in Toronto and a doctorate in economics at Manchester (1986–9), on a Commonwealth scholarship. He returned to academic posts at the University of Swaziland and moved back to South Africa on transformation and joining the South African Reserve Bank in 1995, becoming deputy governor in 2001.

The journalist may be more influential than the politician; CSFP has produced some of them. Charles Krauthammer, in an unusual career, did a BA in politics at McGill and a BPhil at Oxford in political science (1970–1) before changing direction and qualifying as a medical doctor and psychiatrist. He moved back towards politics in 1978 as science adviser to Jimmy Carter in Washington, later moving to journalism and to the right: a syndicated column in the *Washington Post* won him the Pullitzer prize and his writings placed him as one of the most influential journalists arguing the neocon agenda.[55] Edward Greenspon, building on a career as an investigative student journalist at Carleton University, went to work at the *Lloydminster Times* on the borders of Alberta and Saskatchewan. He escaped the cold with a Commonwealth scholarship to do a master's in economics and politics at the London School of Economics, returning in 1986 to the *Globe and Mail*. Following spells as a business journalist to London, which surprisingly included reporting from Timisoara on the fall of Ceausescu, he was back in Canada in 2002 with promotion to editor in chief of the same paper.[56] One other scholar, who went to Canada, unusually combined influence within government and, after retiring from government service, through journalism outside. Brian Egner was a colonial civil servant, originally from the Isle of Man, working in the Bechuanaland protectorate, now Botswana, and went to study economics at the University of British Columbia in Canada in 1962. In a long career, during which he took out Botswana citizenship, he held key posts at various times in the ministry of local government and lands and as director of information. On retirement he became an economic consultant and, from being a forthright commentator while within government, became even more vociferous outside, backing moves to establish an independent newspaper, *The Examiner*, alongside the government *Botswana Daily News*.[57]

Politicians, journalists and bankers are not the only leaders in public life. Civil servants—including those who have remained in government service as well as those who made new careers outside such as Nicholas Frederick and Brian Egner—also belong in the gallery of the influential, and they too are among the plan's alumni. Appropriately enough, Tony Humphries, who went from Britain to Nigeria as a Commonwealth scholar in 1973, found himself in the FCO's Commonwealth coordination department thirty years later.[58] With the civil servants, too, belong the many university staff members who have played a role in public affairs as well as within academe. Some 45 per cent of alumni surveyed in 2008 reported that they had, in one way or another, been "influencing government thinking and policy".[59]

Poets and painters

The plan never set out to produce a quiver-full of poets but they were within the founding fathers' vision. The Indian delegation reminded the Oxford conference that "the fine arts, literature, humanities and other cultural subjects like archaeology and anthropology cannot be neglected" while the Canadians specifically referred to the humanities in arguing that the plan should "embrace all recognized academic disciplines".[60] Developing-country poets would, today, have to demonstrate the developmental relevance of their work if they were applying to Britain and, in practice, the handful of internationally known scholar poets came to do something else. Kamau Brathwaite, for example, did a doctorate in history at Sussex in the late 1960s, with one year of this funded by the commission. His book, *The development of Creole society in Jamaica, 1770–1820*, which grew out of his thesis, was a major contribution to Caribbean history and to its historiography. "His achievement does not only lie in his contribution to knowledge production, but it lies even more in the fact that through his powerfully imaginative reworkings of ideas about Jamaican/Caribbean cultural history, he opened a door where there had appeared to be an impenetrable brick wall".[61] On returning to the University of the West Indies Brathwaite continued his academic career as a historian but became increasingly well known also as a poet and for his argument for the use of "nation language" in poetry, drawing from the oral traditions and rhythms of Caribbean speech.[62] Poetry, in his case, was not far from politics.

It was even closer in the case of Jack Mapanje who did a doctorate in linguistics at University College London (1983) from which he returned to become head of the department of English at Chancellor College in the University of Malawi. His first collection of poems *Of chameleons and gods* appears to have attracted limited attention when first published but was then withdrawn from bookshops in Malawi. In 1987, the Malawi government, then under Banda's authoritarian rule, arrested and imprisoned Mapanje, all without charge or trial. In Britain the scholarship commission "heard with concern" about this in October 1987; they were told, incorrectly, in December that he was to be tried for sedition at a traditional court. The foreign office did not want to be involved. He was not a British citizen and "In any case it would be FCO practice to make representations only after due legal process had been completed", though there was little due process about his incarceration.[63] International protests by Harold Pinter, Wole Soyinka, Susan Sontag, Noam Chomsky and others eventually led to his release—still without charge—and to a life in exile in Britain. He has since taught at the universities of York and of Newcastle on Tyne and continued to publish poetry. This still drew from Malawian oral traditions, but also addressed British as well as African political themes. His most recent

> collection's stories spiral from a tribal court to a Yorkshire beach, from hyenas and jacarandas to the winter of discontent and GNER, but the subject that appears again and again in his conversation, as in his poetry, is the

brutal regime of the Malawian dictator Hastings Kamuzu Banda, and the time Mapanje spent in Malawi's notorious Mikuyu prison. The animation drains from his face, and his small frame becomes still as he touches on the pain of the "three years, seven months, sixteen days and twelve hours"—the words tumble out like a catechism—in the gruelling conditions of a maximum security jail.[64]

Poets may have been funded by accident, as doctorates in history and linguistics are not obvious prerequisites, whereas the plan deliberately chose to fund a number of artists, most of them from the industrialised Commonwealth. Leslie Carlyle's exemplifies a multinational career. She worked at the Canadian Conservation Institute for some twenty-five years, specialising in the materials used by nineteenth-century artists. She did a master's degree at Queen's University before spending three years in Britain doing a doctorate at the Courtauld Institute of Art in 1981. She then came back to Britain in 2005 to take up the post of head of conservation at the Tate.[65] A near contemporary of hers, Stephen Turner, went in the other direction. He was attracted to Canada to do an MA in visual art at Regina in Saskatchewan as "Canada was a place where in terms of research and work everything was possible in a wide optimistic landscape". He was influenced to go by family stories of his uncle who had moved from farming to booze running during prohibition, influenced after he arrived by the Regina Five, a leading group of Canadian abstract artists in the 1960s, and in particular by Ted Godwin one of the five. In assessing its influence on his own art he explained:

> Ted was producing huge abstract "tartan" canvases just before I got to Regina, but when I was there he had retraced his steps to work with the hugeness and emptiness of Canadian landscape for the first time (he still is). These had a big influence on my work and I made large paintings that were abstractions of prairie light and space, of real local colour. I also took from him a sense of his joy in the journey—a feeling for the fleetingness of life and our own temporality—or frailty perhaps—that the paysage is personal, psychological and emotional as much as descriptive. The whole Canadian experience as shared with Ted Godwin, helped me refine and define a lifelong love of nature, place and distinctiveness, and to retain it at the heart of my art through periods when nature has not been at the fashionable end of art. I have never forgotten its importance.[66]

India has steadily provided scholarships for artists from both the developing and the industrialised world. It attracted artists, who went back to professional and academic posts in their home countries, from Kenya, Mauritius, Sri Lanka and Uganda among others. George Kyeyune, for example, with two Commonwealth scholarships studied art at Baroda, and later at the School of Oriental and African Studies in London, and returned to the Margaret Trowell School of Industrial and Fine Arts at Makerere University.[67] In Sri Lanka Kolitha Bhanu Dissanayake returned from doing an MMus in vocal music at the Banaras Hindu University in 1993 and became dean of the faculty of music at the University of Visual and Performing Arts.[68] One British artist who went to India as a Commonwealth scholar in 1988, Mark Cazalet, found that he was not expected, but was untroubled by this as exactly the same thing had happened when he went to study in Paris, and began a rewarding year at Baroda. He attributes much of his development as an artist, and his style as a teacher, to the time he spent there and to the influence of his tutor, Gulam Mohammed Sheikh. On arriving in India he "was determined to branch out from the previous year's work which I had completed in London and explore all the new themes and directions that might develop". Sheikh explained how Cazalet had done this, by starting from the "panorama of the Indian street" where

> Those who venture to wade through the whirling crowds of the bazaars, trains, processions and agitations are struck by the enigma of the flux and its dynamic momentum. Within the year Mark Cazalet has spent in India he has tried to touch the nerve centre of that enigma—somewhat impatiently, even tentatively, but with a great deal of courage and conviction. As a result, the sheer energy of his vision has charged his personal vision to turn commonplace sights into images of a poetic voyage, at once engaging and disturbing.[69]

The poets and the painters, who can stand for others in the fine arts and the humanities, were outside the mainstream of the plan. Their record is important, however, in illustrating the eclectic variety of achievements that has followed from the original decision to set no limits to the plan in terms of subject area or academic discipline.

Was the money well spent?

There is no easy answer. As the plan's purposes have changed so the criteria for its assessment may need to change: investment in the promotion of Commonwealth cohesion, or the cultivation of friends by a member state, or the pursuit of sustainable development, cannot easily be measured with the same yardstick. Doctors, engineers, lawyers and poets, along with university teachers, have different kinds of impact on their society and we cannot compare like with like by looking at reductions in morbidity against measures of good road building or effective governance. One all-purpose measure is to use rate-of-return analysis, assessing the benefits that follow from a programme of education by measuring the increased income of its beneficiaries. While there is extensive literature on rate-of-return analysis to compare domestic returns to different levels of education, and at least one comparative assessment of local and international scholarship programmes, there does not appear to have been any assessment of CSFP using this approach.[70] Rate-of-return analysis is in any case contentious and faces, among other difficulties, the formidable challenge in this case that most costs will be calculated at rich-country prices but benefits, for developing-country scholars working in their home countries, at poor-country ones. Any attempt at cost–benefit analysis, examining the benefits within alumni home countries, would also need to look at the externalities in terms of benefits to awarding-country institutions: universities value able students, benefit from them, and run their own scholarship programmes to attract them.

In the absence of economic data of this kind we cannot answer a number of more detailed questions about effectiveness. We cannot, for example, quantify in terms of increased income, the extra benefit—if there is one of this kind—of spending three years doing a doctorate rather than a master's, or of travelling to a metropolitan country for a year rather than doing a distance-learning course. Decisions on this kind of issue have in practice been made on different criteria. Doctoral scholarships have been sought and awarded, particularly in the sciences, as a necessary part of the professional development of future university teachers. One-year Chevening scholarships, were, in contrast and as noted in chapter 4, seen as being long enough to develop friends for Britain.

An economic appraisal of the plan therefore depends on the evidence, quoted in this chapter and in chapter 7, on scholars' performance, on the cost data, and on more general arguments about the economics of education. The evidence shows that the plan has been efficient in ensuring that its scholars graduate and that many of them return to work in their home countries. The more discursive evidence on their subsequent careers confirms the obvious expectation that postgraduate education is likely to produce benefits for the graduate's career and for society more broadly; these are enhanced where, as with many university teachers, there is a long-term multiplier effect from their own work. Society worldwide funds tertiary education in that belief. If we are concerned with the current developmental agenda, the evidence of correlations between tertiary education and economic growth provides one justification for expenditure on scholarships.[71] Study abroad may, too, have an economic, as well as educational, edge on study at home. Universities, particularly in large countries, have attracted students to courses which would be uneconomic if run on too local a basis: Mauritian medical students have, for example, gone to India, Indian glaciologists to Canada and molecular biologists to Britain in pursuit of specialist expertise. Sound economics in these cases fits closely with the pursuit of academic excellence.

Alongside the evidence on outcomes, some figures are available on the costs of the plan. Using British figures, tables 3.2 and 4.1 showed how the scholarship commission's expenditure rose from £547,300 (2008£7.63 million) in 1966 (by which time it was in full swing) to £16.9 million in 2008. Annual costs per award are estimated to have risen from £1,035 (2008£14,431) in 1966 to £19,937 (2008£24,711) in 2001.[72] A significant proportion of the increase in real terms is to be attributed to the rising level of university fees, which increased as a result of national policy in the 1980s and then, steadily, in the 1990s and 2000s as a result of decisions by individual universities. Britain was able to maintain the number of awards offered only by its programme of diversifying: shorter fellowships, split-site scholarships, and distance-learning awards all have lower unit costs than the narrower range of awards it offered up to 2000.

The costs of the plan have represented a small proportion of aid or foreign affairs expenditure. At the time of the Oxford conference Britain committed itself to spending double the amount on teacher training for the Commonwealth as on Commonwealth scholarships. Three years later the plan was criticised, albeit by an opposition MP, as looking "completely inadequate" in relation to educational needs, particularly in Africa.[73] Up to the early 1990s, expenditure on the plan was a small proportion of total aid expenditure on education and training programmes. The closing down of the technical cooperation and training programme led to a "dramatic decrease" by 1999, from 12,500 down to 1,000 of aid-funded students travelling to Britain with the result that the commission grant was a much higher proportion of total expenditure on tertiary education and training.[74] While, as argued in chapter 4, the expenditure was now more exposed, with its grant from DfID at between £10 million in 2000/1 and £14 million in 2005/6, this figure was slightly more than British aid to Jamaica (£12.7 million in 2005/6), slightly less than that to Honduras (£16.6 million), and can be seen against a total aid expenditure of £6.6 billion.[75] Between 1999 and 2003 the foreign office budget for Commonwealth scholarships varied between £1.75 million and £2.25 million while it spent between £29.4 million and £34.2 million on Chevening scholarships, all against a total budget that reached £1,513 million in 2002/3.[76]

The Canadian figures tell a similar story. Expenditure on the plan rose from Cdn$3.84 million in 1981/2 to $8.05 million five years later (about

2008£4.8 million to £8.7 million). Over the next five years it varied between Cdn$9 million and Cdn$12 million (2008£8 million to £12 million). The cost per award holder was generally in the range Cdn$13,000 to $21,000 (around 2008£17,000). Over the period 1981 to 1992, the whole aid budget rose from Cdn$1,489 million (2008£1,775 million) to $3,184 million (£2,328 million) so that expenditure on the plan kept below a 0.5 per cent of aid expenditure. (Expenditure on other Canadian scholarship programmes rose after 1989 so that CSFP now took less than half of the total.)[77]

Expenditure on Commonwealth scholarships is small beer in relation to aid or diplomatic expenditure generally, or in relation to the vastly greater world expenditure on crossborder study. It can reasonably be set against the evidence on the achievements of scholarship holders. That evidence is robust enough to suggest that the taxpayers who funded Commonwealth scholarships and fellowships got a good return on their investment. In the British case, the commission has maintained a reputation for cost effectiveness by keeping its management costs below 10 per cent.[78] In contrast it has no control over steadily rising university costs, which inevitably constrain the number of awards that can be made.

Conclusion

The evidence is consistent in suggesting simple answers to the opening questions in this chapter. By and large scholars and fellows did go home after their awards. They achieved success in varied careers, exemplified in science, politics and the fine arts. Expenditure on their awards has been a small proportion of government expenditure and the multiplier effects of their achievements, both as university teachers and as entrepreneurs of various kinds, has increased the long-term impact of their work.

The conclusions can be nuanced in at least three ways. First, they are inevitably limited as we know more about the first destinations of alumni than about their long-term careers. Second, the record suggests that an increasing proportion of alumni are now following mobile careers. Whereas young, wandering, scholars always moved from country to country, this has become a common mid-career pattern among academics, and in other parts of both the public and the private sector. CSFP alumni have given a human face to globalisation and may, almost by accident, have helped towards Commonwealth cohesion within their own areas of interest. Third, politics have affected outcomes. The impact of the plan in South Africa, Pakistan and Nigeria, for example, was affected by the periods in which they were within and outside the Commonwealth. The same is more surprisingly true of Tanzania and the Seychelles that had no awards from Britain in the mid-1970s and the early 2000s respectively because of British aid policy. In contrast British policy at least was to continue to offer scholarships regardless of the political standing of a country, provided it managed to remain within the Commonwealth. It awarded scholarships to Malawi even while the commission was protesting at the imprisonment of Mapanje, and to Pakistan when many other funding agencies had ceased doing so. Despite its political status, northern Cyprus has benefited from the plan; there is a sad irony in being able to point, as evidence for the plan's long-term political influence, to a minister within a government that no Commonwealth country recognises as legitimate.[79] The decision to avoid political tests, other than that of Commonwealth membership, has had beneficial consequences for individuals, surprising ones for individual countries.

Chapter Nine

Conclusion

In assessing the plan and moving from chronicle to explanation, we need to ask how and why it has changed and survived. For it seems to have done so against the odds, over a period in which the Commonwealth has lost its political and economic significance. The explanation can start by looking at the achievements of the plan and at changes in its practice, set against changes in the structure and politics of the Commonwealth and of its member states.

The number of scholars and fellows has risen, though not spectacularly. There were less than 400 award holders in 1960, one-third of them from the colonies, 1,000 within five years. In 2008, there were between 1,500 and 2,000. Any assessment of the Commonwealth scholarship and fellowship plan needs to start from the fact that it has continued to provide awards over fifty years and throughout the Commonwealth to scholars and fellows selected because of their academic capacity. On the face of it, the plan has changed less than the Commonwealth itself.

The achievements of the plan are set out in chapters 7 and 8. Although the data are incomplete, the evidence is solid enough to show that the plan has produced graduates, with masters and doctorates, and done so with acceptable success rates. Probably a majority of scholars, and the huge majority of fellows, have returned home, as was always intended by the countries that nominated them and those that funded them. Many have become academic leaders, some leaders in other spheres, a handful political leaders. The record can stand against the accusations that the plan is an over-academic irrelevance. Selection by academic merit seems to have served it reasonably well. It is more difficult to establish how far they became lifelong friends of the countries where they studied; unreasonable to assume that they created a sense of Commonwealth cohesion when the term was undefined fifty years ago and is almost unheard in political dialogue today.

People and programmes, the educational essence of the plan, have changed over the fifty years. Women are still in a minority among scholars and fellows but have increased from about 12 per cent to about 45 per cent of the total. Scholarships are now almost entirely for postgraduate degrees, except for a small handful of students from territories with no national university, a minority of the awards in India, and a Canadian student-exchange programme for the Caribbean.[1] Technical awards, which in their time took east African technicians to Pakistan and west African hockey coaches to India, have fallen away. New subjects have come into the plan: there were few awards in computer science in the early years and none in nanotechnology. Canada has flirted with distance learning and Britain seems to have adopted it as a regular part of its programme. Although Britain continued to provide mid-career fellowships, those designed for high-status academics, once offered by half a dozen countries, did not survive budget cuts around the Commonwealth in the 1980s.

Changes in the geography of the plan take us into its politics. At its establishment reciprocity was seen as an aim, even perhaps a condition of success. Award holders might in principle come from and travel to any country of the Commonwealth that produced able students or could provide university places. In practice, awards offered by developing Commonwealth countries were never popular, either to other developing or to industrialised countries. By 2008 the great majority of scholars and fellows were travelling to just four countries—Britain, Canada, India and New Zealand. The principle of reciprocity was respected but rarely given the backing of sanctions: the major awarding countries did not say that, respecting the principle, they would make awards only to citizens of countries that themselves offered them. The major exceptions have affected rich-country exchanges so that, for example, Canada decided to stop offering awards to Australia when it withdrew its awards.

Two policy changes have influenced the geography. First, there has been a shift by Britain and Canada of resources towards Africa, as its needs have attracted growing international concern. Second, once Australia left the plan, the proportion of scholars travelling between the industrialised countries fell by one half from around 25 per cent of the total to 12 to 13 per cent. By 2009, the plan had become predominantly a mechanism to bring scholars and fellows from the developing Commonwealth to Britain and Canada and, as such, for more than 85 per cent of the total, something indistinguishable from an overseas-aid programme.

These changes mean that in recent years the plan has become more homogeneous in the direction of travel, but more heterogeneous in terms of its programmes. Britain had by 2009 some six types of award: scholarships (which were sometimes split between regular and academic staff scholarships), split-site scholarships, shared scholarships, distance-learning scholarships, academic fellowships and professional fellowships, and made a small number of these within institutional capacity grants, a seventh and cross-cutting category. The introduction of shorter fellowships and part-time, distance-learning awards meant that, for the same money, the commission was able to make more awards.

The Commonwealth-wide total of 1,560 award holders in 2005/6, the last year for which figures were available at the time of writing, suggests the glass was half as full again as the founding fathers had in mind at the beginning, but still one quarter empty when viewed against a targeted figure of over 2000. While the plan has changed and survived, it has done so at a modest scale. But perhaps that is the oddity when set against the changes in the Commonwealth discussed in chapter 5. The first scholars moved within a Commonwealth that was almost coterminous with the sterling area, and one that was widely accepted as a bulwark against the Soviet bloc. The Commonwealth itself was expected to have a grand, though changed, future. The next generation of scholars, twenty-five years later, moved within a world in which the Commonwealth's defining quality was its opposition to apartheid. Those moving in the present century have done so in a world that has outlived the sterling area, the Soviet Union, and apartheid; instead regional trading groups, and until 2008 a neoliberal consensus on free trade, dominated the economy.

The record provides answers to our opening questions—what was CSFP for, how has it changed, what has it achieved—and possible responses to the criticism of northern domination, elitism, and bias. In any formal definition of purpose the plan was for the international education of a carefully selected group of the academically able. It has enabled that process of education, on a scale determined by the resources provided by governments, and done so with success. At the same time it has met some of the consequent expectations of politicians and civil servants, who at various stages and in several countries, wanted it to produce political leaders, and of university teachers and administrators who wanted it to develop more of their own kind. Long-standing ambivalence, about the extent to which it was for the support of development in the south, has been resolved so that many of its awards in recent years have been unequivocally for development. As for northern domination, it is inescapable that the huge majority of awards are made as a result of decisions taken in the north, and that for some southern scholars a Commonwealth scholarship has been a route to a northern career. At the same time, those running the plan in the north could point towards their efforts to match their policies with evidence of southern interests and towards their consistent encouragement to scholars to go home. As their background changed, from ruling the raj to working in development and teaching in overseas universities, so the decisions made by commissioners in Britain have been informed by a different kind of experience of the south. As for bias and elitism, which go hand in hand, the plan has certainly provided access to an elite and there have been accusations that awards have sometimes been open only to existing members of one. Those accusations have to be set against measures to ensure or at least promote equity. Cronyism may have produced some scholars; there is no evidence that it has been the norm.[2] The tendency of those making awards in the north has been to select in such a way that women form a higher proportion of those offered scholarships than of those nominated for them.

Many of the particular achievements of the plan are the result not of deliberate or evolving intent but almost of its absence. For much of its history it is as if, once launched, the rolling stone of the plan needed to gather no moss of policy: the founding principles and the process of seeking academic excellence could define its trajectory. There have been unintended, perhaps surprising, consequences in relation to both the geography of awards and the disciplines of award holders. The quest for individual academic excellence meant that awards were always scattered. As argued in chapter 6, where there have been significant groups of alumni, as at Makerere, or in some faculties in Barbados, or at a handful of institutions in India, this has been the result of happy accident and not of deliberate planning in the interest of institutional development. The plan has seldom targeted particular institutions or disciplines. Then, still on geography, the early decision that scholars in any part of the Commonwealth should be able to compete on equal terms has, in practice, led to remarkable privilege for small states. They have been generously rewarded for going to the effort of creating a nominating machinery to recommend candidates: there was never a conscious decision that Malta should have 220 scholars and India 2,200 for a population nearly 3,000 times as great. Choices about which discipline to support have, for their part, been affected by the original decision to offer awards in all areas, by government policies in choosing whom to nominate, by the recent move towards a developmental agenda, and above all by individual preferences. One consequence of that process has been a steady drift away from the pure sciences and the humanities; insofar as the plan has in practice been a means of forming the next generation of university teachers this may be seen as an unhappy narrowing as well as an unintended outcome. In contrast, while there are inevitably problems of definition, and leaving aside the catch-many term of education, Britain appears to have funded more engineers and lawyers than any other occupational group, without any deliberate decision to do so.

The combination of intended and unintended consequences makes it possible to conclude, positively but simply, that the plan's alumni, and their host societies, have benefited from its existence. It has done what it set out to do. When it has been reviewed, by the Commonwealth Secretariat, by ministers of education, and by individual governments, plaudits have outweighed criticisms, and affirmations of support have been stronger than proposals for change of direction. There remains a separate question, not about the impact of individuals, but about the politics and survival of the plan.

In the post-Soviet world, international student mobility has grown so rapidly that by 2000 there were already some two million students studying abroad with the number projected to double by 2015.[3] Full-cost fees, that were predicted to bring a permanent decline in the movement of Commonwealth students, and seriously weaken the Commonwealth as an institution, have not brought about at least the former. The robustness of international study, and the comparative ease with which at least the more privileged among young scholars have been able to finance themselves, both suggest that scholarship programmes may no longer be necessary. The growth of postgraduate higher education in the south, to the point where universities can nurture their own future academics, would add weight to cost-cutting arguments against providing scholarships. (Or they might have done: the argument that access to international education for able students can safely be left to market forces looks increasingly implausible in 2009.) How then have Commonwealth scholarships survived?

Beyond the evidence of the achievements of its alumni, the survival of the plan can be explained in terms of governments' political values, of the plan's adaptability, of its autonomy, and of its bilateral status.

First, governments like scholarships, and politicians of most parties see them as a valuable political gesture. As British relationships with China were improving in the mid-1990s the conservative government introduced a programme of Sino-British scholarships. In 1999, the labour prime minister launched a strategy to increase the number of international students with a planned—though not achieved—fifty per cent increase in the number of Chevening awards.[4] When the Australian government withdrew its support from the plan, it did so not from scepticism about the value of scholarships but in the interest of having a single brand and of focusing them on Asia and the Pacific. India has seen the plan as something to be maintained. The proposal to cut scholarship funding in Canada provoked, apparently convincing, arguments about their political benefits. Their value is enhanced in that they bring identifiable benefits, and perhaps long-term friends, for expenditure that is modest as a proportion of aid or diplomatic budgets. The maintenance of the plan in Britain, without any major increase in its budget in real terms from the mid-1990s to the mid-2000s, suggests a careful or tacit view that it was worth supporting even if not worth expanding.

Second, the plan has proved adaptable, as it needed to be, against changes in the Commonwealth. This did not protect it in Australia or New Zealand where regional priorities trumped Commonwealth memories in the 1990s. In Britain, it responded, sometimes rather late, to the changing discourse about international students. In the 1980s, as discussed in chapter 4, it was shielded from the debates about full-cost fees and their impact which was conducted partly in terms of Commonwealth values but, at least as much, about economic benefit to Britain. In the 1990s the foreign office became clearer in its wish to find leaders, with the hope of gaining friends for Britain. As for international development, the commission slowly moved from an acceptance that one might ask about the pertinence of scholars' interests to national needs on to a redefinition of its criteria for making awards. With a definition that matched DfID's own interests, and a slew of programmes that demonstrated its willingness to change, it was able to make its case to that ministry in 2000. New programmes, and a vigorous defence of the old, brought new funds. The weakness of the position was demonstrated when the foreign office decided that awards to the industrialised Commonwealth no longer fitted its priorities. In another change to the discourse, the universities, and their parent department, provided a new source of funding for a different, though in practice long-standing, reason—British university interests: universities wanted the best students and this was a means of getting them. The plan that was set up within a rhetoric of international cooperation, and in the interest of a Commonwealth-wide sharing of resources, had survived by changing its functions to ones of supporting aid and assisting universities in their own international competitiveness.

In Britain, adaptation of the plan's purposes has been accompanied by changes in its working practices. The Nolan procedures for public appointments meant that the three most recent chairs of the commission all held university posts, as well as having international development experience, whereas their predecessors included three politicians, two diplomats, and a businessman. Applicant commissioners, like applicant scholars, have had to demonstrate the strength and relevance of their background. One consequence of this, and of the appointment of an executive secretary who wanted to change the plan, was a growing professionalism by the commission: its meetings have rubberstamped less, debated more. Issues of principle, on which there used apparently to be sufficient consensus for them not to need discussion, have taken up its time. There have been losses as well as gains in the commission's political, and perhaps academic, capacity in this process: patronage made it easier to appoint the influential to the commission and to locate potential commissioners in a particular discipline without the chanciness of advertising.

Third, the independence of the commission in Britain and of advisory committees in the other industrialised countries have helped to create independent constituencies that could act on behalf of the plan. New Zealand vice-chancellors supported the continuation of the plan when government withdrew its direct funding. In Britain, the commission's independence irritated the Commonwealth office in its first year and the development ministry within ten years of its establishment. The heavyweights in its membership were seen as a reason to leave it untouched even when government expenditure was under attack. In Britain and Canada alike, members of the commission and of the scholarships committee were active in opposing the cuts in expenditure announced in 2006 and 2008. In each case, too, the independence of the plan, and interest by its administrators in its alumni, meant that there was also an outer-track constituency of current and former scholars willing to make the case for the plan and its survival. In contrast the Australian history establishes that independence is not a sufficient condition for survival.

Fourth, one of the oddities of the plan is that it is both multilateral in its intentions and financed as a set of bilateral agreements. Its Commonwealth-wide status brings it the political advantage of getting the attention of education ministers every three years, and sometimes the attention of heads of government, while the accident of timing has limited the Commonwealth Secretariat's role to one of monitoring. If the secretariat had existed in 1959, it might have owned the plan from the outset. As a result, its funds have not depended on the degree of support member states wanted to give the secretariat, but on bilateral decisions that reflected their own national interests. India has continued to provide scholarships for reasons of its own national policy. Bilateral funding is no defence against the loss of Commonwealth reciprocity but has provided a mechanism for the plan to have survived, though with changed purposes and a reduced number of countries offering awards.

Political status, adaptability, a measure of independence and bilateral funding have been enough to maintain the plan at least in the minority of Commonwealth countries that have provided the majority of its awards. But neither educational programmes nor Commonwealth institutions are guaranteed immortality, or government funding. In the early 1990s, Britain closed down its technical cooperation and training programme, which was eight times as large as its contribution to the plan, and went on a decade later to close down the Commonwealth Institute, which had a history that went back to the Imperial Institute of 1887, and a purpose-built headquarters opened by the Queen in 1962. Successive crises—of student mobility in the 1980s, budget cuts in Britain and Canada and the withdrawal of Australian and New Zealand government support in the 1990s, funding uncertainties in Britain and Canada in the 2000s—all these suggest that survival has been a near-run thing.

We can only speculate whether its founders would be encouraged that the plan has survived, in the way that it has, or disappointed in the way it has changed. Sonny Ramphal warned in 1986 that "the rich industrialized countries of the North have still not been able to find a way of speaking and acting across the divide from the impoverished South". He staked a claim for the Commonwealth as "part keeper of the grail of internationalism—one of the world's custodians of the ethic of international co-operation".[5] For its 25,000 alumni the scholarship plan has been a practical demonstration of that internationalism. The recent refocusing of its awards—the development agenda—has increased its evident relevance to poverty in the south. The plea for speaking across the divide, even the pursuit of that long-forgotten Commonwealth cohesion, remain as aspirations for whatever future it may have.

APPENDIX: STATISTICAL TABLES

Table A.1: Scholarships taken up by nominating country

	1960 & 61	1962	1963	1964	1965	1966	1967	1968	1969	1970	1971	1972	1973	1974
Australia	28	27	28	26	36	28	40	37	21	35	34	42	29	37
Bangladesh													16	29
Botswana														
Britain	22	23	25	31	25	26	22	30	31	28	22	31	20	31
Brunei				2		1		1			1			
Canada	23	38	29	41	38	30	42	39	37	35	41	45	40	35
Cameroon														
Caribbean	18	34	34	40	36	33	52	32	33	30	36	27	37	31
Cyprus		3	4	4	5	3	5	2	7	5	6	3	4	3
Gambia	1	2	1		2	1	2	2	2	2	2	3	2	5
Ghana	6	13	10	3	2	13	13	6	17	10	10	13	11	12
Gibraltar	1	1	2	1	2			1			1	1		
Hong Kong	8	14	10	13	17	14	11	12	11	9	13	15	14	11
India	54	67	63	66	70	48	62	46	43	54	54	46	49	61
Kenya	7	14	9	8	13	8	10	7	7	15	3	8	9	19
Lesotho										2		1		1
Malawi				1	1	2		2	3	2	8	4	4	4
Malaysia	10	15	9	11	9	9	11	11	11	12	10	8	17	12
Maldives														
Malta	3	1	3	4	4	4	5	2	4	5	6	2	2	4
Mauritius	3	15	12	11	11	17	14	8	12	9	9	6	8	10
Mozambique														
Namibia														
New Zealand	17	20	15	13	14	18	13	15	16	20	12	17	12	21
Nigeria	20	19	23	11	35	20	23	27	36	29	28	29	35	49
Pacific	6	6	7	11	5	12	10	5	5	12	13	10	15	13
Pakistan	28	35	24	34	37	28	29	29	43	35	28	25		
PNG												1		
Seychelles				1		1	1	1	2	1	1	3	1	
Sierra Leone	2	7	4	3	6	4	12	4	5	8	4	5	5	4
Singapore	11	5	6	8	9	9	10	10	12	8	9	13	9	9
South Africa	19	21	1											
Sri Lanka	11	13	14	17	18	21	25	18	13	15	14	14	19	14
Swaziland	4	1	5	3		2	1	2						1
Tanzania	5	13	10	10	2	7	4	4	6	3	4		11	4
Uganda		9	1	8	3	11	10	6	9	7	3	13	5	5
Zambia					3	4	1	2		1	2	6	2	7
Zimbabwe	10	10	9	9	10	5	10	10	19	17	12	10	12	11
Others	18	2			1	2	2							
Total	335	428	358	390	414	381	440	371	407	407	386	401	389	442

Appendix

	1975	1976	1977	1978	1979	1980	1981	1982	1983	1984	1985	1986	1987	1988	1989
Australia	34	22	22	25	26	19	27	35	23	31	41	39	38	34	39
Bangladesh	41	20	26	31	29	17	24	32	25	44	38	55	44	36	42
Botswana	1	4	2		2	2		4	4	2	1	3	3	2	2
Britain	23	20	19	17	28	18	22	18	18	21	23	20	25	19	25
Brunei			1		1			1							
Canada	45	33	35	33	45	31	33	29	47	46	54	54	47	43	51
Cameroon															
Caribbean	49	34	32	40	36	24	30	36	45	50	49	67	61	43	60
Cyprus	6	5	10	6	6	8	6	8	5	10	8	11	10	10	8
Gambia		3	4	4	2	3	3	5	5	4	4	5	4	3	3
Ghana	16	13	12	19	12	10	14	22	19	16	19	38	21	19	16
Gibraltar	2		1	1	1	2	2	1	2	2	1	2	1	3	
Hong Kong	13	13	12	12	10	10	12	15	15	16	15	14	15	9	10
India	63	39	33	60	46	36	24	51	56	61	41	66	63	50	60
Kenya	10	8	12	16	17	13	10	11	12	14	12	20	19	14	24
Lesotho		2	1		3	1		1	4	4	2	6	3		6
Malawi	5	7	2	3	5	3	3	6	6	3	8	6	7	6	6
Malaysia	22	21	15	17	15	7	6	15	12	25	15	12	8	3	10
Maldives											1	3	3		1
Malta	5	6	5	6	7	7	4	7	6	9	10	7	6	4	12
Mauritius		8	16	13	14	12	7	14	14	9	9	14	13	16	13
Mozambique															
Namibia															
New Zealand	12	9	9	10	19	12	10	13	22	15	16	17	21	20	20
Nigeria	36	24	22	19	27	25	21	36	35	45	39	56	42	45	52
Pacific	13	15	9	16	6	8	13	16	10	18	11	15	11	9	7
Pakistan															
PNG	2	3	4	3	6	3	6	1	5	3	6	4	3	3	8
Seychelles			2	1					4	2	1	3	1	1	2
Sierra Leone	8	6	7	10	5	6	4	6	2	7	6	8	5	6	3
Singapore	11	8	7	8	10	9	5	9	11	8	5	6	6	3	6
South Africa															
Sri Lanka	15	16	21	20	21	12	17	22	27	23	17	36	26	22	19
Swaziland		1	1			1				1	5	3	5	3	3
Tanzania	3	12	14	7	3	4	3	13	5	12	10	31	16	19	22
Uganda	6	7	9	5	2	3	8	20	9	15	13	19	19	16	14
Zambia	8	5	3	5	8	9	7	10	13	10	8	18	12	12	6
Zimbabwe	17	10	6	9	7	12	4	9	6	11	4	11	18	5	11
Others			1	1	1			1							
Total	466	375	374	417	420	327	325	467	467	537	492	669	576	478	561

Learning Abroad

1990	1991	1992	1993	1994	1995	1996	1997	1998	1999	2000	2001	2002	2003	2004	2005	2006	Total
17	26	34	41	14	17	40	6	35	23	10	6	33	26	21	24	19	1295
41	39	35	29	22	16	15	20	18	16	21	17	14	23	26	47	41	989
4	1	3	1	1	3		6	5	2	4	2	2	6	5	2	6	85
13	21	21	20	4	6	5	16	11	19	13	14	4	10	16	29	28	933
							1					1	1	1	1	1	14
37	48	45	47	22	43	54	13	39	42	17	11	34	36	31	27	29	1714
								1	9	9	8	2	7	7	6	2	51
54	65	60	58	41	39	17	46	33	53	99	44	21	48	46	38	44	1935
7	7	5	8	4	6	5	4	3	7	6	6		2	1	2		244
2	2	4	3	1	3		5	6	5	5	6	3	4	4	3	6	141
18	21	21	18	11	9	8	12	14	13	20	16	14	16	34	12	11	673
1	1			1	2		1	2	1	1			2		1		44
8	6	8	9	3	5	1											403
53	55	58	61	55	47	38	40	19	21	29	25	22	26	65	87	45	2278
10	22	13	16	8	12	7	16	7	10	14	7	7	52	42	39	48	679
3	1	4	1	1	2		5	5	3	4	3	2	2	2	3	2	80
4	6	2	2	2	3	3	8	1	3	8	5	4	7	6	16	17	204
7	7	11	3	7	6	8	6	3	4	9	9	5	1	10	8	5	467
1	2	2	1	2	1			4	3	8	7	4	8	7	9	10	77
3	7	8	7	4	4	6	4	5	6	5	6	3	3	2	4	2	229
8	6	14	11	11	8	7	10	11	11	3	5	3	9	7	5	10	456
										1		1		1		1	4
			2		2	1	4	5	1	5	2	1	1	3	8	11	46
14	15	19	16	7	4	8	9	12	16	8	8	15	12	8	9	6	634
43	36	38	32	27	37	18					11	12	26	25	22	21	1256
2	7	2	1	3	5	3	3	6	7	4	5	5	3	7	8	7	385
	12	23	19	19	9	9	22	15	13	17	3	5	10	34	16	23	624
4	3	4	4	3	3	2	5		1	3		1	3	2	3	1	103
1	2	1	2	2		2	2		2	1	1	3	4			2	54
10	10	8	8	3	4	2	4	7		4	8	3	4	8	12	6	263
6	3	2	3	2	5	3	3			2	3		1	2	2	3	280
						2	24	29	36	44	20	24	41	46	38	41	386
17	19	19	17	11	11	9	13	13	15	8	9	8	15	14	16	11	765
4	1	1			1	1	2	2	1	5	2	3	3	7	2	3	80
11	22	10	15	8	9	5	9	3	10	9	11	10	19	19	49	20	496
13	8	13	14	8	9	5	10	14	15	11	10	10	18	17	17	13	460
6	5	6	6	4	8	5	9	4	5	10	8	10	12	28	15	30	333
12	16	16	11	5	4	5	6	4	5	12	8	7	14	7	1	1	428
1	1	1	14	95	31	31	1										204
435	503	511	500	411	374	325	345	336	378	429	306	296	475	561	581	526	19792

Note: Dates are for year ending.

Appendix

Table A.2: Scholarships taken up by hosting country

	Australia	Botswana	Britain	Brunei	Canada	Ghana	Hong Kong	India	Jamaica	Malaysia	Malta	Mauritius	New Zealand	Nigeria	Pakistan	Sierra Leone	S Africa	Sri Lanka	Tanzania	Trinidad &Tobago	Zimbabwe	Total
1960/61	38		178		101		2			3			10				1				2	335
1962	44		232		103			22		4			8	2	2			2	2		3	428
1963	38		187		91		2	20		3			11	1	2				2		1	358
1964	26		219		84		2	22		4			13	7	3			3				390
1965	27		241		99		1	19	1	5			7	4	7						5	414
1966	46		191		83	2	3	26	1	6			10	8	2			2			1	381
1967	30		257		105	4	2	20	1	1	1		7	4	4	2		2	2			440
1968	37		217		79	1	1	14	1	1			9	5	2	2		4	2			371
1969	29		238		89		3	21		3			8	4	7	1		4	1			407
1970	30		237		88	2	3	21	1	2			9	4	5	2		4	1			407
1971	32		242		76		1	20		2			7	3				2		1		386
1972	23		229		111	nir	4	19	1	2			6	5				5		nir		401
1973	45		230		70	nir	3	20	nir	1			10	4				5				389
1974	29		238		108	6	2	35	1	2			9	6						1		442
1975	38		292		88	nir	3	24	nir	nir	1		10	11								466
1976	29		218		74	5	3	20	1	1			13	8				3				375
1977	48		190		73	3	3	31		5			11	5				4				374
1978	22		258		87	1	2	28	1	2			11	3						2		417
1979	28		264		84	nir	4	25		nir			14	nir				nir		1	1	420
1980	23		218		34	1	3	25					13	3				7				327
1981	36		182		62		3	20	1	1	1		12	1				6				325
1982	35		281		109		4	16	1	4			16					1				467
1983	47		271		101	nir	8	18	nir				13	6				3				467
1984	55		362		87		3	12	1	nir			10	2		1		1		3		537

Learning Abroad

Year	C1	C2	C3	C4	C5	C6	C7	C8	C9	C10	C11	C12	C13	C14	C15	C16	C17	C18	C19	C20	Total
1985	46		319		82	nir	4	17				17	3				3		1		492
1986	47		381		195		4	22	nir			16	1				1		2		669
1987	36		318		163		3	31	nir			17	4				2		2		576
1988	34		263		137		6	21	1			12	2	nir			nir		2		478
1989	19		369		124		4	24	nir	nir		14	4	nir			nir		2		561
1990	20		286		97	nir	4	18	nir	nir			7	nir	1		nir		2		435
1991	30		309		122	2	2	13	nir			15	8	1	nir				2		503
1992	18		314		134	2	2	19	nir			12	6						4		511
1993	8		297		144		4	23	nir			14	6						3		500
1994	nir		261		88		4	32	1			24			1		1		1		411
1995	nir		297		30			24	1			22									374
1996	nir		264		29			19				13									325
1997	13		223	8	68			24	1			8									345
1998	14		242	7	48			18				7									336
1999	6		249	7	72			25	1			18									378
2000			255	4	145			19				6									429
2001			165	5	87			30	1	6		8							4		306
2002			231	2	20			31		6		6									296
2003	3		374	4	43			29		9		12							1		475
2004			451	6	61			22		10	1	7					1		3		561
2005	4		445	5	73	1		26		10		14							2		581
2006	3	2	384		56			32	1	11		36									526
Total	1136	2	12369	48	4104	30	102	1017	20	104	5	545	137	34	9	2	61	11	39	12	19792

Note: Dates are for year ending.

Appendix

Table A.3: Fellowships taken up by nominating country

Year	Australia	Bangladesh	Botswana	Britain	Cameroon	Canada	Caribbean	Cyprus	Fiji	Gambia	Ghana	Hong Kong	India	Kenya	Lesotho	Malaysia	Malawi	Malta	Mauritius	Namibia	New Zealand	Nigeria	Pakistan	PNG	Samoa	Sierra Leone	Singapore	South Africa	Sri Lanka	Swaziland	Tanzania	Uganda	Zambia	Zimbabwe	Unknown	Total
1960 & 1961	3												1																					1		6
1962	2					1					1										1															5
1963	2			2		3							2																							7
1964	2			4		3				1	1		3																							13
1965	2			7		1							2			2																				14
1966	4			9		6					2		2																							27
1967	9			11		7						1	28								3	3	1			1			5							72
1968	2			8		5	6				1		22								3	1	1				3		5		1	1		1		62
1969	8			6		2	2		1	1	2	2	48								4	3	4				1		5		1	1				89
1970	8			8		7					6		22			1		1			5	2	1				3		4				1			74
1971	13			12		3	3				3	1	55	1		1					4	5	7			1	1		6							113
1972	13			13		2	3				2	7	54	1							2	1	8				3		4		1					117
1973	15			8		4	1		1		4	3	42			2					4	5				1	1		9				1			117
1974	10	9		8		4	2			1	1	3	70			4		1	1		8	6				2	2		7				1			139
1975	8	16		10		1			1		2	4	60								3	9				2	3		8				2			129
1976	8	10		10		2	3				2	1	56	1		4					4	11				1	2		6				1	2		119
1977	3	5		11		2	1				2	4	45			3					2	10				1	2		8				1			94
1978	6	12		14		3					2	2	36	2		2					5	5					3		7							103
1979	4			7		3	1				2	2	44	1		1					1	10					2		6					1		94
1980	4	5	1	9		2	2				1	1	42	1		2	1	1			4	8				1	5		7		2	2	1	1		93
1981	7	6		9		2	2				3	2	19	2		4		1			2	9				3	3		9		2	2				84

192

Learning Abroad

Year	C1	C2	C3	C4	C5	C6	C7	C8	C9	C10	C11	C12	C13	C14	C15	C16	C17	C18	C19	C20	C21	C22	C23	C24	C25	C26	C27	C28	C29	C30	C31	C32	C33	C34	C35	Total
1982	5	9		13		1	2				1	7	37	2			4				1	9					3		11		3		1			109
1983	6	6	1	8		2	3				1	4	32	4			3	1			4	10					2		5		2	1				93
1984	3	11		10	3	3	3				2	8	45	1			10				1	18							9		1	4				131
1985	10	5		6	7	3	3	1			6	7	29				9				2	12					3		9							112
1986	4	7		8	5	6	7				4	8	34	1		2	5	1			3	23							11	1	5	3		1		137
1987	8	11		8	6	5	5	1			5	3	43	2			8	1	1		3	24				1	3		12		4	2				151
1988	9	7		5	5	5	4				5	5	29	1			3	1			2	22			1	1			9		3	1				111
1989	3	7		4	2	4	2				3	3	36	3			8					24				1	1		16		7	1	1			122
1990	6	8		2	3	4	3				1	4	35	2			8	1	1		2	18					6		8		2	2	1			113
1991	5	6		4	3	3	2				4	4	29	1			11	1			2	27					1		6		2	3				116
1992	4	7		2	2	2	1				3	3	28	2	1		9	1			1	25							12							92
1993	2	7		5	4	4					3	4	29	5			3				1	21	5				2		12		2	3	1		3	108
1994	2	3		5	1	2					2	2	31	1			5	1	1		2	13	3						7		3	2		1		87
1995	1	8		1	3	2	1				2	1	38	6			7	1	1		1	18	3			2			14			1				112
1996	4	8		3	1	1					1	1	24	1			7		1		1	7	2			2	4		8		2	2				81
1997		14		1		2					2	1	15	2			6					3	1					1	6			1		2		66
1998		8									2		36				5	1				7							6							81
1999		13		2				1			1		33	3			6					9					3		8		3	2		2		88
2000		10		2		1					2		36	4			8	1				7			1		3		7		5	1	1			87
2001		8		2		1					4		30	2	1		2										5		5		5	2				75
2002		9		1		1					2		28	2			3					7	1				3		9	1	3	1	1			69
2003		5		4		2					6		39		1		4	1	2			5	7				2		8	2	1					100
2004		9	1			5				4	6		41	4			8	2				6	8	1		1		1	10	1		3	2			125
2005		9	1			8				3	11		30	8	2			1				9	5			1			11	1	4	4	1			132
Total	200	276	5	254	14	106	88	2	6	9	108	95	1440	68	3	5	168	15	14	4	81	393	95	3	1	19	82	46	310	6	53	49	27	17	3	4069

Note: Dates are for year ending.

Table A.4: Fellowships taken up by hosting country

Year ending	Australia	Britain	Canada	India	New Zealand	Zimbabwe	Total
1960 & 61	2				3	1	6
1962	1	3			1		5
1963	3	2			2		7
1964	4	5		1	2	1	13
1965	5	3		1	5		14
1966	7	4	7	3	6		27
1967	6	50	9	2	5		72
1968	3	47	7		5		62
1969	5	74	6	3	1		89
1970	9	54	8	2	1		74
1971	9	91	8	1	4		113
1972	10	100	4		3		117
1973	7	101	7	1	1		117
1974	7	118	11	1	2		139
1975	7	112	7	2	1		129
1976	5	107	5		2		119
1977	6	79	7		2		94
1978	7	84	7		5		103
1979	5	83	5		1		94
1980	7	81	3		2		93
1981	6	68	8		2		84
1982	9	92	6		2		109
1983	6	81	5		1		93
1984	5	115	8		3		131
1985	6	94	8	3	1		112
1986	5	118	8	3	3		137
1987	6	132	8	2	3		151
1988	3	97	8	1	2		111
1989	2	113	7				122
1990	4	102	6	1			113
1991	4	106	6				116
1992	3	82	7				92
1993	3	99	6				108
1994	2	79	6				87
1995	2	106	4				112
1996	3	75	3				81
1997		64	2				66
1998		81					81
1999		88					88
2000		87					87
2001		75					75
2002		69					69
2003		100					100
2004		125					125
2005		132					132
Total	184	3578	207	27	71	2	4069

Table A.5: Total number of awards held by awarding country - selected years

Year ending	Totals						
	Australia	Britain	Canada	India	NZ	Other	Total
1961	40	178	101	0	13	9	341
1966	87	512	301	64	34	42	1,040
1971	113	618	240	49	32	31	1,083
1976	104	703	286	80	26	34	1,233
1981	133	554	211	86	36	28	1,048
1986	161	1,000	407	61	76	26	1,731
1991	120	970	464	75	49	30	1,708
1996	382	781	368	90	65	7	1,693
2001	0	599	344	30	47	20	1,040
2006	3	1,172	201	83	70	31	1,560

Source: Tables A1-A5 include data from CSFPAR (all awards for years ending 1961 to 1996), "ACU Submission, 14, 15, 16 CEM" (for year ending 1997 up to year ending 2006 for non-UK scholarship awards and UK scholarships from year ending 1997 to year ending 2000), ACU database (for years ending 2000 to 2006 for UK scholarship awards), "ACU Submission, CEM 14" (years ending 1997 to 2000 for fellowship awards), "ACU Submission, 14, 15, 16 CEM" (years ending 2000 to 2005 for non-UK fellowship awards), ACU database (years ending 2000 to 2005 for UK fellowship awards).

NOTES

Introduction

[1] 1 CEM, 3, 17, 6
[2] "North" and "south" are used as shorthand even though this moves Australia and New Zealand, uncomfortably and ungeographically, to the north.

Chapter One: Launch: Planning and Implementing

[1] Woanacott, "Tariff policy", 127-8
[2] Garner, *Commonwealth office*, 378-9
[3] Treasury note, 1.8.1958, NA, DO 35/8478
[4] Miller, *Survey of Commonwealth affairs*, 283; Makins, 1.8.1958, NA, DO 35/8478
[5] Shepherd, *Macleod*, 164
[6] Hyam, *Britain's declining empire*, 311
[7] Heinlein, *British government policy*, 303
[8] Curtis, interview
[9] McIntyre, "Commonwealth legacy", 698; Macmillan listed three London clubs in *Who's Who* (Carlton, Beefsteak, Buck's) but neither the exclusive Boodle's nor the Royal Automobile Club.
[10] Low, *Eclipse of power*, 330
[11] Note of discussion with Professor Sundaram, 6.11.1958; Cockram, note, 14.11.1959, NA, DO 35/8152
[12] Memoranda by Australia, Britain, Canada, India, NA, DO 35/8163
[13] Smith, "Universities and the Commonwealth" (Address to AUBC 8th quinquennial congress, 1.9.1958); Logan heard the speech but did not take in its significance (see chapter 3); Logan to Morris, 13.10.1958, LP, 78 2 1 1
[14] Curtis, interview; "Committee on scholarship and fellowship scheme: Composition and terms of reference", 15.7.1959, NA, DO 35/ 8163
[15] Cockram to Lintott, 5.11.1958, NA, DO 35/8152
[16] THBS draft notes for Dr Sidney Smith for a Commonwealth Scholarship Plan, May 1958
[17] Smith, "Universities and the Commonwealth" (Address to AUBC 8th quinquennial congress, 1.9.1958)
[18] Symons, interview
[19] 1 CEM, 4
[20] Ibid., 18

[21] Ibid., 6
[22] Symons, interview
[23] 1 CEM, 19
[24] Paper CSC 1/66, CSCM, 25.1.1966
[25] Jean-Louis, *Canada–Caribbean distance education scholarship programme*; 43
[26] 11 CEM, 29
[27] CSCAR 6, 10
[28] CSFPAR 5, 14
[29] In my eyes and those of Richard Siaciwena, its long-time director, it was an unfortunate and inappropriate model to follow.
[30] Paper CSC 29/67, CSCM, 28.11.1967; paper CSC 44/72, CSCM, 5.12.1972
[31] CSCAR 21, 5; paper CSC 13/81, CSCM, 30.6.1981
[32] Paper CSC 1/66, CSCM, 25.1.1966
[33] CSCAR 43, 9
[34] CSCAR 45, 6-7
[35] Held et al., *Global transformations*, 170

Chapter Two: Purposes: The Plan in its Context

[1] 1 CEM, 18
[2] Ibid., 11
[3] Morgan, *Guidance towards self-governance*, 318-9
[4] Carr-Saunders, *New universities*, 31
[5] Ashby, *Universities: British, Indian, African*, 216
[6] Morgan, *Origins of policy*, 109-10
[7] Whitehead, "Sir Christopher Cox"
[8] PDL, 5.2.1963, col. 528-30; Iredale, *Power of change*, 1
[9] Carr-Saunders, *New universities*, 226
[10] Sherlock and Nettleford, *University of the West Indies*, 117
[11] Ibid., 100-1
[12] Tilak, "Financing", 51
[13] Chanana, "Accessing higher education", 127
[14] Esi Sutherland-Addy quoted in Ajayi et al., *African experience*, 203-4
[15] World Bank, *Education in sub-Saharan Africa*, 79
[16] Commission for Africa, *Our common interest*, 137
[17] Chitnis, "Gearing a colonial system of education", 402
[18] Altbach, "Dilemma of change", 24
[19] World Bank, *Higher education*, 15
[20] World Bank, *Constructing knowledge societies*, 3
[21] Stone, "Social control"
[22] Hellyer, interview
[23] Long to Caine, 23.3.1995, CSCM, 25.4.1995
[24] Williams, *Policy for overseas students*, 157
[25] Auletta, "Retrospective view of Colombo Plan", 48-51

²⁶ Lulat et al., *Governmental and institutional policies*, 21
²⁷ Eliutin, "International activity",156; UNESCO *Statistical yearbook*
²⁸ Maxey, *Student mobility on the map*, 45, Rao, *Brain drain*, 50
²⁹ S. Mathai, Special addresses, 3 CEM, 19
³⁰ Ashby to Blount, 19.5 1959, LP, 78.2.1.1
³¹ British government brief, 1962, LP, 138, file 2
³² 2 CEM working papers, LP, 138, file 2
³³ "Preliminary draft agenda for 6th Commonwealth educational conference", UTA, A79-0051, box 38
³⁴ CSCAR 34, 8
³⁵ Rev 2, 19
³⁶ Lintott, minute, 9.1.1959, NA, DO 35/8151
³⁷ CSCAR 44, 8, 11; Stafford, *Caribbean*
³⁸ 3 CEM, 15
³⁹ Draft brief, 12.5.1964, NA, BW 1/455
⁴⁰ 3 CEM, 120
⁴¹ Niven, interview; Stafford, *Caribbean*
⁴² PDC 25.11.1959, col. 422-3
⁴³ Lintott to high commissioners, 30.7.1059, NA, DO 35/8147
⁴⁴ 6 CEM, 152
⁴⁵ "ACU Submission 16 CEM", 9

Chapter Three: Britain: Establishing the Plan

¹ Morris to Logan, 14.10.1958, Logan to Laithwaite, 15.10.1958, LP, 78 2 1 1
² Rumbold, brief for Commonwealth Relations Secretary, 27.6.1958, NA, DO 35/8477
³ Conclusions of official steering group, 18.7.1958, NA, CAB 130/148
⁴ "Brief on training of Commonwealth students in UK", 4.9.1958, NA, CAB 130/149
⁵ Morris to Logan, 14.10.1958, LP 78 2 1 1
⁶ "Cost of UK educational assistance to the Commonwealth", 2.3.1959, NA, CAB 134/1495
⁷ "Minutes of ministerial committee on Commonwealth trade and economic conference", 1.9.1958, NA, CAB 130/148
⁸ "Report by official committee on educational facilities within the Commonwealth", 1.7.1959, NA, CAB 134/1495
⁹ Hennessy, *Having it so good*, 42
¹⁰ "Draft cabinet memorandum for Future Policy Study", 30.7.1959 and Cabinet memorandum, 24.2.1960, in Hyam and Louis, *Conservative government*, 64, 94
¹¹ He was reporting on discussions at the CRO in which he had been making the ACU's case as a Commonwealth body; Aitken to Logan, 6.6.1959, LP, 78 2 1 1
¹² Second draft report part III, 22.5.1959, NA, DO 35/8156; Paper CEC 59/10, 29.6.1959 and cabinet committee minute 3.7.1959, NA, CAB 134/1495

[13] At this time Sir Eric, later Lord Ashby; Ashby to Blount 19.5.1959, LP, 78 2 1 1
[14] Lintott to Logan, 5.6.1959, LP, 78 2 1 1; Lintott to Aitken, 5.6.1959, Aitken to Lintott 6.6.1959, NA, CAB 21/3108
[15] Logan to Garner, 1.1.1969, LP, box 81, file 2 I 7
[16] Meeting note, 18.6.1959, LP 78 2 1 1; Parkinson to King, 11.6.1959, minute, King to Lintott, 15.6.1959, NA, CAB 21/3109
[17] Minutes, CRO Secretary of State, 30.10.1959 and 13.11.1959; Colonial Secretary, 4.11.195; Prime Minister, 22.11.1959, NA, DO 35/211
[18] Prior, "Lumley"
[19] CRO meeting report, 8.10.1959, NA, DO 35/8211
[20] Minutes, Home to Macleod, 18.12.1959; Macleod to Home, 29.12.1959, NA, DO 35/8211
[21] Press notice, 3.2.1960, NA, DO 35/8211; Matthew and Harrison, *ODNB*; *WW*
[22] Temple, interview
[23] Interim committee for CSFP, minute 8, 5.10.1959, minute 4a, 11.11.1959, ACU files
[24] Despatch to high commissioners, 31.10.1959, NA, DO 35/8207; "Note regarding financing of Commonwealth education schemes", undated (mid-October) 1959, NA, DO 35/8208
[25] Commonwealth Scholarships Act, 1959, c.6; "Directions to the Commonwealth Scholarship Commission", CRO, 4.3.1960, ACU files
[26] Ashby to CRO, 14.10.1959 and 23.11.1959, NA, DO 35/8211
[27] CSCM, 9.3.1960
[28] Temple, interview
[29] Agm 1(e), CSCM, 23.2.1960
[30] Agm 12, CSCM, 9.3.1960; M141 (f) 28.2.1961
[31] M125, CSCM, 17.1.1961
[32] Minute, King to Lintott, 11.7.1960, NA, DO 163/15
[33] Cockram to Foster, Agm 48(c), CSCM, 28.6.1960
[34] Agm 4 and paper CSC 19/64, CSCM, 24.11.1964
[35] Goatly to controller, home division, 18.11.1959, NA, BW1/552
[36] Paper CSC 18/62, CSCM, 27.9.1962
[37] M302, CSCM, 27.2.1962; M291, CSCM, 19.12.1961
[38] M64, M65, CSCM, 26.7.1960; M411, CSCM, 27.11.1962; M825, CSCM, 25.1.1966
[39] "Report by official committee on educational facilities within Commonwealth", 1.7.1959, NA, CAB 134/1495
[40] ODA to Temple, 20.2.1974, agm 12 (d), CSCM, 2.4.1974
[41] Philip Goodhart MP, PDC 25.11.1959 col.431-2
[42] Agm 2 (b), CSCM, 11.12.1973
[43] Cockram in M211, CSCM, 20.6.1961; Paper CSC 16/63, CSCM 28.5.1963; agm 15, CSCM, 28.11.1967
[44] CSCAR 3, 5
[45] Scarbrough to Duke of Devonshire, M333, CSCM, 22.5.1962
[46] Scarbrough to Sandys, 27.11.1962, NA, DO 163/16

[47] Minute, Pares, 23.11.1952, NA, DO 193/16
[48] Mumford, note, 20.2.1966, NA, OD 17/381
[49] Logan to Martin, 30.10.1964, LP, box 79, file 6
[50] Minutes, Leach to Rednall, 4.10.1965, Dunnill to Cohen, 9.11.1965, NA, OD 17/381
[51] Lannon, interview
[52] Pimlott, *Harold Wilson*, 50
[53] Minute, Mumford to Dunnill, 12.12.1966, NA, OD 17/381
[54] File notes, Thomas, 13.3.1967, 3.4.1967 and 3.5.1967, NA, OD 17/188
[55] Berthoud, *Life of Henry Moore*, 37-45; *Guardian* Obituary 3.5.1996; Temple, interview
[56] Houghton to Prentice, 14.12.1967, NA, OD 40/35
[57] Minute, Dunnill, endorsed Thomas, 21.12.1967, NA, OD 40/35
[58] Minute, Thomas to Cohen, 4.1.1968, NA, OD 40/35
[59] May, "Garner"
[60] Foxcroft, quoted in Harrison-Train, *South Africa*; Luntz, interview
[61] M794, CSCM, 23.11.1965
[62] Temple to Mark, 26.3.1969, LP, box 81 file 3 1 7
[63] Hart, *Aid*, 253; minute, Thomas, 12.7.1968, NA, OD 40/32; minute, Stewart to Samples, 10.7.1968, NA, FCO 13/70; Direction, M794, CSCM, 6.10.1968
[64] Note of discussion, 1.9.1968, NA, OD 40/34
[65] Note of ODM meeting, 7.7.1967, LP, 81 5 1 6 general correspondence, part 1
[66] Cox to Butterworth, 20.9.1969, NA, OD 40/34. There is a note on the file that the words "a significant reality" are an inference against a gap in the transcription.
[67] Paper CSC 9/70, CSCM 21.4.1970; agm 12, CSCM, 21.4.1970
[68] Paper CSC 48/71 and agm 8, CSCM, 7.12.1971
[69] Papers CSC 48/71, CSCM, 7.12.1971; CSC 39/74, CSCM, 17.12.1974; CSC 15/78, CSCM, 4.7.1978
[70] Paper CSC 21/69, CSCM, 8.7.1969; agm 7, CSCM, 7.12.1971; Jones to CSC, 26.1.72 and agm 4, CSCM, 28.3.1972
[71] CSCM, 2.7.1974; 1.7.1975; 6.7.1976
[72] White paper *CSFP* (Cmnd. 894),.5; "Note regarding financing", 19.10.1959, NA, DO 35/8208
[73] "Supplementary note, Delegation brief for 3CEM, August 1964", NA, ED 121/1091; Boyle to CSC, 3.7.1964, M622, CSCM, 28.7.1964
[74] "British brief A6, January 1971", LP, box 82 file 2
[75] Robbins, *Higher education*, para. 174-5
[76] PDC 23.2.1967 col. 1981-2044
[77] Agm 3, CSCM, 30.3.1976
[78] Agm 3, CSCM, 6.7.1976; Burr to Garner, 14.1.1977, agm 7, CSCM, 26.4.1977

Chapter Four: Britain: Adapting and Surviving

[1] Layard et al., *Impact of Robbins*, 13

[2] Williams, "Overseas students", 13
[3] Woodhall, "Government policy", 25-6
[4] House of Commons 1st report of education, science and arts committee 1979/80, HC552, viii, para. 18
[5] From this time the records differentiate between ODA and the diplomatic wing, phraseology suggesting that the pukka foreign office might launch into flight, away from their earthbound developmental colleagues.
[6] House of Commons 3rd report of foreign affairs committee 1979/80, HC553; x, para. 17
[7] SCSM 1, i
[8] Williams, "Overseas students", 15
[9] Ibid., 16–17
[10] Garner to Carrington, agm 4 (h), CSCM, 8.7.1980
[11] Ibid.
[12] Agm 8, CSCM, 23.9.1980
[13] ODA to CSC, 9.2.1983, CSCM, 19.4.1983
[14] Iredale, interview
[15] Rev 2, 25
[16] "Financial management review of the Commonwealth Scholarship Commission", ODA, March 1987, CSCM, 31.3.1987
[17] Ibid., para. 31
[18] Ibid., para. 32
[19] Paper 5/86, CSCM, 15.4.1986
[20] Agm 6, CSCM, 15.4.1986
[21] Agm 5, CSCM, 9.12.1987
[22] Agm 2, CSCM, 4.7.1989; agm 2 and paper 20/89, CSCM, 5.10.1989; agm 5 (i), CSCM, 5.12.1989
[23] Hetherington, interview
[24] Lannon, interview
[25] CSCAR; Matthew and Harrison, *ODNB*, *WW*
[26] Green, "Caine"
[27] Temple, interview
[28] Hetherington, interview
[29] Little, interview
[30] Maxey, *Student mobility on the map*, 30
[31] Agm 4 (b) (i), CSCM, 29.3.1988
[32] IWGE, *Education aid*, 14; DfID, *Eliminating world poverty*, 36
[33] ODA, *Into the nineties*, 24; Iredale, *The power of change*; Iredale interview
[34] Agm 5 (a) (i), CSCM 3.7.1990; agm 5 (a), CSCM, 5.7.1994; paper CSC 1/95, CSCM, 4.7.1995; Hetherington, interview
[35] Agm 3 and paper CSC 20/90, CSCM, 4.12.1990
[36] Agm 13, CSCM, 7.7.1992
[37] Agm 6, CSCM, 1.12.1992
[38] CSCAR 34, 8
[39] Rev 3, 4-5

[40] Agm 14, CSCM, 6.7.1993; agm 12, CSCM, 5.10.1993; Iredale, interview
[41] Agm 13, CSCM, 5.10.1993; agm 4, CSCM, 29.3.1994; Hassall report, para. 6.3.2.3
[42] Paper CSC 6/94, CSCM, 5.7.1994
[43] Paper CSC 7/94, CSCM, 5.7.1994
[44] Paper 8/94, CSCM, 5.7.1994
[45] Long to Caine, 23.3.1995, CSCM, 25.4.1995
[46] ODA to Caine, 2.7.1996, paper 12/96, CSCM, 3.12.1996
[47] House of Commons report of foreign affairs committee 1993/94, HC372, *Public expenditure spending plans 1994/95 to 1996/97*, xvi
[48] CSCAR 37, 9
[49] House of Commons report of foreign affairs committee 1995/96, HC45, vol. 2, 15, 134
[50] Harrison, "Changing frameworks", 167
[51] International Development Act 2002
[52] *WW*
[53] Caston report, 14
[54] Caston, interview; Kirkland, interview
[55] CSCAR 43, 8
[56] Caston report, 1
[57] Caston, interview; Kirkland, interview
[58] Caston report, 21-3; CSCAR 43, 9-11
[59] CSCAR 42, 16-17
[60] Personal communication
[61] Personal communication and recollection; Kapuściński, *The soccer war*, 200
[62] House of Commons 13th report of science and technology committee 2003/04, HC133-1, para. 112
[63] CSCAR 48, 52
[64] Miliband to Harpham, 1.3.2008; House of Commons 13th report of science and technology committee 2003/04, HC133-1, para. 123; Harpham to Miliband, 17.3.2008, ACU files
[65] "Comschols—epetition response", http://www.number10.gov.uk/Page16554, (accessed 12.2.2009)
[66] CSC Press release, "Universities welcome scholarships restoration", 16.10.2008; J. Gill, "Government U-turn on Commonwealth scholarships", *Times Higher Education*, 16.10.2008
[67] Maxey, *Update*, 50; Robbins, *Higher education Appendix 2A,* 253-4. Exact comparisons are bedevilled by differing definitions of Europe and changing membership of the Commonwealth.

Chapter Five: Commonwealth: The Plan in the North

[1] Quoted in Barclay, *Commonwealth or Europe*, 17
[2] Quoted in Boyce, *Decolonisation*, 184-5

[3] Louis and Robinson, "The imperialism of decolonization", 473, quoting 1959 government study on "Africa in the next ten years"
[4] Pimlott, *Harold Wilson*, 353
[5] Perkins, *The sterling area*, 55
[6] Barclay, *Commonwealth or Europe*, 182-3; Rooth, "Britain, Europe, and Diefenbaker's proposals", 117
[7] Barclay, *Commonwealth or Europe*, 108; Rooth, "Britain, Europe, and Diefenbaker's proposals", 127
[8] Ramphal, "Foreword" in Springer, *Commonwealth of universities*
[9] Partridge, "Comment", 36-8
[10] Personal communication, A. F. Dunton, June 1965; M373, CSCM, 17.7.1962
[11] "CEC Committee on Commonwealth scholarships and fellowships: Statement by the Canadian delegation", 16.7.1959, NA, DO 35 8/63
[12] Chitty, Note of talk, 6.11.1958, NA, DO 35/8152
[13] Macdermot, Memorandum, 13.5.1959, LAC, RG74, 36-9A-1, vol.1, box 289
[14] Wellington to Ottawa, 30.4.1959, LAC, RG 25, vol. 7893, 14020-C-14-2-40 part 2.2
[15] "UK delegation paper 5: Comments by other countries", July 1959, NA, DO 35/8139
[16] Levi, *Canada*; Rev 1, 10-11; Connell, *Australia*
[17] Small to External Affairs, 25.2.1960, LAC, RG74, 36-9A-2 vol. 1, box 289
[18] Colombo to Ottawa, 25.2.1960, Ibid.
[19] Delhi to Ottawa, 26.3.1960, LAC, RG74, 36-9A-2 vol. 1, box 289, file CSFP—training and secretariat; MacPherson to Berlis, 5.12.1960, LAC, RG25, vol. 433b, file 14020-C-14-5-40, part 1
[20] Rev 1, 10-20
[21] Ault to Berlis, 24.6.1960, LAC, RG74, 36-9A-2 vol. 2, box 289, file CSFP—training and secretariat
[22] Figures for 1964/5, Rev 1, table 4
[23] Rev 1, 4
[24] Ibid., 61
[25] Paper CSC 31/68, CSCM, 2.7.1968
[26] 1 CEM, 5
[27] B. C. Lucia, Personal communication, November 1965
[28] Barclay, *Commonwealth or Europe*, 127
[29] Ibid.,137
[30] Sandbrook, *White heat*, 366
[31] Chalfont, 10-11 October 1967 quoted in Barclay, *Commonwealth or Europe*, 185
[32] Barclay, *Commonwealth or Europe*, 159
[33] Papadakis, "Australia and Europe", 131
[34] MacGuigan, *Inside look*, 100
[35] Cumpston, *Evolution of the Commonwealth*, 108
[36] Ibid., 109
[37] MacGuigan, *Inside look*, 125

[38] 4 CEM, 26-8
[39] 6 CEM, 156
[40] Jennings to GCO 28.1.1970, and to Watson, 5.2.1970, LAC, RG25, vol. 15214, file 55-12-CWLTH vol. 4
[41] "British brief A6, January 1971", LP, Box 82 file 2
[42] Rev 1, 69
[43] Patterson to Bissell, 25.7.1969, UTA, A77-0019, box 21, file AUCC
[44] Connell, *Australia*
[45] AUCC "Proceedings", 1977, vol. 1, 132; 1976, vol. 1, 18-21; CBIE *Annual report*, 1980, 1, 4
[46] 3 SCSM, 6
[47] 6 SCSM, 36
[48] 1 SCSM, 6
[49] Paper CSC 26/80, CSCM 23.9.1980; Harrington, report, 22.8.1980, LAC RG25, vol. 15986, 55-12-CWLTH, vol. 14
[50] Cavan, Memo to AUCC, 25.5.1983, UTA, A84-0016, box 39
[51] MacKinnon to LaChapelle, 3.9.1981, LAC RG25, vol. 15986, 55-12-CWLTH, vol. 14
[52] AUCC board minutes, 6.3.1984, UTA, A90-0021, box 27; Ramphal to minister, 23.2.1984, LAC RG-25. vol. 21173, file 55-12-CWLTH, part 15
[53] Plourde to Catley-Carson, 9.5.1954, LAC RG-25. vol. 21173, file 55-12-CWLTH, part 15
[54] 9 CEM, iii
[55] Ibid., 13. Before UDI the Central African Federation had offered awards.
[56] 10 CEM, 37
[57] Mulroney, *Memoirs*
[58] Evans and Grant, *Australia's foreign relations*, 22
[59] Goldsworthy "Overview", 12-13; Ravenhill, "Australia and the world economy", 107
[60] Mackinnon to Armstrong, 25.4.1984, LAC RG-25. vol. 21173, file 55-12-CWLTH, part 15
[61] Trilokekar, *Federalism*, 157-8; Hellyer and Lawton, interview
[62] Long to Levi, email, 5.8.2008
[63] Trilokekar, *Federalism*, 187-8
[64] Connell, *Australia*
[65] Back et al., *Internationalisation and higher education*
[66] 6 SCSM, 80; 7 SCSM, 75-9
[67] Connell, *Australia*
[68] *Evaluation of CSFP*
[69] Levi, *Canada*
[70] House of Commons report of foreign affairs committee 1995/96, HC45, xvi and vol. 2, 139

Chapter Six: Universities: Expansion in the South

[1] Stafford, *Caribbean*, and personal communication
[2] e.g. *Manchester Guardian* , 25.7.1960
[3] Ajayi et al., *African experience*, 85
[4] Carr-Saunders, *New universities*, 111
[5] PDC 19.11 1962 col. 836
[6] Coleman, *University development,* 306-7; Rev 1, 3
[7] Yee, *Whither Hong Kong*, 255
[8] Saraf, "Higher education", 284, 277
[9] Thompson et al., *Higher education*, 240; Rev 1, 25; Ibid., 39
[10] CSFPAR 11, 15-16
[11] Court, "Higher education in east Africa", 465; Working party meeting, 16.1.1962, LP, 138 file 3; CSFPAR 15, 21
[12] 6 CEM, 157
[13] 3 CEM, 4, 16; NA, BW 1/455
[14] Dhanarajan, interview
[15] Rev 1, 61-5, 24; agm 6, CSCM, 2.2.1974
[16] Court "Higher education in east Africa", 467; the dates are implied, not stated, in the chapter.
[17] Email, J. Mwakali to Lawrence, 9.9.2008
[18] Rev 1, 25, 62
[19] Rev 2, 19
[20] Ibid., 21
[21] Perraton, *Open and distance learning*, 4
[22] Rev 3, 10
[23] Paper CSC 10/84, CSCM, 28.6.1984
[24] Levi, *Canada*
[25] Magagula, "Benefits and challenges"
[26] Moja, "Policy responses", 37-8
[27] Sicherman, *Becoming an African university*, 128-34
[28] Tan "Singapore", 189-92; French, "Reform in Hong Kong", 161-74; Lee, "Malaysian universities", 222-39
[29] Powar, "Introduction", xiii
[30] Caston report, Appendix 2
[31] Ibid.
[32] Day, *Evaluating the impact*
[33] Rev 3, 23
[34] CSCAR 44, 7
[35] Romalis, *Barbados and St Lucia*
[36] CSFPAR 10, 9
[37] "Note by the Indian delegation", 17.7.1959, NA, DO 35/8163
[38] Levi, *Canada*

[39] CSCAR 48, 40-1
[40] Personal information
[41] Jean-Louis, *Evaluation report*, 5
[42] Jean-Louis, *Evaluation report*; see also DFAIT, *Canada Caribbean programme*; Perraton, *Open and distance learning*, 118-19
[43] M. Hamilton, personal communication; Brandon, *New external providers*, 20
[44] Caston report, 21-2
[45] CSCAR, 43, 10-11; Perraton, "Access"
[46] Caston report, 22
[47] Raza, *Pakistan*
[48] Badat, interview

Chapter Seven: Experience: The Scholars' and Fellows' Story

[1] Rev 3, 14–15
[2] Rev 1, 45
[3] Thompson, *Statistical briefing paper*, 52–3
[4] CSCAR 38, 21; ACU database
[5] Robbins, *Higher education, Appendix 2A*, 43; HESA *Students* 1996/7 and 2005/6 table 2b
[6] Thompson, *Statistical briefing paper*, 27
[7] Rev 1, 44
[8] Landsberg, M. "Canada works stubbornly for human rights", *Globe and mail* 26 April 1986: A8.
[9] Rev 3, 19
[10] "ACU Submission 16 CEM", 9
[11] Scarbrough to Sandys 16.10.1960, NA, DO 163/15
[12] Nesbitt to Ritchie, 26.11.1964; Ritchie to Moran, 27.11.1964; Moran to Ritchie, 2.12.1964, LAC, RG-25, vol. 15986, file 55-12-CWLTH
[13] Harrison-Train, *South Africa*
[14] Johnston to Lintott, 6.7.1959, NA, DO 35/8135
[15] Colombo high commissioner to Ottawa, 14.3.1961, LAC, RG74, 36-9A-1, vol. 3, box 289
[16] M985, CSCM, 25.9.1967
[17] Temple, interview
[18] Papers CSC 27/74, CSCM, 24.9.1974; CSC 40/74, CSCM, 17.12.1974; CSC 13/75, CSCM, 1.7.1975
[19] Papers CSC 7/76, CSCM, 30.3.1976; CSC 11/86, CSCM, 15.11.1986
[20] Hassall report, para. 6.2.2.3
[21] Agm 9, CSCM, 29.3.1994
[22] Paper CSC 7/94, CSCM, 5.7.1994
[23] Paper CSC 2008/28, CSCM, 9.12.2008

[24] Raza, *Pakistan*; Jodhka and Raina, *India*, and personal communication; Harrison-Train, *South Africa*
[25] CSCAR 43, 3
[26] John Harington, *Epigrams*, book 4
[27] CSFPAR 2, 17
[28] Note of discussion, B. Cockram, 17.6.1959, NA, DO 35/8135
[29] CSCAR 11, 4
[30] Professor D. H. Jennings, agm 9, CSCM 7.7.1992
[31] Lawton, interview
[32] PDC 19.11.1962 col. 836
[33] 3 CEM, 14; "Report of committee A", 3CEM
[34] 6 CEM 29, 160, 31; Rev 2, 9
[35] Rev 3, 14
[36] Balakrishna, "The major source countries", 76–81
[37] Data from Indian Council for Cultural relations, email U. Rawal to author 27.3.2009
[38] CSFPAR 31, 15; CSFPAR 33, 9
[39] Data from ICCR, email, U. Rawal to author, 27.3.2009
[40] CSCAR 37, 9–10
[41] Personal information on FCO; personal communication, Gail Larose, 5.8.2008
[42] Rev 1, 46
[43] CSCAR 46, 29
[44] CSFPAR 2, 15
[45] Raza, *Pakistan*
[46] CSFPAR 12, 71–2; http://www.iccrindia.org/scholarships.htm (accessed 11.3.2009)
[47] M483, CSCM, 28.5.1963
[48] Email, Jiggins to Lawrence, 9.9.2008
[49] p'Bitek, *Africa's cultural revolution*, 10–13
[50] Email, Sandy to Lawrence, 23.7.2008; Misra, interview
[51] Levi, *Canada*; email, Campbell to Lawrence, 29.7.2008
[52] Paper 28/61, CSCM, 28.11.1960
[53] Agm 12a, CSCM, 8.7.1986
[54] CSCAR 43, 4
[55] Dalley, interview
[56] Paper CSC 21/67, CSCM, 25.9.1967
[57] Berridge, interview
[58] Paper CSC 21/67, CSCM, 25.9.1967
[59] Paper CSC 25/63, CSCM, 26.9.1963
[60] Banting, interview
[61] Paper CSC 28/80, CSCM, 23.9.1980
[62] Personal recollection
[63] Bain, interview, Banting interview, Jayatilaka, interview,
[64] Berridge, interview
[65] Paper CSC 19/81, CSCM, 6.10.1981

[66] Stafford, *Caribbean*
[67] Email, J. Driver to Levi, 11.8.2008
[68] Agm 12 (d), CSCM, 18.4.1989
[69] Fuller, interview
[70] M957,CSCM, 23.5.1967
[71] Agm 14 (c), CSCM, 2.4.1985
[72] Crapper, *Review of stipends*, 10-14, 21-4
[73] Director, Universities Department to Joint Secretary, 13.1.1967, agm 14, CSCM, 28.11. 1967
[74] HC Accra to AUCC, 19.6.1985, LAC, RG-25, vol. 25794, file 55-12-CWLTH, part 17
[75] Paper 12/89, CSCM, 18.4.1989
[76] Paper CSC 28/66, CSCM 21.9.1966
[77] Agm 10(e), CSCM, 8.10.1968
[78] Email, Kuri to Lawrence, 3.8.2008
[79] Paper CSC 22/65, CSCM, 22.9.1965
[80] Eta, interview
[81] Rao, *Brain drain*, 147
[82] Email, Mashologu to Lawrence, 24.7.2008
[83] Paper CSC 26/71, CSCM, 21.9.1971
[84] Paper 28/66, CSCM, 21.9.1966
[85] Kanyeihamba, interview
[86] Personal recollection, Hornsey, spring 1960
[87] Quoted in Sandbrook, *White heat*, 637; CSCM, 20.6.1961
[88] Paper CSC 22/65, CSCM, 22.9.1965
[89] Paper CSC 25/63, 26.9.1963
[90] Ibid.
[91] Paper CSC 29/78, CSCM, 25.9.1978
[92] Paper CSC 20/82, CSCM, 5.10.1982
[93] Countries, numbers and subjects are from various years of CSFPAR, unless separately referenced.
[94] Chivers, interview
[95] Humphries, interview
[96] Paper CSC 27(b)/86, CSCM, 7.10.1986
[97] Paper CSC 10/86, CSCM, 15.4.1986
[98] Humphries, interview
[99] Paper CSC 27/86, CSCM, 7.10.1986
[100] M827, CSCM, 25.1.1966
[101] Paper CSC 8/76, CSCM, 30.3.1976; paper CSC 50/76, CSCM, 6.7.1976
[102] Paper CSC 31/85, CSCM 10.12.1985
[103] Email, Jiggins to Lawrence, 9.9.2008
[104] Agm 9(b)(ii), CSCM, 5.7.1994
[105] 6 CEM, 157
[106] Memo, Catley-Carson to minister, J7.7.1984, LAC, RG-25, vol. 22134, file 55-12-CWLTH, part 16

[107] Papers CSC 5/85, CSCM, 2.4.1985; CSC 22/89, CSCM, 5.10.1989
[108] Papers CSC 5/85, CSCM, 2.4.1985; CSC 22/89, CSCM, 5.10.1989; agm 7, CSCM, 6.7.1999; CSCAR 40, 14; paper CSC 2008/11, CSCM, 13.5.2008

Chapter Eight: Impact: What they did next

[1] Personal information
[2] 2CEM, 21
[3] 9CEM, 13
[4] Tracer study, 11
[5] Day, *Evaluating the impact*, 1
[6] Foster to Logan, 9.12.1964, LP, box 79, file 6
[7] CSCAR 17, 6
[8] LP, 138, file 2
[9] Rev 1, 37
[10] Jodhka and Raina, *India*.
[11] Barr to Lawrence, 21.8.2008; Sandy to Lawrence, 23.7.2008
[12] Harrison-Train, *South Africa*
[13] Rathi, interview; email, Howell to Lawrence 1.8.2008; Guma, interview
[14] Berridge, interview
[15] Christie, interview
[16] M. Watson to J.G. Leonard, 19.3.1974, LAC, TG76, vol. 1164, file 5366-7
[17] Levi, *Canada*
[18] Gibson, interview
[19] Email, Krishnamurti to Levi, 14.8.2008
[20] Email, Mashologu to Lawrence, 24.7.2008; email, Phiri to Lawrence, 2.8.2008
[21] Jayatilaka, interview; email, Hung to Lawrence, 2.8.2008; email, Afonja to Lawrence, 2.8.2008; Cranston, interview
[22] cf. Day, *Evaluating the impact*, passim; J. Kirkland, personal communication, 16.2.2009
[23] Raza, *Pakistan*
[24] Padman, interview
[25] Email, Green to Levi, 11.8.2008
[26] Raza, *Pakistan*
[27] Ibid
[28] Email, Mwakali to Lawrence, 9.9.2008
[29] Ahmed, interview, 20.8.2008
[30] Day, *Evaluating the impact*, 10
[31] Ottawa to Capetown, 3.3.1967, LAC, RG-25, vol. 15213, file 55-12-CWLTH
[32] Stafford, *Caribbean*
[33] Delhi to Ottawa, 18.11.1974; Ottawa to Delhi, 20.11.1974, LAC, RG25, vol. 13159, file 55-12-CWLTH
[34] Goldschlag to LePan, August 1958, LAC, RG25, vol. 7893, file 14020-C-14-2-40, part 1

[35] Lannon, interview; Little, interview
[36] Sharp, interview
[37] Levi, *Canada*, passim, Jodhka and Raina, *India*
[38] ACU, *Directory*
[39] Levi, *Canada*
[40] "Commonwealth scholars from FCO funded countries" (CSC, n.d. (2008))
[41] "Biography for Dr Joe Borg", http://ec.europa.eu.commission_barroso/ borg/profile/index_en.htm (accessed 3.11.2008)
[42] Stafford, *Caribbean*
[43] ACU, *Directory*; http://www.ghanaweb.com/GhanaHomePage/people/ person.php?ID=180 (accessed 28.2.2009)
[44] ACU, *Directory*; http://www.afdevinfo.com/htmlreports/peo/peo_374.html (accessed 28.2.2008)
[45] ACU, *Directory*; http://www.thecommonwealth.org/Internal/ 185198/185199 /185209/hassan_bubacar_jallow__the_gambia/ (accessed 28.2.2009) and http://www.afdevinfo.com/ htmlreports/peo/peo_681.html (accessed 5.3.2009)
[46] ACU, *Directory*; http://www.judicature.go.ug/kanyeihamba.php (accessed 15.04.2008); http://www.africafiles.org/printableversion.asp?id=18801 (accessed 10.2.2009)
[47] Stafford, *Caribbean*; email Stafford to author, 9.2.2008
[48] Levi, *Canada*
[49] ACU, *Directory*; http://www.nationmaster.com/encyclopedia/ Joni-Madraiwiwi/ (accessed 3.11.2008)
[50] ACU, *Directory*; http://www.maldiviandetainees.net/individuals/ 36Munavvar.htm (accessed 9.2.2009)
[51] Day, *Evaluating the impact*, 11
[52] Andrews, *Quotations*, 600
[53] Levi, *Canada*; ACU, *Directory*; email, Ostry to Levi, 28.5.2008
[54] Levi, *Canada*
[55] "Charles Krauthammer", http://rightweb.irc-online.org/profile/1252.html, (accessed 3.11.2008)
[56] "The scoop on Ed", http://www.rrj.ca/issue/2003/summer/403/, (accessed 3.11.2008)
[57] Personal information; "Brian Egner dies", http://www.gov.bw/cgi-bin/news.cgi?d=20030709, (accessed 3.9.2008)
[58] Humphries, interview
[59] Day, *Evaluating the impact*, 10–11
[60] "CEC Note by the Indian delegation on scholarships and fellowships", 17.7.1959; "CEC Statement by the Canadian delegation", 16.7.1959, NA, DO 35/ 8163
[61] Gregg, "Yuh know", 148–9
[62] Brathwaite, *History of the voice*
[63] Agm 19, CSCM, 6.10.1987 and agm 13, CSCM, 9.12.1987
[64] Lea, "Rhyme and treason"
[65] "Van Gogh's paint: Was it special?", http://www.nasonline.org/ site/PageServer ?pagename=Beckman_Fall06event_preseason_Lcarlyle (accessed 6.11.2008)

[66] Emails, Turner to Lawrence, 19.8.2008 and to author, 20.11.2008
[67] ACU, *Directory*; http://sifa.mak.ac.ug/staff_members.html (accessed 28.2.2009)
[68] ACU, *Directory*; http://www.sundayobserver.lk/2008/07/06/imp11.asp (accessed 28.2.2009)
[69] Cazalet, interview; Private view notice, "Mark Cazalet", Gallery 7, Bombay, 1989
[70] Rate-of-return analysis of overseas and local training for east Africa in the 1970s is reported in Maliyamkono et al., *Training and productivity*.
[71] Though the relationships are complex, see Pritchett, "Where has all the education gone?".
[72] Calculations of cost are complicated after this date by the variety of different awards being made.
[73] G. M. Thomson, PDC 19.11.1962 col. 832
[74] Maxey, *Student mobility on the map*, 48; see also chapters 3 and 4.
[75] DfID, *Annual report 2007*, 255-6, 232
[76] CSCAR 41-7; Riverpath Associates, *FCO scholarship review*, 15; *FCO Annual report 2007-8*, 120
[77] Levi, *Canada*. Costs per award holder are estimated by dividing total expenditure by the numbers on award. Conversions have been done by using the exchange rate for the period of expenditure and then using the British RPI to convert to 2008££.
[78] CSCAR, passim
[79] Included in the list of 80 influential scholars produced by CSC in 2008 in its bid to retain FCO funding

Chapter Nine: Conclusion

[1] http://www.scholarships.gc.ca/CUSEP-en.html (accessed 14.3.2009)
[2] In her survey, Stafford (*Caribbean*) found a high proportion of award holders were second-generation middle class. A common pattern was for scholars' parents to have been teachers, their grandparents agricultural workers. Although not a representative sample, many former scholars interviewed by Lawrence, from a variety of countries, had similar backgrounds with parents as teachers and civil servants.
[3] Maxey, *2006 update*, 6–7, citing calculations made before the recession.
[4] River Path Associates, *FCO scholarship review*, 15
[5] Ramphal, "The Commonwealth and common purpose", 11, 14

SOURCES

This book draws from five kinds of original source in addition to the literature cited in the bibliography: archives, published reports, commissioned case studies, correspondence and interviews.

Four sets of archives have been particularly useful: the National Archives in Britain (NA), mainly the series CAB, DO, FO, and OD; Library and Archives Canada (LAC); the Logan Papers, of the former principal of the University of London, Sir Douglas Logan, at the university's Senate House Library (LP); the minute books of the Commonwealth Scholarship Commission in the United Kingdom currently held at the Association of Commonwealth Universities (CSCM). These are generally cited by reference to the date and to the minute number (used for minutes 1 to 1000, reached in 1967), or the agendum number (agm), or to a paper number (e.g. CSC 10/94).

The Commonwealth Scholarship Commission has an unbroken series of annual reports (CSCAR); all have been published by the Commission but reports 1 to 26 (1984/85) were also printed as command papers. Annual reports on CSFP as a whole (CSFPAR) were published by the Commonwealth Education Liaison Committee until no. 7 (1966/67) and then by the Commonwealth Secretariat until no.34 for 1992/3. The ACU then published a single report for the next three years, cited as CSFPAR 35-7. It then produced reports for education ministers' conferences in 2000, 2003 and 2006, cited as "ACU Submission, 14, 15 and 16 CEM". Reports of all Commonwealth education meetings have been published, with the exception of the 13th conference in 1997 (1-16 CEM). The first meeting was entitled "Commonwealth Education Conference"; later meetings are "Conference of Commonwealth Education Ministers". The first three reports were published by the British government as command papers (Cmnd. 841 (1959), Cmnd. 1655 (1962), Cmnd. 2545 (1964)); reports from the fourth conference (1968) on were published by the Commonwealth Secretariat. Other primary material is cited as follows.

ACU, *Directory*	Association of Commonwealth Universities (ACU). *Directory of Commonwealth scholars and fellows, 1960-2002*. London, 2003
Caston report	Caston, G. *CSFP and international development: Report of a review by the Commonwealth Scholarship Commission in the United Kingdom*. London: CSC, 2000
Hassall report	Hassall, C. H. *Review of the Commonwealth Scholarship and Fellowship Plan (UK): Report and recommendations to the FCO*. n. p. (? London: Overseas Development Administration), 1993
PDC	Hansard: Parliamentary debates, House of Commons
PDL	Hansard: Parliamentary debates, House of Lords
Rev 1	Commonwealth Secretariat. *Commonwealth Scholarship and Fellowship Plan: Ten year review 1960-70* (first draft). London, n.d. ?1972
Rev 2	Commonwealth Secretariat. *Commonwealth Scholarship and Fellowship Plan: Report of the second ten year review committee*. London, 1982
Rev 3	Commonwealth Secretariat. *Commonwealth Scholarship and Fellowship Plan: Report of the third ten year review committee*. London, 1993
1 to 7 SCSM	Commonwealth Secretariat. *Commonwealth Standing Committee on Student Mobility - 1st to 7th reports*, London. 1982—1992
Tracer study	Niven, A. *Commonwealth Scholarship and Fellowship Plan: Tracer study*. London: Commonwealth Secretariat, 1989

Statistics on the plan are drawn from five sources: the two series of annual reports (CSCAR and CSFPAR); reports put to the 2000, 2003 and 2006 ministerial conferences; a statistical annex to Rev 3 (Thompson, *Statistical briefing paper*); a database held by ACU. There are discrepancies between these sources, which may be explained by errors in transcription, by differences between reporting years and academic years, and by differing definitions (e.g. for any one year and country, there can be differences between the number of awards accepted and the number of scholars taking them up). The tables in the appendix have attempted to reconcile these but there remain minor discrepancies between the totals there and those in some tables within chapters. These are not large enough to invalidate conclusions drawn.

Six country case studies and one thematic case study were carried out. They are as follows and are to be made available through http://www.stedmunds.cam.ac.uk/vhi.

Connell, H. *Australia: The CSFP*
Harrison-Train, C. *South Africa: The CSFP*
Jodhka, S. S. and Raina, D. *India: The CSFP*
Levi, C. *Canada: The CSFP*
Stafford, P. *The Caribbean: The CSFP in Barbados and St Lucia*
Raza, R. *Pakistan*: *The CSFP*
Darnbrough, M. *Medical awards in the CSFP*

Interviews and correspondence were generally undertaken by the author, by Suzanne Lawrence, the Commonwealth Fellow working on the project in Cambridge, and by the case study writers. Interviews quoted in the text were undertaken as shown below by Candice Harrison-Train (CH-T) in South Africa, Surinder Jodhka and his associates (SJ) in India, Suzanne Lawrence (SL) in Britain and Canada, and Hilary Perraton (HP) in Britain. The interview with the late George Curtis was recorded in Vancouver by Winnie L. Cheung.

Kazi Ahmed (SL, 20.8.2008), Saleem Badat (CH-T, 5.6.2008), Sir George Bain (SL, 23.9.2008), Keith Banting (SL, 27.8.2008), Sir Michael Berridge (SL, 4.3.2008) Geoffrey Caston (HP, 24.7.2008), Mark Cazalet (SL, 23.2.09), David Chivers (SL, 25.9.2008), Renfrew Christie (CH-T, 19.8.2008), Ross Cranston (SL, 18.3.2008), George Curtis (Winnie L. Cheung,11.10.2005), Jeff Dalley (SL, 22.8.2008), Gajaraj Dhanarajan (SL, HP, 19.12.2008), Jerome Obi Eta (SL, 7.1.2009), Danielle Fuller, (SL, 25.2.2009), Lorna Gibson (SL, 20.8.08), Xolile Guma (SL, 15.9.2008), Michael Hellyer and William Lawton (SL, HP, 18.1.2008), Peter Hetherington (HP, 8.9.2008), Kate Hofmeyr (CH-T, 9.6.2008), Tony Humphries (SL, 3.3.2008), Roger Iredale (HP, 21.3.2007), Ayal Jayatilaka (SL, 7.2.2008), George Kanyeihamba (SL, 6.1.2009), John Kirkland (HP, 20.8.2008), Frances Lannon (SL, HP, 22.11.2007), Angela Little (HP, 8.4.2008), Harold Luntz (CH-T, June 2008), Sanghamitra Misra (SL, 18.8.2008), Alastair Niven (HP, 5.5.2007), Rachael Padman (SL, 15.2.2008), Ravi Rathi (SJ, 23.5.2007), Andrew Sharp (SL, 2.9.2008), Tom Symons (HP, 7.5.2008), Edgar Temple (SL, HP, 2.9.2008)

REFERENCES

Ajayi, J. F. A., Goma, L. K. H. and Johnson, G. A. *The African experience with higher education*. Accra: Association of African Universities, 1996

Altbach, P. G. "The dilemma of change in Indian higher education." in Chitnis and Altbach, *Higher education reform*

Altbach, P. G. and Umakoshi, T. (ed.) *Asian universities: Historical perspectives and contemporary challenges*. Baltimore: Johns Hopkins, 2004

Andrews, R. *The new Penguin dictionary of quotations*. London: Penguin, 2006

Ashby, E. *Universities: British, Indian, African*. London: Weidenfeld and Nicolson, 1966

Auletta, A. "A retrospective view of the Colombo Plan: Government policy, departmental administration and overseas students." *Journal of higher education policy and management* 22, 1 (2000): 47-58

Back, K., Davis, D. and Olsen, A. *Internationalisation and higher education: Goals and strategies*. IDP Education: Canberra, 1996 (www.dest.gov.au/archive/highered/eippubs/eip9615/front.htm; accessed 28.11.08)

Balakrishna, K. N. "The major source countries for international students." in K.B. Powar (ed.) *Internationalisation of Indian higher education*. New Delhi: Association of Indian Universities, 2001

Barclay, G. St J. *Commonwealth or Europe*. St Lucia: University of Queensland Press, 1970

Berthoud, R. *The life of Henry Moore*. London: Faber, 1987

Boyce, D. G. *Decolonisation and the British empire, 1775-1997*. Basingstoke: Macmillan, 1999

Brandon, E. P. *New external providers of tertiary education in the Caribbean*. Caracas: International Institute for Higher Education in Latin America and the Caribbean, 2003

Brathwaite, E. K. *History of the voice: The development of nation language in anglophone Caribbean poetry*. London: New Beacon Books, 1984

Carr-Saunders, A. M. *New universities overseas*. London: Allen and Unwin, 1961

Chanana, K. "Accessing higher education - the dilemma of schooling: Women, minorities, scheduled castes and scheduled tribes in contemporary India." in Chitnis and Altbach, *Higher education reform*

Chitnis, S. "Gearing a colonial system of education to take independent India towards development." in Chitnis and Altbach, *Higher education reform*

Chitnis, S. and Altbach, P. G. *Higher education reform in India: Experiences and perspectives*. New Delhi: Sage, 1993

Coleman, J. S. *University development in the third world: The Rockefeller Foundation experience*. Oxford: Pergamon, 1993

Commission for Africa. *Our common interest*. n.p., 2005

Cotton, J. and Ravenhill, J. (ed.). *Seeking Asian engagement: Australia in world affairs 1991-95*. Melbourne: Oxford University Press, 1997

—. *The national interest in a global era: Australia in world affairs 1996-2000*. Melbourne: Oxford University Press, 2001

Court, D. "Higher education in East Africa." in K. W. Thompson, B. R. Fogel and H. E. Danner (ed.) *Higher education and social change: Promising experiments in developing countries (vol. 2: Case studies)*. New York: Praeger, 1977

Crapper, D. *Review of stipends and allowances paid by DfID and the FCO to students and trainees under TCT and scholarship schemes*. London: DfID, 2003

Cumpston. I. M. *The evolution of the Commonwealth of Nations 1900-1980*. Canberra: Cumpston, 1997

Day, R. *Evaluating the impact of Commonwealth scholarships in the United Kingdom: Results of the alumni survey*. London: Commonwealth Scholarship Commission, 2007

Department for International Development (DfID). *Eliminating world poverty: Making globalisation work for the poor (White Paper Cm 5006)*. Norwich: Stationery Office, 2000

Department of Foreign Affairs and International Trade (DFAIT). *Canada-Caribbean distance education scholarship programme* (Powerpoint presentation at Commonwealth of Learning), n.d

Eliutin, V. P. "The international activity of Soviet higher education." *Soviet education* 27, 9-10 (1985): 121-57

Evaluation of the Commonwealth Scholarship and Fellowship Plan and Government of Canada Awards 2002 (http://www.dfait-maeci.gc.ca/department/auditreports/evaluation/evalCSFP02-en.asp; accessed 15.12. 2007)

Evans, G. and Grant, B. *Australia's foreign relations in the world of the 1990s*. Carlton: Melbourne University Press, 1991

French, N.J. "The reform of higher education in Hong Kong." in D. C. B. Teather (ed.) *Higher education in a post-binary era: National reforms and institutional responses*. London: Jessica Kingsley, 1999

Garner, J. *The Commonwealth Office 1925-68*. London: Heinemann, 1978

Goldsworthy, J. "An overview." in Cotton and Ravenhill, *The national interest*

Green, A. "Sir Michael Caine." in Matthew and Harrison, *ODNB*

Gregg, V. M. "Yuh know bout Coo-coo? Where you know bout Coo-coo?" in V. A. Shepherd and G. L. Richards (ed.) *Questioning Creole: Creolisation discourses in Caribbean culture*. Kingston: Randle / Oxford: Currey, 2002

Harrison, M. "Changing frameworks and practices: The new Department for International Development of the United Kingdom." in K. King and L. Buchert (ed.) *Changing international aid to education: Global patterns and national contexts*. Paris: UNESCO, 1999

Hart, J. *Aid and liberation: A socialist study of aid policies*. London: Gollancz, 1973

Heinlein, F. *British government policy and decolonisation 1948-65*. London: Frank Cass, 2002

Held, D., McGrew, A., Goldblatt, D. and Perraton, J. *Global transformations: Politics, economics and culture*, Cambridge: Polity, 1999

Hennessy, P. *Having it so good: Britain in the fifties*. London: Allen Lane, 2006

Higher Education Statistics Agency (HESA). *Students in higher education institutions*. Cheltenham, 1996-

Hyam, R. and Louis, W. R. *The conservative government and the end of empire 1957-1964—Part I: High policy, political and constitutional change*. London: Stationery Office, 2000

Hyam, R. *Britain's declining empire: The road to decolonisation 1918-1968*. Cambridge: Cambridge University Press, 2006

International Working Group on Education (IWGE). *Education aid policies and practices*. Paris: IIEP, 1995

Iredale, R. *The power of change*. London: ODA, 1992

Jean-Louis, M. *Canada-Caribbean distance education scholarship programme: evaluation report*. Vancouver: Commonwealth of Learning, 2001

Kapuściński, R. *The soccer war*. London: Granta, 2007

Layard. R., King, J. and Moser, C. *The impact of Robbins*. Harmondsworth: Penguin, 1969

Lea, R. "Rhyme and treason." *Guardian*. 31.8.2007

Lee, M.N.N. "Malaysian universities: Toward equality, accessibility, and quality." in Altbach and Umakoshi, *Asian universities*

Louis, W. R. and Robinson, R. "The imperialism of decolonization." *Journal of imperial and Commonwealth history* 22, 3 (1994): 462-71

Low, D. A. *Eclipse of power*. Cambridge: Cambridge University Press, 1991

Lulat, Y. G-M., Altbach, P. G. and Kelly, F. H. *Governmental and institutional policies on foreign students: An overview and bibliography*. Buffalo: Comparative Education Center, SUNY at Buffalo, 1986

MacGuigan, M. *An inside look at external affairs during the Trudeau years*. Calgary: University of Calgary Press, 2002

McIntyre, W. D. "Commonwealth legacy." in J. M. Brown and W. R. Louis (ed.) *The twentieth century (Oxford History of the British Empire vol. 4)*. Oxford: Oxford University Press, 1999

Magagula, C. M. "The benefits and challenges of cross-border higher education in developing countries." *JHEA/RESA* 3,1 (2005): 29–49

Maliyamkono, T. L., Ishumi, A. G. M., Wells, S. J. and Migot-Adhola, S. E. (ed.) *Training and productivity in eastern Africa*. London: Heinemann, 1982

Matthew, H. C. G. and Harrison, B. (ed.) *Oxford dictionary of national biography: From the earliest times to the year 2000*. (*ODNB*) Oxford: Oxford University Press, 2004

Maxey, K. *International student mobility in the Commonwealth: An update*. London: Council for Education in the Commonwealth, 2003

—. *International student mobility in the Commonwealth: 2006 update*. London: Council for Education in the Commonwealth, 2006

—. *Student mobility on the map: Tertiary education in the Commonwealth on the threshold of the 21st century*. London: UKCOSA, 2000

May, A. "Saville Garner." in Matthew and Harrison, *ODNB*

Miller, J. D. B. *Survey of Commonwealth affairs 1953-69*. London: Royal Institute of International Affairs / Oxford: Oxford University Press, 1974

Moja, T. "Policy responses to global transformation by African higher education systems." in P. T. Zeleza and A. Olukoshi (ed.) *African universities in the twenty-first century (Volume I: Liberalisation and internationalisation)*. Dakar: CODESIRA, 2004

Morgan, D. J. *Guidance towards self-government in the British colonies 1914-71 (The official history of colonial development: vol. 5)*. London: Macmillan, 1980

—. *The origins of British aid policy 1924-45 (The official history of colonial development: vol. 1)*. London: Macmillan. 1980

Mulroney, B. *Memoirs 1939-1993*. Toronto: McClelland and Stewart, 2007
Overseas Development Administration. *Into the nineties: an education policy for British aid*. London, 1990
Papadakis, E. "Australia and Europe." in Cotton and Ravenhill, *The national interest*
Partridge, P. H. "Comment." in E. L. Wheelwright (ed.) *Higher education in Australia*. Melbourne: F. W. Cheshire, 1965
p'Bitek, O. *Africa's cultural revolution*. Nairobi: Macmillan, 1973
Perkins, J. N. O. *The sterling area, the Commonwealth, and world economic growth*. Cambridge: Cambridge University Press, 1970
Perraton, H. "Access to international postgraduate study: the role of distance-learning scholarships." EDEN Conference, UNESCO, Paris, 20-22 October 2008
—. *Open and distance learning in the developing world (2nd edition)*. London: Routledge, 2007
Pimlott, B. *Harold Wilson*. London: HarperCollins, 1992
Powar, K.B. "Introduction." in Z. S. Shafi (ed.) *Reforms and innovations in higher education*. New Delhi: Association of Indian Universities, 2001
Prior, K. "Lawrence Lumley." in Matthew and Harrison, *ODNB*
Pritchett, L. "Where has all the education gone?" *World Bank economic review* 15, 3 (2001): 367-92
Ramphal, S. "The Commonwealth and common purpose." in R. Maltby and P. Quartermaine (ed.) *The Commonwealth: A common culture*. Exeter: University of Exeter, 1989
Rao, G. L. *Brain drain and foreign students: A study of the attitudes and intentions of foreign students in Australia, the USA, Canada, and France*. St Lucia: University of Queensland Press, 1979
Ravenhill, J. "Australia and the world economy 1991-95." in Cotton and Ravenhill, *Seeking Asian engagement*
River Path Associates. *The FCO scholarships review*. (n.p.) (?London: Foreign and Commonwealth Office), 2003
Robbins, Lord (Chairman) *Higher education (Report of committee appointed by the prime minister) Cmnd. 2154*. London: HMSO, 1963
Romalis, C. *Barbados and St Lucia: A comparative analysis of social and economic development in two British West Indian islands* (PhD thesis). St Louis Missouri: Washington University, 1969
Rooth, T. "Britain, Europe, and Diefenbaker's trade diversion policies, 1957-58." in B. Buckner (ed.) *Canada and the end of empire*. Vancouver: UBC Press, 2005

Sandbrook, D. *White heat: A history of Britain in the swinging sixties*. London: Little Brown, 2006

Saraf, S. N. "Higher education and five year plans: Policies, plans and perspectives." in A. Singh and G. D. Sharma (ed.) *Higher education in India: The social context*. Delhi: Konark, 1988

Shepherd, R. *Iain Macleod*. London: Hutchinson, 1994

Sherlock, P. and Nettleford, R. *The University of the West Indies: A Caribbean response to the challenge of change*. London: Macmillan, 1990

Sicherman, C. *Becoming an African university: Makerere 1922-2000*. Trenton: Africa World Press

Springer, H. E. *The Commonwealth of universities: The story of the Association of Commonwealth Universities 1963-88*. London: ACU, 1988

Stone, L. "Social control and intellectual excellence." in N. Phillipson (ed.) *University, society and the future*. Edinburgh: Edinburgh University Press, 1983

Tan, J. "Singapore: Small nation, big plans." in Altbach and Umakoshi, *Asian universities*

Thompson, S. *Statistical briefing paper: CSFP third ten-year review*. London: Commonwealth Secretariat, 1993

Tilak, J. B. G. "Financing higher education in India." in Chitnis and Altbach, *Higher education reform*

Trilokekar, R. D. *Federalism, foreign policy and the internationalization of higher education: A case study of the International Academic Relations Division, Department of Foreign Affairs and International Trade, Canada* (EdD thesis). Toronto: Ontario Institute for Studies in Education, 2007

Unwin, J. and Humphreys, S. *Preliminary country report—Uganda*. London: Commonwealth Scholarship Commission, 2007

Whitehead, C. "Sir Christopher Cox." in Matthew and Harrison, *ODNB*

Williams, G., Kenyon, M. and Williams, L. (ed.) *Readings in overseas student policy*. London: Overseas Students Trust, 1987

Williams, L. "Overseas students in the United Kingdom: Some recent developments." in Williams et al. *Readings*

Williams, P. 1982 *A policy for overseas students: Analysis, options, proposals*. London: Overseas Students Trust, 1987

Woanacott, R. J. "Tariff policy." in L. H. Officer and L. B. Smith (ed.) *Canadian economic problems and policies*. Toronto: McGraw Hill, 1970

Woodhall, M. "Government policy towards overseas students: An international perspective." in Williams et al. *Readings*

World Bank. *Constructing knowledge societies: New challenges for tertiary education.* Washington D.C., 2002
—. *Education in sub-Saharan Africa: Policies for adjustment, revitalization, and expansion.* Washington D.C., 1988
—. *Higher education: The lessons of experience.* Washington D.C., 1994
Yee, A. H. *Whither Hong Kong: China's shadow or visionary gleam?* Lanham: University Press of America, 1999

INDEX

academic advisers 41-2, 64, 76
— excellence 30-1, 42-3, 50, 58, 70, 75, 79, 103-4, 118, 165, 175, 181-2
achievements *see* careers
Afonja, A. 161-2
Africa, awards to 72. 134, 180
age of scholars 125-6
Ahmed, K. 164
aid policy 68-9, 180
Aitken, R. 37
allowances *see* children's allowances, marriage allowances, stipends
alumni 65, 75, 108-9, 168
Ameyaw-Akumfi, C. 166-7
Anguilla 135
Anthony, K. 167
Ashby, E. 31, 37-8, 40, 42, 43
Asquith commission 21
Association of Commonwealth Universities ix, 35, 37-8, 42, 92, 130
Association of Universities and Colleges of Canada (AUCC) 92, 96
Aston University 104
Athabasca University 119
Australia 1, 26, 27-8, 32, 50, 81-99, 125-7, 140, 146-7
policy 7-9, 14, 31, 81-99
scholars and fellows from 14, 17, 32, 44, 125-7, 140, 143, 158, 162, 163, 166
scholars and fellows to 2, 10, 12, 15, 123, 146-7, 168
withdrawal of support 2, 14, 183-4

Australian Development Assistance Agency (ADAB, AusAid) 92, 97
awards 11-18
academic 12, 17, 18, 53, 71, 104-5, 128
by developing countries 33, 133-4, 137, 144
direction of travel 123-6, 131-4, 180
duration 44, 46, 71, 86, 135-6
master's and doctoral 71, 75, 135
medical 12, 17-18, 32, 46, 111, 115-17, 127, 137
undergraduate 31, 41, 86, 103 135, 180
Badat, S. 122
badgers, rabid 78
Bahamas 76, 94
Bahr, G. C. 159
Bangalore University 115, 117
Bangladesh 54, 96, 102, 120, 129, 134, 149, 163-4, 169
Bangladesh University of Agriculture and Technology 120
bankers 169
Barbados 32, 64, 101, 110-13, 166, 168, 182
Basu, P. 115-16
Battersea Technical College 40
Bechuanaland 46, 170
Beckles, H. 112
Beeby, C. 86-7
Behari, S. 117
Belize 158
Bernard, L. 166
Berridge, M. 141, 160

bias 2-3, 32, 111, 121, 127-31, 181-2
bilateral nature of CSFP 1, 10, 90. 183-5
bonding 158
Borg, J. 166, 168
Botswana 14, 170
Boyle, E. 55
brain drain 2, 32, 118, 155-7, 181-2
Brandis, G. 166
Brathwaite, K. 139, 171
Brathwaite, W. 112
British Academy ix
British Council 37-8, 40, 42, 44, 65, 69, 72, 129, 145, 149
Brunei 76
Butt, N. 121-2
Butterworth, J. 53
cable network 6
Caine, M. 67, 74
Campbell, R. 140
Canada ix, 1-3, 5-8, 14, 19, 30, 81-99, 134
　distance learning programme 12, 118-19, 152
　finance of plan 86, 94, 96-7, 143, 175-6, 183
　policy 8-12, 31, 81-99. 128, 135-6, 169, 164-5, 180
　scholars from 158, 166, 168-170, 172
　scholars and fellows to 15, 26-7, 34, 45, 112, 116, 123-7, 132, 139, 142-5, 161, 172
Canadian Bureau for International Education (CBIE) 96
Canadian International Development Agency (CIDA) 91-2, 96, 168
careers of scholars 159-73
Caribbean 3, 12, 19, 22, 72, 82, 89, 110-13, 118-19, 123-4, 171, 180
Carleton University 170
Carlyle, L. 172
Carnegie foundation 101, 107
Carney, M. 169

Carr-Saunders, A. 21-2
Carter, J. 169
cash limits 57-8, 61, 65
Castle, B. 49
Caston report 120
Caston, G. 74-5, 77
Cazalet, M. 173
Central African Federation 1, 9, 15-17
Ceylon 9, 10, 45, 85, 129, 133 *see also* Sri Lanka
Chainama College 120
Cham Tao Soon 140
Chelsea College 112
Chevening awards 61, 78-9, 174, 175, 183
children's allowance 44-6, 55, 143-6
Chinese University of Hong Kong 102
Chomsky, N. 171
Chunga, P. 18
Churchill, W. 6, 39, 81
civil service training 7-8, 30, 84-5, 102-5, 161, 170
Clarke, D. 112
Clegg, A. 15
cold war 6-7, 27, 95
Colombo Plan 5, 27, 84, 87, 92
colonial policy 5-7, 19-22, 52
Commission for Africa 23
Committee of Vice Chancellors and Principals 35, 68, 74
Common Market 5, 88 *see also* European Economic Community
Commonwealth 2, 60-1, 81-99
　attitudes towards 6-7, 72-3, 79, 87-90, 99
　cohesion 27-8, 31, 36-7, 43, 58, 79, 87, 162, 173, 176, 179, 186
　links 5, 61-2, 87-90, 99
　trade 5-6, 82-3, 88-9
　trade conference *see* Montreal conference

Commonwealth education
  conference
  1959 Oxford 1, 7, 9–11, 17, 19,
    33-4, 36, 40-2, 58, 83-7, 170-1,
    175
  1962 New Delhi 28, 155
  1964 Ottawa 55, 104, 133
  1971 Canberra 57, 91, 155
  1974 Jamaica 103-5, 133-4,
    151
  1977 Accra 134
  1980 Colombo 61-2, 63, 93
  1984 Cyprus 93-4, 155
  1990 Barbados 69, 73
  1994 Islamabad 97, 110
  2006 Cape Town 2006 14, 28
Commonwealth Fund for Technical
  Cooperation 134
Commonwealth Institute 186
Commonwealth of Learning 95,
  118-19
Commonwealth relations office 32,
  35-8, 41, 43, 48, 49, 129, 132
Commonwealth Scholarship
  Commission 2-3, 11-12, 35-80
  chair 38-9, 49-51, 66, 67, 74,
    77
  directions to 41-3
  established 37-40
  evaluation programme 109,
    155-7, 162
  finance 14, 55-8, 62-6, 69, 72-
    3, 76-7, 78-9. 174-5
  influence 62, 73, 78, 185
  membership 38-40, 47-9, 66-7,
    74, 76-8, 184-5
  policy 31-2, 41-6, 50, 54-5, 69-
    76, 119-21, 130-1, 180-1
Commonwealth scholarship
  committees 2, 11, 30, 85, 91,
    94, 97, 118, 128, 160, 185
Commonwealth Scholarships Act
  41-2
Commonwealth Secretariat ix, 2,
  11, 54, 63, 70, 89, 90, 95, 97,
  127, 183, 185

Commonwealth shared scholarships
  76
Commonwealth Standing
  Committee on Student Mobility
  60, 92, 93
Commonwealth Universities'
  Congress 8, 35
communism 6–7, 82 *see also* cold
  war, Soviet bloc
Cornelius, J. 166
cost effectiveness 173-6
Cox, C. 21, 53
Cranston, R. 162, 166
Crosland, A. 57
Cullen, M. 166
Curtis, G. 7, 8–9, 85
Cyprus 7, 76, 82, 124, 129, 137,
  140-1, 177
Dalhousie University 168
Davies, P. Maxwell 15
Debnath, C. 32
decolonisation 5-7, 24, 52, 81-2
department for international
  development 73-8, 131, 162,
  175, 184
department of innovation,
  universities and skills 79
Dhanarajan, G. 104
Diefenbaker, J. 5-6, 28
disadvantaged students 10, 131
discrimination 55, 129, 146-8, 166
Dissanayake, K. B. 173
distance learning 3, 12, 68, 70, 110,
  118-121, 127, 132, 180
Dodd, W. 62-3
Dominica 103, 118
Dorothy Hodgkin awards 26
east Africa 9, 45, 103, 105, 133,
  137, 180
economic appraisal 173-6
— development 22, 24-6, 31, 50,
  84, 108
Eden, A. 37
Egner, B. 46, 170
elitism 2-3, 32-3, 181-2
ERASMUS 28

European Economic Community 35, 83, 88
Evans, G. 95-6
experiences during awards 139-51
Falkland Islands 135
fellowships 1-3, 15-18, 34, 85, 86-7, 95, 96-7, 105, 113, 127-8, 135, 180
 academic 30, 63, 75, 163
 professional 18, 75, 76, 131, 135
 types of 15-18
field work 31, 43-4, 54, 69, 105-6, 142
Fiji 27, 148, 168
finance 14, 55-8, 62-6, 69, 72-3, 76-7, 78-9, 86, 94, 96-7, 142-5, 173-6
fine arts 91, 137, 148, 150,170-3
Ford foundation 101, 107
foreign and Commonwealth office 57-8, 60-1, 63-4, 71-2, 73, 76, 78-9, 135, 162, 165, 166, 171
francophonie 95, 99
Fraser, M. 90, 95
Frederick, N. 167, 170
Freedman, C. 169
Fulbright awards 32, 98
Gambia 135, 167
Garner, Lord 5, 51, 57
gender 3, 33-4, 70, 77, 107, 125-7, 161, 179
Ghana 2, 5, 9, 10, 14, 18, 22, 31, 33, 82, 88, 125, 130, 133, 145, 166-7
Gibson, L. 161
Godwin, T. 172
Goodridge, R. 112
Green, M. 163
Greenspon, E. 170
Guma, X. 160, 169
Guyana 67, 89, 94, 148
Hall, P. 39-40
Harkness awards 32
Harpham, T. ix, 77
Hart, J. 52

Hassall, C. 70-1, 72, 130
Heath, E. 88, 89
Hetherington, P. 66, 67
Hinshelwood, C. 40
Home, Lord 38-9, 40
Hong Kong 1, 12, 14, 22, 60, 85, 71, 96, 102, 104, 107-8, 125, 133, 144, 150, 161
Houghton, D. 49-51
housing 147-8
Howell, E. 159-60
Humphries, T. 170
Hung Wan Chung 161
Hunte, K. 112
Imperial College 115
India 2, 7-8, 11, 19, 23-4, 32, 39-40, 81, 82, 87, 102, 108, 109, 113-18, 130, 131, 136-7, 145, 163, 182, 183-5
 African students in 36, 124, 172-3
 awards offered by 9, 12, 15, 17, 19, 27, 33, 113, 124, 133-5, 137, 148-50, 172-3, 175, 180
 scholars and fellows from 17, 31,50, 71, 113-18, 128, 129-30, 136-7, 140, 148, 158, 159, 161, 164
 state agricultural universities 117
inflation 56, 143-4
institutional capacity grants 110, 180
institutional development 104-7, 110, 119-121
International Council for Canadian Studies 96
internationalism 8–9, 160, 184, 186
Inter-University Council 53
Iredale, R. 62, 70, 72
Jadhavpur University 117
Jallow, H. B. 167
Jamaica 14, 110, 112, 119, 134, 171, 175
Jayatilaka, A. 161
Jefferson, T. 169

Jiggins, J. 137, 150
JLN Technological University 115
Jomo Kenyatta University 120
journalists 169-70
Kantharia, C. V. 116
Kapuściński, R., 78
Kapuya, J. 167
Karachi Polytechnic 137
Keele University 77, 112
Kenya 31, 71, 94, 102, 103, 107, 120, 148, 172
Kenyaihamba, G. 167, 168
Khan, A. A. 169
Khan, G. M. 163
Khan, I. 163
Kilmuir, Lord 48-9. 51
Kirkland, J. ix, 74-5, 79
Krauthammer, C. 169-70
Krishnamurti, C. 161
Kulkarn, A. V. 116
Kumasi College of Technology 22
Kyeyune, G. 172-3
Lakshmanan, A. V. 115
Lannon, F. 49, 66
Laval University 167-8
Lawton, W. 132
lawyers 21, 51, 136, 165-7, 182
leaders 9, 27, 32, 71, 76, 79, 165-70, 179, 181, 184
Leeds Metropolitan University 120
Lesotho 147, 161
Lewis, A. 22-3
Ligenga, L. 168
Lintott, H. 8, 38
Little, A. 67
Logan, D. 35-6, 43-50, 53-54, 57, 66, 158
London School of Economics 170
London School of Tropical Hygiene 77
London South Bank University 77
Louisey, P. 167-8
Loveridge, A. 54
Lugard, F. 102
MacArthur foundation 107
McGill University 112, 168, 169

Mackenzie, N. 8
Macleod, I. 6, 38, 39-40
McMaster University 163
Macmillan, H. 6–7, 28, 35, 48, 89
Madraiwiwi, R. 168
Magagula, C. 107
Makerere University 105, 107, 164, 167, 173, 182
Malawi 18, 101, 168, 171-2, 177
Malaya 1, 7, 9, 22, 60, 87, 108, 133
Malaysia 8, 19, 24, 27, 45, 60, 64,102, 103, 106, 108, 133, 134, 147-9
Maldives 134, 135, 168
Malta 48, 76, 124, 166
Mapanje, J. 171-2, 177
marketing of education 28, 118
Marlborough House 42, 89, 90
marriage allowance 34, 42, 44-6, 50, 54-5, 86, 140, 142-5
— of scholars 145, 158-9
Marshall commission 11, 37, 78
Marshall, W. 101, 112
Mascoll, C. 168
Mashologu, M. 147, 161
Maudling, R. 83
Mauritius 14, 27, 134, 148, 164, 172
medical adviser 41, 43, 129-30
Memorial University 119, 132
Mewsigye, J. 32
ministry of overseas development 49-51, 52-3, 57-8, 60
Misra, S. 140
Mohan, P. 140
Montreal conference 1, 5-8, 9, 35-6, 40, 83-4, 147
Montserrat 103
Morris, P. 38
Morrison, H. 38
Mount St Vincent University 119
Mulroney, B. 95
multilateralism 1, 9, 10, 185
Munavvar, M. 168
Mwakali, J. 163-4
Mwansa, K. 167

Narayanaswami, P. 115
Ndlovu, L. 107
New Zealand 1, 2, 3, 7, 11, 14, 30, 50, 63, 81-99, 143, 166, 184, 186
    scholars from 44, 125-7, 132, 134, 141, 146, 165
    scholars and fellows to 9, 11, 12, 15, 113, 127, 139, 180
    vice-chancellors 14, 97, 185
Nigeria 101, 105, 107, 129, 133, 176
    scholars from 134, 145, 161
    scholars to 14, 33, 133, 149, 170
Niven, A. 33, 145
Nolan rules 74, 184-5
nominating agencies 1, 11, 12, 30, 42, 61, 75, 128-31, 182
Northern Ireland 147
Nuffield Foundation ix, 101
numbers of awards 9, 11-14, 64, 91, 93-4, 97, 103, 123-8, 133-4, 179, 181
origins of CSFP 8-10
Ostry, J. 169
outcomes 103-22, 140-1, 151-2, 155-177, 179-183
overseas development administration 60, 61-4, 70, 71-2, 73
overseas student policy 14, 57, 59-61, 68, 71, 92, 97
Oxford conference *see* Commonwealth education conference
Padman, R. 163
Pakistan 7, 10, 19, 31, 33, 34, 101, 102, 131, 136-7, 145, 150,
    politics and 52, 87, 149-50, 159, 176-7
    scholars from 7, 12, 121-2, 132, 163
    scholars to 14, 41, 133, 180
Pandurangappa 115
Papua New Guinea 94, 96, 142

Parkinson, N. 38
p'Bitek, O. 139-40
Peddie, Lord 21
Phiri, S. 161
Pinter, H. 171
pledges of scholarships 8, 14, 19, 85, 86, 94, 133
Pode, J. 40
poets 170-3
prejudice *see* discrimination
Prentice, R. 50-1
principles 10-11, 99, 117, 182
Punjab Agricultural University 117
Punjab University 114
purpose
    Canadian view of 8, 98
    of awards 1, 3, 18, 25-8, 43-4, 62, 69-70
    of plan 10, 19-34, 50-1, 53, 84-5, 91-2, 183-5
Pym package 60-2, 93
Pym, F. 60-61
quality of applicants 44-5, 75
Queen's University 168, 169, 172
quotas 41, 52, 130-1, 135
Raka, M. 114
Ramphal, S. 60, 89-90, 94, 95, 186
Rathi, R. 159
reciprocity 28, 84-5, 98, 180, 185
Reddy, A. S. 115
relevance 31-2, 50-1, 53-4, 62, 69-70, 91, 164-5
return to home country 2, 32-3, 155-62, 179, 181-2
Rhodes scholarships 32, 34, 44, 84, 165
Rhodes University 122
rich-country exchanges 26-7. 32-3. 83-7, 91, 98-9, 125, 139, 157-8, 180
Robbins committee 57, 59, 127
Rockefeller Foundation 87, 101, 105, 107
Rose, G. 112
Royal Society 48, 160

Royal Technical College, Glasgow 40
St Edmund's College ix
St Helena 135
St Kitts 158
St Lucia 119, 164, 167-8
St Vincent 119
Sandy, J. 140, 159
Sandys, D. 147
Scarbrough, Lord 38-9, 42, 46, 47, 77
science and technology 76, 78-9. 85. 91. 101, 111, 114-8, 136-7, 162-5, 182
selection procedures 1, 19, 32, 41-2, 76, 128-31. 179
sex discrimination act 55
Seychelles 135, 177
Sheath, H. 15-17
Sheikh, G. M. 173
Shivashankaran, S. 116
Short, C. 73-5
Sierra Leone 14, 64, 140, 145, 150, 159
Singapore 19, 24, 71, 76, 87, 96, 104, 106-8, 125, 140
Sinker, P. 38
Sloman, A. 62, 66
small states 14, 82,111, 123, 137, 158, 164, 165, 167-8, 182
Smith, A. 89
Smith, S. 8-9, 11, 35
Sontag, S. 171
South Africa 1, 12-14, 23, 51-2, 58, 89, 95, 122, 128-9, 131, 133, 147, 159, 169, 176
Southern Rhodesia 52, 87, 89, 129, 141, 160 *see also* Zimbabwe
Soviet bloc 27, 36-7, 81-3, 87, 181
Societ Union 27, 95, 181
Soyinka, W. 149, 171
split-site awards 31, 54, 69-70, 75, 101, 128, 135-6, 164, 175, 180
Sree Chitra Tirunal Institute 117
Sri Lanka 33, 102, 103, 107, 109, 134, 137, 140, 145, 147, 148, 149, 158, 161, 172-3, *see also* Ceylon
sterling area 5, 37, 82-3, 88, 181
stipends 33, 42, 46, 142-5, 149
student fees 26, 57, 60-3, 68, 73, 92-3, 97
— mobility 26-8, 36, 60, 68, 80, 90, 92-3, 134, 183
subject areas 9-10, 41-2, 84, 135-9, 162-173, 182
success rates 65, 151-2, 179
survival of CSFP 183-5
Swaziland 107, 160, 169
Syers, C. 48
Symons, T. 8–9, 11
Tamakloe, W. 18
Tanzania 19, 52, 88, 102-05, 167, 177
targeting of awards 53, 105-7, 110-11, 113-14, 118
Tate, M. 166
teacher training 9, 35-6, 175
technical assistance 5, 28, 84
technical cooperation and training programme 21, 68, 185-6
Temple, E. 40, 42, 50, 52, 63, 67, 106, 129
ten-year review 28, 128
  first 54, 91, 102, 103, 104, 127, 158
  second 63-4, 93, 105-6
  third 69-70, 106, 109-10, 125, 155-7
Thatcher, M. 58, 60, 89, 90, 95
third-country awards 63, 105-6
Thomas, J. H. 51
tracer study 155-7
treasury 5-6, 46, 54
Trent University 8
Trinidad 8, 12, 14, 23, 110, 140, 163-4
Trudeau, P. 90, 95
Turks and Caicos 160
Turner, S. 172

Uganda 13, 14, 23, 32, 52, 102-3, 105, 139, 148, 150, 163-4, 167, 171
United States of America 27, 81, 83, 88, 89, 101, 111, 161
Universiti Sains Malaysia 104
universities *see also* individual universities
   Africa 19-24, 80, 106-7
   Asia 106-8
   Australia 83
   Britain 19, 26-7, 68
   Canada 19, 84
   developing country 19-25
   expansion 19-25
   Hong Kong 22
   India 19, 23, 103, 108, 113-18
   Malaysia 22, 24
   Pakistan 19, 136-7
   Singapore 24
   South Africa 19, 23
university
   expansion 19-30, 59, 80, 101-22, 183
   fees *see* student fees
   staff 12, 17, 32, 103-110
University of Adelaide 168
— of Agricultural Sciences Bangalore 117
— of Alberta 161
— of Birmingham 37, 109, 167
— of Botswana and Swaziland 169
— of British Columbia 8, 161, 170
— of Calgary 164
— of Cambridge 37, 40, 67, 83, 85, 101, 112, 114, 132, 140, 141, 159, 160, 161, 163, 165, 166
— of Dhaka 164
— of East Africa 22, 102-3, 105
— of Edinburgh 115, 142, 166
— of Essex 62
— of Ghana 21
— of Hong Kong 144
— of Ibadan 149
— of Kerala 104
— of Leeds 112, 140
— of London 22, 35, 54, 72, 120, 171
— of Malawi 171
— of Malaya 108
— of Malta 166
— of Manchester 40, 112, 169
— of New Brunswick 94
— of New England 17
— of New South Wales 32
— of Newcastle 171
— of Nottingham 141
— of Oxford 17, 40, 51, 66, 74, 82, 83, 85, 115, 132, 140, 141, 142, 162, 166, 169
— of Pretoria 120
— of Saskatchewan 140
— of Southampton 159
— of Stirling 120
— of Sunderland 120
— of Surrey 164
— of Sussex 17
— of Swaziland 107, 169
— of the South Pacific 74
— of the West Indies 22-3, 101, 104-5, 110-13, 119, 121, 164, 167, 171
— of Toronto 8
— of Visual and Performing Arts 173
— of Wales 166, 167
— of Warwick 114, 167
— of Western Cape 122
— of York 122, 171
— of Zambia 17, 161, 167
Vickers, J. 33
Wakhlu. O. 109
Walker, M. 58, 67
West Indies *see* Caribbean, University of the West Indies
Whitlam, G. 90, 92
Wickramasinghe, A. 109
Wilson, H. 49, 82, 88, 89
World Bank 23-5, 106, 169
Zambia 17, 105, 120, 161, 167
Zimbabwe 52, 58, 90, 94, 107, 129, 150, 158

DATE DUE